NEW TESTAMENT CHRISTIANITY
FOR AFRICA AND THE WORLD

NEW TESTAMENT CHRISTIANITY FOR AFRICA AND THE WORLD

Essays in honour of Harry Sawyerr

EDITED BY
MARK E. GLASSWELL
AND
EDWARD W. FASHOLÉ-LUKE

London
SPCK
1974

First published in 1974
by SPCK
Holy Trinity Church
Marylebone Road
London NW1 4DU

Printed in Great Britain by
William Clowes & Sons, Limited,
London, Beccles and Colchester

SBN 281 02783 8

CONTENTS

54212

THE CONTRIBUTORS

C. K. BARRETT   Professor of Divinity, University of Durham; Fellow of the British Academy

C. E. B. CRANFIELD   Reader in Theology, University of Durham

KWESI A. DICKSON   Professor of the Study of Religion, University of Ghana, Legon

NILS A. DAHL   Professor of New Testament in the Divinity School and Fellow of Branford College, Yale University

IEUAN P. ELLIS   Lecturer in Theology in the Department of Theology, University of Hull; formerly Lecturer in Theology, Fourah Bay College

E. W. FASHOLÉ-LUKE   Senior Lecturer in Theology, Fourah Bay College; Dean, Faculty of Arts, University of Sierra Leone

MARK E. GLASSWELL   Lecturer in Theology, Fourah Bay College

S. L. GREENSLADE   Canon Residentiary of Durham Cathedral 1943–58; Lightfoot Professor of Divinity, University of Durham 1943–50; Van Mildert Professor of Divinity, University of Durham 1950–58; Regius Professor of Ecclesiastical History, University of Oxford and Canon of Christ Church 1959–72; Fellow of the British Academy

D. R. JONES   Canon Residentiary and Sub-Dean of Durham Cathedral; Lightfoot Professor of Divinity, University of Durham

NOEL Q. KING   Professor of History and Comparative Religion, University of California, Santa Cruz; formerly Professor of the Study of Religion, University of Ghana, Legon and Makerere University, Uganda

OLOF LINTON   Professor of New Testament, University of Copenhagen 1949–69

MATEI MARKWEI   Lecturer in Religious Knowledge, Head of Department, and Chaplain, Milton Margai Teachers' College, Sierra Leone

C. F. D. MOULE   Fellow of Clare College and Lady Margaret Professor of Divinity, University of Cambridge; Fellow of the British Academy

vii

P. E. S. THOMPSON   Chaplain and Part-Time Lecturer in Theology, Fourah Bay College

H. E. W. TURNER   Canon Residentiary and Sub-Dean, Durham Cathedral, and Van Mildert Professor of Divinity, University of Durham till 1973. Canon Emeritus from 1974

H. W. TURNER   Lecturer in Religious Studies, University of Aberdeen; formerly Lecturer in Theology, Fourah Bay College

A. F. WALLS   Senior Lecturer and Head of Department of Religious Studies, King's College, University of Aberdeen

MAX WARREN   General Secretary of the Church Missionary Society 1942–63; Canon and Sub-Dean of Westminster 1963–73; Hon D.D. University of Sierra Leone

TABULA GRATULANTIUM

His Excellency Dr Siaka Stevens
President of the Republic of Sierra Leone
and Chancellor of the University

Mr S. A. S. Adams, Principal, Milton Margai Teachers'
College, Freetown
The Rev. Dr James B. Adamson, Rockford, Ill.
Professor J. F. Ade Ajayi, Vice-Chancellor, University of Lagos
The Rev. E. A. Adeolu Adegbola, Institute of Church and
Society, Ibadan, Nigeria
The Rev. D. Anderson, Watford, Herts
The Rev. Professor G. W. Anderson, University of Edinburgh
Mr G. S. S. Anthony, Vice-Principal, Milton Margai Teachers'
College, Freetown
The Rev. Canon J. H. Armstrong, York
The Rev. Dr W. L. Avery, Fourah Bay College

The Rev. Professor C. S. Baëta, University of Ghana
Mr Max Bailor, Albert Academy, Freetown
The Rev. Professor R. S. Barbour, University of Aberdeen
The Hon. J. Barthes-Wilson, Freetown
The Rev. Père Pierre Benoit, o.p., Jerusalem
The Rev. Dr R. J. W. Bevan, Grasmere, Westmorland
The Rev. Père M.-E. Boismard, Jerusalem
Dr Gerald Bonner, University of Durham
The Rev. Professor Gerald L. Borchert, North American
Baptist Seminary, Sioux Falls, South Dakota
The Rev. Professor Schuyler Brown, New York
Professor F. F. Bruce, Buxton, Derbyshire
The Rev. Professor T. A. Burkill, Salisbury, Rhodesia

The Rev. Professor Allen Cabaniss, University of Mississippi

The Rev. Canon B. Carr, All Africa Council of Churches, Nairobi, Kenya
The Rev. Dr J. Walter Cason, Chicago
The Rev. Canon R. E. Cant, York
Dr D. Christopherson, Vice-Chancellor, University of Durham
The Rev. John Cockerton, St John's College, Durham
Mr Justice C. O. E. Cole, Chief Justice of Sierra Leone
Mr E. Cole, Ministry of Education, Freetown

The Rev. F. R. Dain, Kenyatta University College, Nairobi; former Principal, Fourah Bay College
Professor Frederick W. Danker, Concordia Seminary, St Louis
Professor David Daube, University of California
The Rev. G. Henton Davies, Principal Emeritus, Regent's Park College, University of Oxford
Mr Justice P. R. Davies, Speaker of the House of Representatives and Chancellor of the Province of West Africa, Freetown
The Rev. Rupert E. Davies, Bristol
S. Exc. Mgr Albert Descamps, Louvain
Professor K. Dike, Harvard University
Mrs Gloria Dillsworth, Freetown
The Rev. H. O. Duncan, Bishop Middleham, Co. Durham

The Rt Rev. J. R. Elisée, Bishop of the Gambia and the Rio Pongas
The Rev. Professor C. F. Evans, University of London

The Rev. T. F. Fabiyi, Ado-Ekiti, Nigeria
The Rev. Dr Gordon D. Fee, University of Illinois
The Rev. John Charles Fenton, St Chad's College, Durham
Dr Ruth Finnegan, The Open University, Bletchley, Bucks
Professor Fred L. Fisher, Golden Gate Baptist Seminary, Mill Valley, Calif.
The Rev. Dr W. H. Fitzjohn, High Commissioner of Sierra Leone to Nigeria
The Rev. Dr Haakon Flottorp, Kristiansand, Norway
Professor Dr Werner Foerster, Münster
The Rev. D. B. Foss, Fourah Bay College

The Rev. Dr R. S. Foster, St Deiniol's Library, Hawarden,
  Chester; former Chaplain, Fourah Bay College
Dr J. Fugate, Kalamazoo College, Kalamazoo, Mich.
Mr Christopher Fyfe, University of Edinburgh
The Rev. Dr C. Gaba, University of Cape Coast
Mr M. R. O. Garber, former Registrar, Fourah Bay College
Mrs Cassandra Garber, Freetown Secondary School for Girls
The Rev. Dr L. A. Garrard, Reading
The Rev. A. Gelston, University of Durham
Professor Dr H.-W. Gensichen, Heidelberg
The Rev. Père A. George, Saints-Foy-les-Lyon, France
Professor A. Geyser, University of Witwatersrand
The Rev. H. M. Gibson, Glasgow, formerly Lecturer at Fourah
  Bay College
Mrs Ingrid V. Gibson, Glasgow, formerly Lecturer at Fourah
  Bay College
Mr W. H. Glasswell, Darlington, Co. Durham
Mrs W. H. Glasswell, Darlington, Co. Durham
Professor Dr J. Gnilka, Münster
Dr J. J. Grant, University of Durham, former Principal,
  Fourah Bay College
The Rev. Professor Holt H. Graham, Minneapolis
The Rev. Canon E. M. B. Green, St John's College, Notting-
  ham

Professor Dikran Y. Hadidian, Pittsburgh Theological Seminary
Dr P. E. H. Hair, University of Liverpool, formerly Lecturer at
  Fourah Bay College
The Rev. Canon R. J. Hammer, Queen's College, Birmingham
The Rt Rev. R. P. C. Hanson, University of Manchester
Mrs E. A. Harris, Dover, Kent
The Rev. P. G. S. Harrison, Beverley, Yorks
Mr V. J. Hastings-Spaine, Sierra Leone Grammar School
Professor Dr Günter Haufe, Greifswald Universität, East Ger-
  many
The Rev. Professor J. Heywood-Thomas, University of
  Nottingham
The Rev. Canon J. P. Hickinbotham, Wycliffe Hall, Oxford
The Rev. Professor A. J. B. Higgins, St David's University
  College, Lampeter, Cards

Dr F. L. Hilliard, University of Birmingham, former Principal, Fourah Bay College

Miss A. E. Hirst, Deal, Kent, formerly Lecturer at Fourah Bay College

Dr M. D. Hooker, University of Oxford

The Rt Rev. J. L. C. Horstead, former Principal, Fourah Bay College, and former Archbishop of West Africa

Mrs Olive Horstead, Loughborough, Leics, formerly Lecturer at Fourah Bay College

The Rev. J. L. Houlden, Cuddesdon College, Oxford

The Rt Rev. J. W. A. Howe, Secretary General, Anglican Consultative Council, London

Miss Christian Howard, York

The Very Rev. John C. Hughes, Leicester

The Rev. Dr Philip E. Hughes, Rydal, Pennsylvania

The Rev. Professor B. Idowu, University of Ibadan

The Rev. F. N. Jasper, Frimley, Surrey, formerly Lecturer at Fourah Bay College

The Rev. Dr Sherman E. Johnson, Mansfield, Ohio

Professor Eldred Jones, Fourah Bay College

The Rt Rev. Percy J. Jones, formerly Assistant Bishop of Sierra Leone and Dean of the Cathedral

The Rt Rev. S. I. Kale, Bishop of Lagos

Mr Abdul Kanu, Union College, Bunumbu

Dr and Mrs John Karefa-Smart, Harvard University

The Ven. M. Keili, Archdeacon of Bo, Sierra Leone

The Ven. T. B. King, Archdeacon of Freetown

Professor Robert A. Kraft, University of Pennsylvania

Professor Dr Georg Kretschmar, Ottobrunn, West Germany

Dr K. H. Kuhn, Durham

Professor Y. Kumazawa, Tokyo

The Rev. Professor G. W. H. Lampe, University of Cambridge

Professor Xavier Léon-Dufour, Lyon

The Librarian, Columbia Theological Seminary, Decatur, Georgia

The Librarian, Fourah Bay College

The Librarian, University of Durham
Professor K. Little, University of Edinburgh
Dr Henrick Ljungman, Karlstad, Sweden
Professor Dr E. Lövestam, Lund, Sweden
Mr H. M. Lynch-Shyllon, Freetown

The Rev. Dr J. D. McCaughcy, Ormond College, Parkville, Vic.
Mr C. P. McConnachie, C.B.E., Castle Douglas
The Rt Hon. Malcolm Macdonald, O.M., Chancellor, University of Durham
The Rev. Dr G. W. MacRae, Harvard University
Professor Dr J. Mánek, Prague
The Rev. Dr John Marsh, Cumberland
The Rev. Dr I. Howard Marshall, University of Aberdeen
The Rev. Professor Ralph P. Martin, Pasadena, Calif.
Professor Goro Mayeda, Tokyo
Sir Louis N. Mbanefo, Kt
The Rev. Professor John Mbiti, Makerere University, Uganda
Professor Bruce M. Metzger, Princeton Theological Seminary
Dr Robert P. Meye, Oak Brook, Ill.
Professor John Meyendorff, New York
The Rev. Canon D. R. Michell, Leicester
Professor P. S. Minear, Yale Divinity School
The Rev. Dr Leon Morris, Ridley College, Parkville, Vic.
Professor Dr Jac. J. Müller, Stellenbosch
Dr E. Munck, Aarhus

The Reverend I. Ndanema, Fourah Bay College
The Rt Rev. Stephen Neill, University of Nairobi
The Rt Rev. Lesslie Newbigin, Bishop in Madras
Dr Davidson Nicol, C.M.G., United Nations, New York, former Principal of Fourah Bay College
The Rev. Robin Nixon, St John's College, Durham
The Rev. Peter Nober, Pontificio Instituto Biblico, Rome

The Rev. Dr E. G. O'Collins, S.J., University of Cambridge
The Rev. D. C. Okeke, University of Aberdeen
The Rev. G. E. Okeke, Trinity College, Toronto
The Rev. J. P. C. Okeke, Onitsha, Nigeria
The Rt Rev. T. Olufosoye, Bishop of Ibadan

The Very Rev. G. L. O. Palmer, Dean of St George's Cathedral, Freetown
The Rev. Vincent Parkin, University of Belfast
The Rev. Harold J. Parks, London
Professor Jaroslav Pelikan, Yale University
Professor J. R. C. Perkin, Acadia University, Wolfville, Nova Scotia
Professor Dr Rudolf Pesch, Frankfurt
Professor J. Peterson, Fourah Bay College
The Rev. D. E. Phipps-Jones, Hatfield, Herts
Mr J. Pobee, University of Ghana
Professor Dr Petr Pokorný, c.sc., Prague
The Rev. Professor T. E. Pollard, Knox College, New Zealand
Dr A. T. Porter, Vice-Chancellor, University of Sierra Leone
The Hon. S. A. J. Pratt, Freetown

The Rt Rev. Dr J. A. Ramsbotham, Hexham, Northumberland
The Rt Rev. Ian Ramsey [R.I.P.], late Bishop of Durham
The Rev. Professor J. K. S. Reid, University of Aberdeen
Professor Dr K. H. Rengstorf, Münster
The Rev. Professor John Reumann, Philadelphia
The Rt Rev. J. R. Richards, Aberystwyth, Cards
The Very Rev. Alan Richardson, Dean of York
Professor Harald Riesenfeld, Uppsala
The Rt Rev. D. W. B. Robinson, Moore Theological College, Sydney
The Rev. Canon P. J. Ross, Bishop's Chaplain, Sierra Leone
Professor Dr Eugen Ruckstuhl, Lucerne
The Rev. Dr H. O. Russell, Kingston, Jamaica

Professor Dr Y. Herman Sacon, Tokyo
Professor Martin H. Scharlemann, Concordia Seminary, St Louis
Professor Dr Heinrich Schlier, Bonn
Professor Dr Wilhelm Schneemelcher, Bad Honnef, West Germany
The Rev. Dr B. Schneider, o.f.m., Tokyo
Professor Dr H. Schürmann, Erfurt, East Germany
Professor J. H. Schütz, University of North Carolina
Professor Dr Benedikt Schwank, o.s.b., Beuron, West Germany

The Most Rev. M. N. C. O. Scott, Archbishop of West Africa
Professor Jaak Seynaeve, République de Zaïre
The Rev. Dr S. von Sicard, Selly Oak Colleges, University of
  Birmingham
Sierra Leone Library Board, Freetown
The Rev. Stephen S. Smalley, University of Manchester
Professor Newman D. J. Smart, Fourah Bay College
Professor D. Moody Smith, Duke Divinity School, Durham,
  North Carolina
Professor Josef Smolik, Prague
The Rev. Père C. Spicq, Fribourg, Switzerland
Dr R. Stavig, Kalamazoo College, Kalamazoo, Mich.
Professor Krister Stendahl, Harvard University
The Very Rev. Professor James S. Stewart, Edinburgh
The Rev. Dr William Stewart, Edinburgh
Professor Dr G. Strecker, Göttingen
Professor Dr Peter Stuhlmacher, Tubingen
The Reverend J. P. M. Sweet, University of Cambridge

The Rev. Canon J. V. Taylor, Church Missionary Society,
  London
The Rev. Theophilus M. Taylor, Topsham, Vermont
Professor T. W. Thacker, University of Durham
Dr A. T. Thomas, former Chairman of College Council,
  Fourah Bay College
Professor M. E. K. Thomas, Vice-Principal of Fourah Bay
  College
Mrs S. O. Thompson, Fourah Bay College
Dr M. E. Thrall, University College of North Wales, Bangor
Mr Bankole Timothy, Anglo-American Corporation in London
Dr phil. habil. Kurt Treu, Berlin
The Rev. Fr D. Tutu, Theological Education Fund, London

Professor Dr W. C. van Unnik, Bilthoven, Holland
Dr Johannes Alexander van Wyk, Teologiese Skool, Sovenga,
  South Africa
The Rev. Fr T. Paul Verghese, Orthodox Seminary, Kerala,
  India
The Rev. Dr Lukas Vischer, Geneva

ACKNOWLEDGEMENTS

Thanks are due to the following for permission to quote from copyright sources:

Cambridge University Press: *Oedipus and Job in West African Religion*, by Meyer Fortes

The Clarendon Press, Oxford: *Epicurus, the extant remains*, by Cyril Bailey
Lutterworth Press: *John Venn and the Clapham Sect*, by M. M. Hennell

The Pall Mall Press: *Christianity and the New Africa*, by Beetham

Penguin Books Ltd: *Lucretius on the Nature of the Universe*, translated by R. E. Latham (Penguin Classics 1951), copyright © R. E. Latham 1951

S.C.M. Press Ltd: *The Primal Vision: Christian Presence amid African Religion*, by J. V. Taylor

Sheed and Ward Ltd: *John Wesley in the Evolution of Protestantism*, by Maximien Piette

Thanks are also due for permission to quote from the unpublished 'Christian Theology in Africa' by Donald R. Jacobs, and from the late Bishop T. S. Johnson's manuscript 'Biographical Notes', and for use of material from the archives of the Church Missionary Society.

The Editors wish to thank all those who have helped with the preparation and completion of this volume, in particular the publishing staff of SPCK; Dr Raymond Foster, the Society's editorial director from 1971 to 1973, and a former Chaplain of Fourah Bay College; and Mrs D. King, clerk of the Department of Theology at Fourah Bay, who assisted with the typing.

HARRY SAWYERR'S
PUBLISHED WRITINGS

BOOKS

The Springs of Mende and Conduct. Sierra Leone University Press, Free-town, 1968 (with W. T. Harris).

Creative Evangelism. Lutterworth Press, London, 1968.
God: Ancestor or Creator? Longmans, London, 1970.

ARTICLES

'The African Adventure', *East and West Review*, London, 1948, pp. 110–13.

'Prepositions and Post-positions in the Mende Language', *Sierra Leone Studies* (1957), pp. 209–20.

The Temptations of Jesus, Aureol Pamphlets, no. 1. 1957.

'Was St Paul a Jewish Missionary?', *Church Quarterly Review* (1959), pp. 457–63.

'Sacrificial Rituals in Sierra Leone', *Sierra Leone Bulletin of Religion*, vol. 1, no. 1 (1959), pp. 1–9.

'Traditional Sacrificial Rituals and Christian Worship', *Sierra Leone Bulletin of Religion*, vol. 2, no. 1 (1960), pp. 18–27.

Editor, *Evangelism*, Aureol Pamphlets, no. 2. 1960.

Editor, *Christian Theology in Independent Africa*, Aureol Pamphlets, no. 3 (1961), and contributor of chapter 'Church and State in Independent Africa'.

'The Marcan Framework', *Scottish Journal of Theology*, vol. 14, no. 3 (1961), pp. 279–94.

'Do Africans Believe in God?', *Sierra Leone Studies* (1961), pp.148–67.

'The Supreme God and Spirits', *Sierra Leone Bulletin of Religion*, vol. 3, no. 2 (1961), pp. 41–55.

'The Dogma of Super-Size I', *Sierra Leone Bulletin of Religion*, vol. 4, no. 1 (1962), pp. 41–51.

'The Basis of a Theology for Africa', *International Review of Missions* (1963), pp. 266–78.

'The Dogma of Super-Size II', *Sierra Leone Bulletin of Religion*, vol. 5, no. 1 (1963), pp. 1–18.

Christian Stewardship, Aureol Pamphlets, no. 4. 1963.

'The University and the Sixth Form in West Africa', *Journal of West African Education* (1963), pp. 159–62.

'Science and Superstition', *Sierra Leone Science Association Bulletin*, vol. 1, no. 2 (1963), pp. 17–26.

'Disɔŋ: A Kroo Rite', in association with A. W. Sawyerr, *Sierra Leone Bulletin of Religion*, vol. 5, no. 2 (1963), pp. 47–54.

'Sin and Forgiveness in Africa', *Frontier* (1964), pp. 60–3.

'Ancestor Worship I: The Mechanics', *Sierra Leone Bulletin of Religion*, vol. 6, no. 2 (1964), pp. 25–33.

'Christian Evangelistic Strategy in West Africa', *International Review of Missions* (1965), pp. 343–52.

'Sierra Leone's Marriage Laws Amendment Acts 1965', *Sierra Leone Bulletin of Religion*, vol. 7, no. 1 (1965), pp. 22–7.

'The Sense of Concreteness in Yoruba Worship', *Sierra Leone Bulletin of Religion*, vol. 7, no. 1 (1965), pp. 13–22 (with T. F. Fabiyi).

'Graveside Libations in and near Freetown', *Sierra Leone Bulletin of Religion*, vol. 7, no. 2 (1965), pp. 48–55.

'Grundlagen einer Theologie für Afrika', *Theologische Stimmen aus Asien, Afrika und Lateinamerika*, Band I, ed. Gensichen, 1965 (German version of 'The Basis of a Theology for Africa', 1963).

'Is Universal Education a Christian Conception?', *Studies in Education*, ed. Marjorie Reeves (Geneva 1966), pp. 54–67.

'The Role of a University of Sierra Leone—a Projection', *Sierra Leone Journal of Education*, vol. 1, no. 2 (1966), pp. 11–16.

'Ancestor Worship II: The Rationale', *Sierra Leone Bulletin of Religion*, vol. 8, no. 2 (1966), pp. 33–9.

'More Graveside Libations in and around Freetown', *Sierra Leone Bulletin of Religion*, vol. 8, no. 2 (1966), pp. 57–9.

'Confessing the Faith Today: The Witnessing Scene—Africa' (John R. Mott Lecture, Hong Kong, October 1966), *South-East Asia Journal of Theology* (1967), pp. 71–88.

Fondements d'une Théologie pour l'Afrique', *Flambeau* (1967), pp. 194–207 (French version of 'The Basis of a Theology for Africa', 1963).

'Two Short Libations', *Sierra Leone Bulletin of Religion*, vol. 9, no. 1 (1967), pp. 34–7.

'A Sunday Graveside Libation in Freetown, after a Bereavement', *Sierra Leone Bulletin of Religion*, vol. 9, no. 2 (1967), pp. 41–55.

'ŋgewɔ and ŋgawu: An Essay in detection of the origins of the Mende concept of God', *Sierra Leone Bulletin of Religion*, vol. 9, no. 2 (1967), pp. 66–73.

'The Practice of Presence', *Numen*, vol. XV, Fasc. 2 (1968), pp. 142–61.

'The University in Contemporary Independent West Africa I: Cloister or Market Place?', *West African Journal of Education*, vol. 12, no. 3 (1968), pp. 191–5.

'The University in Contemporary Independent West Africa II: Caveats', *West African Journal of Education*, vol. 13, no. 1 (1969), pp. 28–32.

'Sacrifice', *Biblical Revelation and Traditional Beliefs*, ed. K. A. Dickson and P. Ellingworth (London 1969), pp. 57–82.

'Le Sacrifice' (French version of the preceding), C. L. E. Yaounde 1968.

'Theological Faculty Conference for Africa: A Personal Comment', *Africa Theological Journal*, no. 3 (Makumira, Tanzania, 1970), pp. 11–16.

'Ancestor or Creator God?', *Présence Africaine* (Paris 1970), pp. 111–27 (also in Report of Second International Africanists Congress, Dakar 1967, pp. 283–300).

'The Significance of the Western Education Experience for Africa', *West African Journal of Education*, vol. 15, no. 1 (1971), pp. 45–9.

'What is African Theology?', *Africa Theological Journal*, no. 4 (Makumira, Tanzania 1971), pp. 7–24.

'Education for Adjustment', *Report of Conference on National Education in Sierra Leone* (Extra Mural Department Publication, Fourah Bay College).

'The Significance of the Numbers Three and Four among the Mende', *Sierra Leone Studies*, vol. 26 (1972), pp. 29–33 (with S. K. Todd).

'Salvation Viewed from the African Situation', *Présence* (World Student Christian Federation, Nairobi 1972), pp. 16–23.

'Persons in Relationship', *Présence Africaine* (Paris 1972), pp. 189–204.

'The African Concept of Death', *A New Look at Christianity* (World Student Christian Federation, Geneva 1972), pp. 22–34.

'Creating the African University', in two parts, *Sierra Leone Journal of Education*, vol. 7, no. 2 (1972), pp. 43–51; vol. 8, no. 1 (1973), pp. 31–6.

Editor, *Sierra Leone Bulletin of Religion*, 1962–8.

General Editor, Aureol Pamphlets, from 1960.

An Appreciation

MICHAEL RAMSEY
Archbishop of Canterbury 1961–74

I first knew Harry Sawyerr when he came to Durham to read for the Honours School of Theology in the 1940s. He quickly made it plain that he had a lively mind, a good grasp of theological significance, and a keen sense of humour which gave its own delight to intellectual collaboration. He and his wife Edith radiated happiness amongst a wide circle of friends. Harry gave much to Durham and helped Durham to give what it could to him for the service of West Africa.

As a student he responded to the traditions of accurate scholarship and linguistic concern which Durham has always maintained. He had also a sense of history which enabled him to discuss problems in a wide perspective, and while his teachers and fellow-students knew only the English and European scenes he made no secret of the fact that he was glancing all the time at the meaning of it all for African people and culture. When he returned to Fourah Bay and set out on his long career of teaching and writing, it became fascinating to watch, in the subjects on which he wrote, the interplay of the Durham and the West African interests. He knows that Christianity is greater and more widespread than any of its cultural forms, and it is this which makes his work lively and creative.

Harry Sawyerr's writings, in biblical scholarship, in educational strategy, and in African interpretation of theology, are a remarkable testimony to a mind which retains scholarly activity amidst all the pressures of a teacher and administrator. But his loving care for persons and his interest in affairs are such that he would not have been happy in the role of a pure academic. So, scholar, writer, and teacher as he is, he has gone from strength to strength in educational leadership—as Fourah

Bay College became the University College and the University College became the University and the Principal became the Vice-Chancellor. It is fortunate, I am sure, for Sierra Leone that in the transition from what was once a little missionary college near the edge of the water to the comprehensive academic institution on the top of the hill there was on the scene one who, like Harry Sawyerr, understands the historic past of Christianity in his country as well as the immense opportunities of the future.

This volume is a tribute of admiration and gratitude from friends, colleagues, and fellow-workers. It reflects something of Harry Sawyerr's own range of interests, and by winning many readers it will serve the causes of learning and religion to which his life has been devoted.

Introduction

MARK E. GLASSWELL
E. W. FASHOLÉ-LUKE

The idea of a volume of essays in honour of Harry Sawyerr goes back to the awareness that he had effectively ceased to be in charge of the Department of Theology at Fourah Bay College in 1968, when he became Principal of the College, and that he had reached his sixtieth birthday the following year. The award of an honorary D.D. by the University of Durham, his beloved Alma Mater, came as a fitting tribute in 1970 and marked a lifetime's service already to Fourah Bay College and the newly established University of Sierra Leone in general, and the Department of Theology in particular. Yet Harry Sawyerr moved on to further service to Higher Education in Sierra Leone, not only as Principal of Fourah Bay College till 1974, but as Vice-Chancellor of the University of Sierra Leone from 1970–72. It was, however, to mark what he had already achieved in terms of theology as distinct from what he might still achieve in terms of university administration that the idea of a theological tribute came some years ago to the present Editors, as well as to the Reverend Matei Markwei, to whom this Festschrift owes much. As soon as the idea was put to likely contributors it began quickly to grow into a reality. The names of the distinguished contributors to the Festschrift as well as those of the many who have had their names included in the *Tabula Gratulantium* indicate both what a happy conception the Festschrift to Harry Sawyerr was, and also the high esteem which both scholars and ecclesiastical leaders around the world had for him. It is also notable as being the first in honour of an African theologian.

Harry Alphonso Ebun Sawyerr was born on 16 October 1909 and spent part of his boyhood at Boma Sakrim, deep in the heart of Mende country, where his father, the Reverend O. A. D. Sawyerr, served as a missionary and pastor. It is to this background that Harry Sawyerr owes his deep knowledge of Mende language, religion, and culture, as well as his sympathy with, and understanding of, traditional African religious thought and practice *vis-à-vis* Christianity. He has never lost contact with this background, even though he went to school in Freetown and did his undergraduate work at Fourah Bay College. Evidence of this can be seen in his three books: *Creative Evangelism, God: Ancestor or Creator?*, and *Springs of Mende Belief and Conduct*, as well as in the numerous articles that he has published in local and international Journals.

After completing his studies at Fourah Bay College, then affiliated to the University of Durham, and spending some time on the staff of the College as Tutor, as well as obtaining the M.A. and M.ED. degrees of the University of Durham, he proceeded to Durham in 1945 to study theology at St John's College, and this association with Durham at first hand was a mile-stone in his life. From 1948, and since 1962 as Professor of Theology, he devoted his life to theological study and teaching, with a view particularly to its relevance to the African setting he knew so well, against the background of world-wide Christianity. He has therefore not only taken a leading role in local church affairs, but also, as a member since 1962 of the World Council of Churches Commission on Faith and Order and in the following year as a member of its working Committee, he has played a distinctive role in the affairs of world Christianity. Harry Sawyerr has also travelled widely to attend conferences and to give lectures in connection with his theological and educational interests, as well as carrying a heavy load, until very recently, in the day-to-day lecturing and administration in his own College. His enthusiasm for hard work, in which he does not spare himself, has benefited also many of his students, and his friendly and cheerful disposition has encouraged countless numbers who have come into contact with him. But he has never been afraid of controversy where he felt himself to be and most often proved himself to be in the right, and when issues of principle were at stake. What his exertions have cost him he never shows, and he is never too busy to deal with the personal problems of any person seeking his guidance and help. In all he has been upheld domestically by the strength of an equally active and amiable wife.

Because of Harry Sawyerr's first prize in the Thomas Cochrane Essay Competition for West Africa (British and French) in 1960 for an essay entitled 'How can the Church in Africa be both African and yet world-wide', the theme of these essays was obvious. But the varied subjects show how many facets come into the issue with regard to the concerns and interests of Harry Sawyerr. He is a long-standing and respected member of the *Studiorum Novi Testamenti Societas*, and was at one time a regular attender at its meetings, and several essays in this Festschrift centre on the New Testament, which he interpreted for many generations of African students, with special attention to St Mark's Gospel and Pauline theology. But his whole approach to evangelism and theology has been based on the Scriptures and a revelation going back to Hebrew and Jewish religious concepts of the Old Testament. So an essay on 'The Inspiration of Scripture' is a fitting beginning. However, the fact that he found in the concept of sacrifice a significant point of contact for linking the African religious experience with biblical revelation and the Christian gospel, demanded the inclusion of a second essay on 'The Anatomy of Sacrifice', written by one of his pupils, as an examination of one of his cherished beliefs that in the concept of sacrifice we have a bridge between African traditional beliefs and the heart of the Christian message. This is the point of his High Anglican liturgical approach.

The christological basis of the gospel and its suitability to all nations, including African ones, are obvious truths, but they need constant reaffirmation and they ought to be expounded anew for each generation. Harry Sawyerr's faithfulness to the message of the universality of the gospel centred on Jesus Christ is notable and acknowledged by several contributions by leading British and European New Testament scholars. But also his love of the intricacies of Pauline theology is fully attested, not only in terms of Paul's own conceptions at the time (see the contributions of C. F. D. Moule and C. E. B. Cranfield) but also in terms of modern understanding of its tenets in new situations (see the contribution of H. E. W. Turner). In all this, Durham and Fourah Bay College, a former outpost of that University, are at one, even in the persons of some of the contributors. Thus Durham as a point of contact for the meeting of minds on theological issues has been true of Africa in the person of Harry Sawyerr as it had been of Erasmus. A former successor of the earlier Prince Bishops in the person of the present Archbishop of Canterbury thus fittingly graces this Festschrift with a personal appreciation of the work of a former pupil.

In terms too of the missionary situation in which Harry Sawyerr was brought up from earliest childhood it is still *Ecclesia Anglicana* which provides a link, as much at home, in the person of Harry Sawyerr, in West Africa, from Boma Sakrim to St George's Cathedral, Freetown, where Harry Sawyerr has been a Canon since 1961, as in North-Eastern England. It is therefore right to recognize how all this came about as the contributions of Max Warren and Andrew Walls, a former colleague of Harry Sawyerr at Fourah Bay College, remind us, as well as to consider why it had not occurred earlier with regard to the famous North African Church, as does the contribution of another former colleague, Ieuan Ellis. The active presence of a rival force and another religious influence, that of Islam, is also rightly seen as relevant to the situation in which the African Christian theologian must work and which provides him with his point of reference in Christian and world history as well as in African history. This Noel King's contribution provides. Harry Sawyerr has always been conscious of all these factors while remaining faithful to all the influences which have contributed to his own theological development, including the influence of the local Assistant Bishop, T. S. Johnson, who is the subject of Matei Markwei's contribution.

Harry Sawyerr has also of course sought to exercise a positive influence of his own on the local church, by training most of its present clergy and ministers, including the present Archbishop of West Africa. The regular Easter Vacation Course for clergy and ministers and the continuation of the Licence in Divinity Course, mainly for ordinands, are two witnesses to his concern in this direction, and he has never envisaged the Department of Theology in isolation from the needs of the Church, as a means whereby future clergy can mix both socially and intellectually with those destined for secular callings, and thus have a fuller appreciation of the world outside the Church. His attempts to relate University and Church are not always appreciated or understood but they witness to a genuine and real concern for the good of both. He has at the same time never disparaged the simple faith or contribution of those not so well endowed academically or intellectually and has sought to fit them in, so that they may have a broader vision for themselves, and also to spread the perspective of the training programme itself. Harry Sawyerr's idea of the central role of the Theology Department in this may at times be disputed, but no one can doubt that he has brought it and the Church into fruitful relation and dialogue, overcoming in the process some unwillingness at times. All this fits with his concern for Christian Education in the fullest and widest sense, and it is one which will affect future development for some time to come, not least through his former pupils, whatever changes may follow. Amidst his many duties he has found time as Examining Chaplain to the Bishop of Sierra Leone to interview candidates for Holy Orders and to mark their work.

But ultimately, it is to the question of the African contribution to theology that Harry Sawyerr has led the way, as the proper response to all that has gone before elsewhere, so that two streams can meet and flow together. The advantages of this for those of other backgrounds are fittingly depicted by Harold Turner, another former colleague; and a representative of another West African situation, Kwesi Dickson of Ghana, reinforces the necessity of this for the further development of Christianity to the benefit of Africans. It is left to one of the Editors, a former pupil of Harry Sawyerr, to show how in one instance a traditional Christian doctrine, fully affirmed and developed, can be the framework for the African's rediscovery of his own traditional beliefs in a Christian setting, and indeed in Christ, which will benefit not only the African Church, but the world-wide Church. Thus two streams can be seen as compatible and their future merging can be envisaged to the mutual strengthening of African and universal Christianity, each yet remaining authentic as well.

May Harry Sawyerr's vision indeed become a full reality and it is our humble hope that this Festschrift will be a small contribution to that end and therefore a fitting tribute to the man whose name it bears.

The Inspiration of Scripture

D. R. JONES

It is convenient to speak of a *mythological* idea of inspiration both in the Old Testament and in Greek thought, despite continuing lack of precision in the use of the term myth. The term is used here in the sense of an extended symbolism which interprets universal truths or experiences of this world in terms of personal divine actions. This is itself an extension of the myth which tells of events at the origin of the universe. This kind of personalized explanation of empirical phenomena furnishes the oldest description of prophetic inspiration before it has become subject to theological refinement. The phenomenon with which we are concerned is that of the religious man who believes he is sent by God to speak God's word. He believes that his message and the expression of it is given to him in thought or vision or word. The phenomenon of an external constraint is to be found in classes of men in other religions with sufficient frequency to suggest that it is a characteristic of human society that such men shall appear here and there, now and then, like the poet or artist or musician. The poet or the artist or musician appears perhaps more often and consistently. But though the *content* and object of their sensitivity is different, there is similarity in the psychological description of this sensitivity. It is no accident that the term inspiration is widely used of poets who compose out of a mysterious sense of compulsion, and whose sensitivity relates not only to the content of their composition but also to the expression of it in words.

The purpose of this essay is to examine the idea of inspiration as it is received and modified in the Old Testament, with the aim of distinguishing between careful theological description and intuitive mythological description of a phenomenon of religion. The mythological idea may be discerned within the Old Testament in the story of Saul's encounter with a company of prophets (1 Sam. 10). 'The spirit of God suddenly took possession of him, and he prophesied among them.' No doubt we are to understand that Saul was subject to a kind of ecstasy or prophetic rapture. The explanation of this in terms of group psychology is of course modern. The old idea was that the spirit responsible for the behaviour of the prophets also took hold of Saul and turned him into another man. The association of the coming of the spirit with gifts of prophecy remains close despite the paucity of references. Balaam uttered his oracle when 'the spirit of God came upon him' (Num. 24.2). Hos. 9.7 refers to a prophet as an אִישׁ הרוח, not inaccurately translated in NEB as 'inspired seer' after LXX ἄνθρωπος ὁ πνευματόφορος. Micah claims to be 'filled with the Spirit of the Lord' (3.8). (If this is a gloss, the gloss still significantly illustrates the conception. I believe with Lindblom that the text may stand.) There may well be a rare allusion to this work of the spirit in Jer. 4.11, if the passage is translated:

> The spirit has come to me in fulness;
> now I will speak to them of judgement.

Isa. 48.16 is perhaps too doubtful a passage to illustrate the thought of 2 Isaiah. But a later prophet of the same school is explicit:

> The spirit of the Lord God is upon me
> because the Lord has anointed me (61.1).

cf. also the close association of spirit and word in 59.21:

> My spirit which is upon you, and my words which I have put in your mouth, shall not depart out of your mouth.

Ezekiel attributes his message to spirit possession in 11.5,24 and 37.1. Zechariah explains degenerate or false prophecy as due to possession by unclean spirits. But perhaps most eloquent of what came to be the accepted view is the eschatological conception of Joel 2.28. In the age to come the Lord will pour out his spirit on all flesh so that the prophecy now confined to the few will become a universal possession. This idea is reflected in a different way in the narrative of Num. 11 which incidentally shows the high value put by Israel on prophetic ecstasy. 'Would that all the Lord's people were prophets, that the Lord would put his spirit upon them!' In the Old Testament the activity of the spirit is stressed at the beginnings of prophecy and in the eschatological hope. With the major prophets it is undeniably muted. There is nothing in Amos, 1 and 2 Isaiah; there are disputed passages or passages of ambiguous interpretation in Hosea and Jeremiah; but there are enough references to show that the idea was alive, and to raise the question why the prophets are so little concerned to refer to the activity of the spirit as a primary factor in their prophetic experience. To this question Lindblom answered, because their thought was essentially theocentric. This answer is inadequate. It is highly doubtful whether any of the prophets would have set the activity of the spirit *against* that of the Lord; and the period of most marked theocentricity led to an emphasis on intermediaries and periphrases for God. The question remains unanswered.

A similar problem arises in the New Testament, as Professor C. K. Barrett showed in his book *The Holy Spirit and the Gospel Tradition* (London 1947). St Luke clearly understands the appearance of the Christ to be attended by manifest signs of the spirit. The birth narratives abound with references to the spirit. The phenomenon of spirit possession follows upon Pentecost (Acts 2) which restored the lost gift of prophecy as a charisma upon the Church (Acts 11.28; 13.1–2; 15.32; 19.6; 1 Cor. 12.28; 14.2ff, 32; Eph. 3.5; 4.11; 1 Tim. 4.1; 1 Thess. 5.19). The gift, however, was not universal. Pentecost was the sign of the end, not the end itself. There were those who undervalued the gifts of the spirit and were prepared to 'stifle inspiration' (1 Thess. 5.19). On the other hand, St Paul found it necessary also to lay down the principle that 'it is for prophets to control prophetic inspiration' (1 Cor. 14.32). The emergence of the Church and the reawakening of prophecy was accompanied by spirit-activity, as the birth of Old Testament prophecy was attended by phenomena of the spirit. But in the life and teaching of Jesus there is little or nothing. Jesus seems not to have envisaged a community thus endowed with the

spirit. No undisputed sayings point to such a gift. Dr Barrett's
own explanation is that the silence of Jesus was self-imposed,
like the secret of his Messiahship. It was necessary for him,
as for the prophets, to avoid confusion with ecstatic and non-
moral prophets; but primarily silence was necessary because
the expectation of Messiah involved the expectation of gifts
of the spirit. In him the indwelling spirit was *veiled* and it was
part of his vocation of poverty to live with the absence of signs
of the spirit.

This explanation is of course hypothetical. It may, however,
be possible to formulate the answer more fully by means of the
modern distinction between the mythological and the theological. Much of the language is capable of either a mythological
or a theological interpretation, and assuredly it was underlying
mythological assumption which encouraged the more extreme
theories of both personal and verbal inspiration. Already in the
Bible itself there is evidence that the language of inspiration
was carefully controlled in a number of ways so that it might
become the vehicle of serious theological affirmation.

1. It is controlled by the phenomenon of which it is the
description. Conspicuously we see this in the major prophets
and in Jesus. It is thus implicitly recognized that the language
of inspiration is symbolic, that the language does not necessarily
do justice to the experience, and, unqualified, may distort the
experience. *By not using* the language of inspiration at crucial
points, the Bible thus declares that this language is relative,
that the language must be determined by the reality and not
allowed, so to speak, to have an independent and unearthed
life of its own. It is the sheer authenticity of the life of the
prophets and of Jesus which renders claim to spirit possession
unnecessary and misleading.

2. It is controlled by the substitution of other language for
the same phenomenon. Thus, for example, the Old Testament
speaks of the effect of the Lord's *hand* upon the prophets and
there is no discernible difference between the significance of
the hand and of the spirit. (1 Kings 18.46; 2 Kings 3.15; Isa.
8.11; Ezek. 1.3; 3.14,22; 8.1; 33.21f; 37.1.) Ezekiel who
refers more than any other prophet to spirit-phenomena also
refers more than any other prophet to the hand of the Lord as a

synonym of his spirit. The symbolic nature of the language is
thus drawn out.

3. It is controlled by shifting attention from the psychological
state (ecstasy, etc.) to communication. The prophet is primarily
a messenger with a message, not primarily a spirit-phenomenon
requiring interpretation. Therefore, although the initiative may
be said to be that of the spirit of the Lord, it may equally be
said to be the word or the wisdom of the Lord.

4. It is controlled by the extension of the use of the word
spirit, so that the idea of spirit-possession becomes secondary.
Thus רוח, while retaining its basic meaning 'wind' or 'breath',
came to be used as a synonym of נשמה indicating the principle
of life which man shares with the animal world, and without
which he has no vitality or existence; also of a disposition or
mood; or of the skill of a craftsman. On the other hand, the
word רוח lent itself to a theological usage which may be summed up under the title 'creator spirit'. I do not myself doubt
that in Gen. 1.2 רוח אלהים is to be translated 'spirit of God', not
'mighty wind' as is favoured by NEB. The idea of the activity
of God in creation by his spirit is found in Pss. 33.6 (parallel
with 'word'); 104.30, and is implicit in the breathing of God, by
which he gave man 'the breath of life' and so made him a
'living soul' (Gen. 2.7). The association of spirit with the
creative wisdom of God is explicit in Wisd. 7 and with the
re-creation of God's people in Ezek. 37. Thus the spirit of God
was understood to be the crucial factor in both the creation and
the renewal of the world. The silence of the major prophets in
respect of the idea of spirit possession, together with this
determinative development of usage amounts to a theological
reinterpretation of far-reaching importance. When we ask what
the term inspiration means, we may answer that the biblical
usage only onesidedly and therefore erroneously supports the
mythological idea of spirit possession, but taken as a whole
suggests a cluster of ideas and conceptions. It is, on the other
hand, more than a single abstract notion. It is an image,
suggesting: (i) a breath-like activity, all pervasive, coming from
without; (ii) an experience of givenness, of exposure to a
divine initiative; (iii) creativity; (iv) the divine will to renew
the earth and the life of man; (v) (by association) the word of

God as the creative source of all things. The unique value and power of an image is that it can hold together a number of ideas that otherwise fall apart when handled abstractly. Ezra Pound defined the image as 'that which presents an intellectual and emotional complex in an instant of time'. Such is the value of the theologically refined idea of inspiration.

When we turn to the related question of the inspiration of Scripture, it would seem that mythological views have exercised undue influence, and are largely responsible for dictation theories of inspiration. The *Oxford English Dictionary* gives one of the definitions of inspiration as follows: 'a special immediate action or influence of the Spirit of God (or of some divine or supernatural being) upon the human mind or soul: said especially of that divine influence under which the books of the Bible are said to have been written'. Verbal inspiration is further defined as 'the view, according to which every word written was dictated by the Spirit of God'.

Within Scripture itself the *locus classicus* is 2 Tim. 3.16, rendered in the AV 'all Scripture is given by inspiration of God' (πᾶσα γραφὴ Θεόπνευστος—Vulg. 'divinitus inspirata'). In this form it is quoted in the dogmatic constitution on divine revelation of Vatican II. The word Θεόπνευστος is first applied to the New Testament as a whole by Clement, and after him by Origen and Eusebius. But this phrase, as H. B. Swete pointed out many years ago, thus translated supports too dogmatic a conclusion. Largely responsible for the use of the word inspiration among English speaking Christians, it is probably more correctly translated in NEB as: 'Every inspired Scripture has its use for teaching the truth and refuting error, or for reformation of manners and discipline in right living.' The writer's purpose is not to assert the nature of inspiration or to assert that Scripture is free of error or even that all Scripture is inspired, but to teach for what ends the Scriptures were given. Scripture itself, therefore, gives no support to mythological extravagance in the interpretation of the inspiration of the text. The thrust of Scripture is in the direction of the theological refinement we have tried to expound.

Nevertheless mythological tendencies had a continuing history. Direct spirit possession hardly allows for the distortions

of human mediation. Where therefore the idea of spirit possession prevailed, there also dictation theories arose. Such is the
implication of the tale told in 2 Esdras 14 of the inspiration of
Ezra. Ezra's memory was supernaturally perfected by a potion
which seemed like water but had the colour of fire. He was thus
enabled to recite the known Scriptures which were to be
published openly, plus seventy other books to be committed in
secret to the wise. Five scribes were given special understanding
to write down by turns what Ezra recited, even using characters
otherwise unknown to them. A similar tale was told of the LXX,
beginning with the comparatively modest account in the
Letter of Aristeas, where the translators are trained scholars who
agree upon a final text after mutual consultation. But for
Philo the translators are supernaturally protected from error
and the LXX is due not to the human mind but to the direct
intervention of God. Their work was done 'under inspiration'.
For Irenaeus the separation of the seventy translators, yet
producing identical translations, is proof to the heathen that
the Scriptures were translated through the inspiration of God.
Augustine makes use of the same story, remarking that there
was no word of difference because 'there was but one spirit
in them all'.

These stories register a certain kind of approach to the sacred
writings. The character of Scripture as authoritative divine
writings is guaranteed by the immediacy of inspiration obviat-
ing all human refraction of divine truth. What was believed
about translation was believed *a fortiori* about the original
composition of the Scriptures. Philo's notion that a sacred
author was subject to an ecstasy which was the source of
inspiration making him 'a sounding instrument of God,
invisibly played and struck by him', was taken up by the second-
century Athenagoras who thought the Holy Spirit moved the
mouth of the prophets as his own, 'taking away their own
thoughts and playing upon them as a flautist plays upon a
flute'. Augustine was apparently the first to speak explicitly
of dictation: 'the members put down what they know at the
dictation of the Head'. Gregory the Great minimized the function of the authors. They wrote simply as the pen of the Holy
Spirit.

The language of dictation is persistent in Christian theology, even where the more far-fetched mythological accompaniments would be repudiated. We need not trace it in its less objectionable form in the Reformers; in its more extreme forms in Protestant scholasticism or in Roman Catholic definitions up to and including Vatican II. This language is permissible only when it is understood as one analogy among others, requiring corrective. It is safe when it is understood not as cold empirical description from which conclusions may be logically deduced, but as part of a mythology which is as appropriate to poets as it is to prophets. William Blake said: 'I have written this poem from immediate dictation, twelve or sometimes twenty or thirty lines at a time without premeditation and even against my will.' Goethe said: 'The songs made me, not I them: the songs had me in their power.' Dickens said on one occasion when he sat down to his book: 'Some beneficent power showed it all to me.' W. B. Yeats affirmed: 'The poet becomes, as all the great mystics have believed, a vessel of the creative power of God.' A critic wrote of T. S. Eliot: 'His nervous sensibility secretes poetry as infallibly and as automatically as an oyster secretes pearls.' Perhaps most revealing of all is the witness of the agnostic Nietzsche:

> If one had the slightest trace of superstition left in one, it would be hardly possible to set aside the idea that one is the incarnation, mouthpiece and medium of almighty powers. The idea of revelation, in the sense that something suddenly and with unspeakable certainty and purity becomes *visible*, audible . . . simply describes the fact.

The language of inspiration in its most extravagant forms describes not a unique biblical experience but a widespread human phenomenon, and this includes the idea of inspiration as applied to a text.

A satisfactory approach to the inspiration of the text must fulfil three conditions:

1. It must be wholly consistent with the *active* idea of inspiration contained in Scripture. This we have seen to involve a constellation of ideas which make a unity. It is destructive of this idea to isolate the text for separate concentration, as is done by dictation and infallibalist theories. The result, as Karl

Barth saw, is to substitute for the active concept an essentially
passive one, that is to say, the concept not of inspiration but of
inspiredness. The main function of inspiration is thus understood
to be the production of a holy γράμμα. The inspiredness of the
text is identified in separation from the total self-disclosure of the
mystery of God, in which the written text is only a part, even
if it be an important part. As Barth expressed it, 'this is to
transform the statement that the Bible is the Word of God from
a statement about the free grace of God into a statement about
the nature of the Bible as exposed to human enquiry'. The
active idea of inspiration is implicit in the cluster of meanings
which the image of inspiration attracts to itself—pervasiveness,
the divine initiative and givenness, creativity, the divine will
to renew the life of man, its closeness to the idea of the word.
It becomes explicit in the thought of St Paul. For him the
Scriptures are essentially witness to the living God who has
disclosed himself in Jesus Christ. The Scriptures are understood
only in so far as the spirit reveals their truth. The same spirit
who created the witness bears witness to its truth. 'This self-
disclosure in its totality is the Θεοπνευστία'. It is by the same
inspiration that we ourselves are enabled to recognize the truth
of the biblical witness. 'There exists an exact correspondence
between the certainty with which the word of the apostles and
prophets was the Word of God in itself or for them, and the
certainty with which it as such illumines us' (Barth). The line
of inspiration is not complete until faith is evoked by the word
in the believer. The word begins with God and ends with us,
and in the centre is the text. This is in both senses of the word a
moving view of inspiration.

2.   It must be wholly consistent with the phenomenon to
which it relates. Unqualified mythological pictures and
scholastic theories are fatally undermined by the critical and
historical investigation of Scripture. The concept of a holy and
error-free text dictated by the spirit is simply not verified by
examination. Thus understood it ought to be capable of neutral
verification in the hands of men. But whatever else the critical
and historical investigation of Scripture has achieved, it has
demonstrated in every part the human character of the witnesses
and the human character of their work. We now see the Bible

in its setting of history, we distinguish between myth and history, between events and interpretation, between *ipsissima verba* and traditional and conventional attributions. We assume that every man who spoke spoke sense to his contemporaries, not conundrums intelligible only to later centuries. We more and more discover the actual and living conditions of Israelite and Palestinian life, the forms of speech, the presuppositions of thought, the cosmogony, the psychology, the sociology, the realities of existence. All our study is based on the assumption and *increasingly makes sense on the assumption* that everywhere we are presented with the words of men. They are not objectively divine words, nor are some words more divine than others, nor are divine words to be found in a kernel to be distinguished from a dispensable shell. They are all through and through human words. Our understanding of the pervasive character of inspiration together with its active function embracing the total self-disclosure of God to man will not however permit us to set the word of God over against the word of man in opposition. As we confront the utterly human words, which register the way in which God disclosed himself to appropriately sensitive witnesses, it is possible that by the spirit which moves from God through the text to ourselves, the word of *God* may be heard. The empirical phenomenon is the sensitivity of the witnesses to the content of their witness.

3. A viable idea of inspiration must take account of the reciprocity between language and reality. The reality confronting us in the Scriptures is the Eternal God, expressing himself and his will in *this* language, *this* 'fate-laden' language tradition. The word of God to Israel and in Jesus Christ was creative of a new language tradition, and through it is our access to the reality. The poet is sensitive to his sensual experience and to words. So also is the prophet sensitive to the spiritual reality and to the verbal expression of it. Form and content are inseparable. The inspiration of the Bible rests, as Barth says, 'on the relationship of the biblical witnesses to the very definite content of their witness'. Thus, if it is an error to isolate the Scriptures as an objective holy text in terms of inspiredness, it is equally an error to locate inspiration in the witnesses and regard their language as neutral. While, therefore,

it is improper to think of inspiration as meaning that every word is dictated by the spirit of God, nevertheless the idea of *verbal inspiration* is indispensable as pointing to the place of the text in the total, active process of inspiration, and the role of the language tradition in the communication of the word of God.

The Anatomy of Sacrifice
A Preliminary Investigation

P. E. S. THOMPSON

There is already a good deal of literature on the subject of sacrifice both in ancient Israel and among the so-called primitive peoples of the world. The purpose of the present paper is not to suggest any outstandingly new insights but to present evidence which would seem to demand a fresh examination of the subject. It may be that our preliminary investigation would in fact fail to establish a case for re-examination of the subject; but nothing would have been lost in the process. Rather we would hope that the very failure of this attempt would suggest further lines of inquiry along which the subject may be more fruitfully explored leading to more assured results.

One of the theses that Canon Sawyerr has consistently argued concerns the importance of the sacrificial practices of African peoples as a reliable bridge leading from traditional religious practice to the heart of the Christian message. It is the 'open sesame' of the heart of the African to Christian teaching.[1] At the end of this essay, after a penetrating examination of the concepts and ideas associated with the offering of sacrifice in West Africa, he asserts: 'The Christian theologian studying sacrifice in West Africa has the task of finding out the areas in which placation occurs, and those in which *wiping out* a stain does occur in order to present the gospel in a way that can evoke a healthy meaning of the *hilasterion* concept to his audience.'[2]

No one would question the importance of this assertion but there are many large assumptions behind it which need to be carefully examined. To begin with, there seems to be one important difference between the West African rites that Canon Sawyerr discusses and the sacrificial rites mentioned in the Old Testament. Broadly stated it may be put thus: while most of the African rites seem to have a forward-looking reference in so far as they are designed to influence the course of events in the future, those which are mentioned in the Old Testament seem to be retrospective in their main inspiration. That is, the Old Testament sacrifices do not seem primarily to have been offered in order to secure certain benefits in the *future* which was still regarded as indeterminate. They all seem to have reference to an event in the immediate past which is either being acknowledged in thanksgiving or in repentance. We shall elaborate this later on. But for the moment it will suffice to mention the rites discussed on pp. 58–60 in the article mentioned in substantiation of our argument. It is not our contention that these rites in particular comprehend all the sacrificial rites of African peoples: it is simply that they possess a characteristic which seems to find no counterpart in Old Testament sacrifices.

It also seems relevant to pose a further question. How far is it justifiable to compare the significance of the rite of circumcision as practised among African peoples with the same rite as observed among the ancient Israelites? Our argument here is that circumcision from the evidence of the Old Testament seems to have been an *alternative sign* of belonging to the people of God. It came to have great significance later on, but as far as our evidence goes it was not the principal means of being integrated into the people of God. This honour belonged to the Covenant ceremony on Mount Sinai which so far as the records go does not seem to have involved any kind of sacrifice. Circumcision rites may indeed involve some sort of covenant among African peoples, but one can hardly place it in the same context as the Mosaic Covenant on Mount Sinai. The comparison can at best be only formal and superficial.

We pass now to further questions regarding the nature of sacrifice which seem to be important for any discussion of the varied and multifarious rites included by the term. There is no doubt that among the ancient Israelites various attitudes prevailed at different times to the institution of sacrifice-attitudes which can be paralleled among contemporary surrounding peoples and even among the so-called primitive peoples of the modern world. It is equally certain that in ancient Israel unique developments took place within the institution of sacrifice which cannot be paralleled elsewhere.

Why did this happen in Israel and not elsewhere? It would be obvious that this is a very important question which should be answered before we can proceed to build any acceptable bridge between sacrificial rites as observed among African people for instance, and those which we find in the Old Testament. There seems to be a significant problem here. No one who studies the evidence can fail to detect a significant difference of emphasis between the sacrificial cultus of Judaism and the development which led to the conception of Jesus' life and death as a sacrifice, which can produce a statement such as we find in Rom. 12.1. All we are here claiming is that an institution which is widely attested throughout the world was differently developed in various places, and even within the same cultural context led to two widely differing conceptions of the institution. In the one case we have an accentuation and indeed proliferation of sacrifices, and in the other we have the abrogation of sacrifice which paradoxically maintains the all-sufficiency of the one perfect sacrifice, oblation, and satisfaction of the cross. Why? It is the aim of this preliminary investigation to suggest evidence which points to a different approach which may help in framing an answer to these perplexing questions.

We begin first with some methodological considerations. It is widely accepted, for instance, that the sacrificial regulations contained in the Old Testament are a faithful reflection of the practice observed in the Second Temple. Even if we accept that this is based on ancient material, the question naturally arises as to how far this late evidence may be adduced in reconstructing pre-exilic Israelite sacrifice. Is it not possible that the sacrificial regulations which we find in 'P' may contain emphases which were absent from pre-exilic practice? The importance of this question can be seen when we take into consideration the fact that many of the pre-exilic institutions were considerably enhanced in value and significance as a result of the exile experience. Circumcision was one such; the sabbath was another; so was the institution of sacrifice itself.

When once we grant the validity of these considerations, the question inevitably arises whether in seeking to regulate the sacrificial cultus of the Second Temple the priestly writers did not inadvertently present emphases which were peculiar to their time as if they had the sanction of antiquity. Certain indications would seem to point this way. Two of them can be mentioned at once. First of all, there seem to have survived certain descriptions of ancient Israelite sacrificial practice which seem to indicate that sacrifice originally had a simple, undifferentiated character quite distinct from the elaborate sacrificial cultus such as we find in P. Secondly, the emphasis on sin and its expiation which is so prominent in P seems not to have had quite the same prominence in pre-exilic times for the simple reason that this emphasis seems to be absent from the sacrificial practice that we can deduce from pre-exilic times. Not unconnected with this is the fact that the word for 'altar' and the verb usually translated 'sacrifice' both come from a root which simply means 'to slaughter'. Did the usage perhaps originate in a remote past when the slaughtering of animals (their most prized possession) was very rare and occurred only on very solemn occasions when the god was thought to be present in a special manner?

One very important but, it seems, overlooked passage is that which describes Moses' encounter with his father-in-law in the wilderness. The record in Exod. 18 tells us that when Jethro had arrived and Moses had recounted to him 'all that the Lord had done to Pharoah and to the Egyptians for Israel's sake. . . . Jethro rejoiced for all the good which the Lord had done to Israel in that he had delivered them out of the hand of the Egyptians'. Then it was that Jethro 'offered a burnt offering and sacrifices to God (*ᵉlōhîm*), and Aaron came with all the elders of Israel *to eat bread* with Moses' father-in-law before God'. There seems to be no doubt that in the earlier description we can hear the later Israel speaking. If for nothing else the passage seems to be significant for the distinction it makes between 'burnt offering' (*ôlāh*) and sacrifices (*zᵉbhāhîm*) which seems not to be supported by the general phrase 'to eat bread before God' which is used as a synonym for the earlier detailed description. This prompts the question: was there a clear-cut distinction between these two? What does the peculiar phrase 'to eat bread before God' mean? If the *zebhah*, as is generally accepted, involved some kind of fellowship meal, can we assume that the phrase 'to eat bread before God' is a general description of sacrificial practice? It certainly seems a peculiar description which seldom occurs again.[3] My argument is that we should take it seriously as a comprehensive description of sacrificial practice in ancient Israel. If this is granted, then we should like to argue that the earlier statement that Jethro offered burnt offerings and sacrifices to God should not be interpreted in terms of the later differentiated sacrifices of post-exilic Israel, but simply to mean that the normal practice of eating bread before God was followed; in which certain parts were offered to the deity and the rest constituted a fellowship meal in which the offerer, his family, and friends partook. In that case the *'ōlāh* would be a later development of this original undifferentiated sacrificial act. By virtue of this development, it came to be recognized that the deity deserved an offering in his own right which must be made over to him and somehow removed from profane use by being completely burnt up.

We do not claim by any means to have proven our case, but it would seem as if this description of ancient sacrificial practice is crying out for some reasonable explanation. All we are suggesting now is that sacrifice did not begin as a highly sophisticated and completely articulated ritual but as a simple undifferentiated act which contained within itself the seeds of later development such as can be observed not only in later Israel but in all other societies as well. It seems that if we can accept this postulate, then we have gone some way to explain how this universally accepted practice came to lead to different and varied developments in different places. If sacrificial practice developed from an original undifferentiated act, it seems easier to explain how under different stimuli certain emphases developed and led to the observable differences that we have adverted to.

Before we can justify these large assumptions, certain evidence must be presented which seems to suggest that the usual assumptions need to be revised. We have already called attention to the problem of using the evidence of the priestly writers in reconstructing the nature of ancient Israelite pre-exilic sacrifice. Now we must examine the evidence in a little more detail.

The passage relating the actions of Jethro when he met his son-in-law in the wilderness has already been partially discussed. If it is correct that the account reflects genuine ancient

Israelite sacrificial practice, then the absence of those terms which reflect conditions after the Palestinian settlement would be significant. There is no mention of the *minḥāh* which is generally recognized to refer to an offering of wheaten preparations. This absence would not normally be significant, but if the passage really reflects ancient Israelite sacrificial practice, one cannot escape its obvious implications.

This observation gains in weight when we advert to the first recorded sacrifice in the Pentateuch—the sacrifices offered by Cain and Abel. Apart from other considerations this account should certainly be treated as suspect. The fact that the word *minḥāh* occurs with reference to Cain's *sacrifice* alone in the first instance should warn us that there is an implied contrast between the sacrifices natural to an agricultural community and those peculiar to a semi-nomadic one. It is not necessary to develop this point in view of the later prophetic emphasis upon sacrifices. The lesson is obvious; but we shall revert to this later. There seems to be an implied contrast between the sacrifices Israel used to offer in her desert days and those which naturally suggested themselves after her occupation of Palestine. Can we go on to infer that the sacrifices later differentiated into *'ôlāh* and *zebhaḥ* really stem from Israel's antique past? The acceptance of Abel's sacrifice would alone seem to suggest this. If our contentions so far are accepted, it would be further confirmation that the *'ôlāh* was a later development from an originally undifferentiated sacrifice.

There is no reference to a *minḥāh* here, only later in the verse. And there is no suggestion as to how the firstlings and the fat were treated, but surely this is one instance where later practice can be a guide!

When we turn to the other recorded instances of sacrifice the problem seems a little more simplified. The next instance of sacrifice is that of Noah after the flood: 'Then Noah built an altar to the Lord, and took of every clean animal and of every clean bird, and offered burnt offerings on the altar. And when the Lord smelled the pleasant odour, the Lord said in his heart . . .' (Gen. 8.20f).

Much can be made of this passage. But what is of more interest is the fact that this passage as we now have it has been edited by the priestly writers, and more importantly that the sacrifice is offered *after* the scourge of the flood is past. An obvious comparison is to link it with the sacrifice of Utnapish-tim in the Gilgamesh epic. But the contextual ideas are so different that any comparisons would be very misleading. Noah did not offer any sacrifice before the flood abated. Nor did Utnapishtim for that matter! Had he done so, that would have been truly regarded as either a propitiatory or expiatory sacrifice. At least it could then be said that he offered the sacri-fice in order to placate God so that he might cause the flood to cease. The offering of the sacrifice *after* the abatement of the flood seems to demand that we interpret it as 'eucharistic' rather than anything else. It was a thanksgiving for the cessation of the flood and the restoration of normal relations which that betokened. Since we are here dealing with what seems to be primitive notions of sacrifice, ought we not to treat it as a genuine indication of how sacrifice in early Israel was con-ceived? It was a rite *after* the fact rather than before it. That is to say, that sacrifice was not intended to persuade the deity to act in a particular way or to constrain him to act. It was a rite used either to acknowledge the bountiful goodness of a deity or to attest as well as confirm the restoration of normal relations. The religious ideas of Israel's ancestors so far as we can deduce them seem to fit in well with this.[4] If our interpretation so far is correct, then we can begin to understand how certain emphases developed in the institution of sacrifice which have since engaged the attention of different scholars: gift—commun-ion—expiation—propitiation. What is later differentiated into various types of sacrifice seems originally to have been one undifferentiated act which had all these elements built-in because of the differing and varied occasions to which it was applied; and which therefore made possible all the observable developmental differences.

Before we proceed further however, we must substantiate our argument by further references. It would be tedious to examine in detail all the descriptions of sacrificial occasions that we have in the Old Testament, so we shall select a few to illustrate the point. It can be fairly claimed that there are no descriptions of sacrifice in the Old Testament which suggest that sacrifice was offered in order to procure a boon from a deity. Here it is important to set sacrificial acts within the context of ideas that prevailed rather than view them from the standpoint of modern ideas. For instance, we cannot doubt that there was an accepted procedure when a man or a community wanted to approach God. To a modern observer some parts of this would appear as a sacrifice and he may even be tempted to interpret it as a gift to procure the god's favour or simply in terms of later developed sacrificial ideas. Similarly it cannot be doubted that whenever a community came together for whatever reason there were certain procedures necesssarily to be followed. We can say with reasonable certainty that part of that procedure involved the preparation and sharing of food. If animals were slaughtered they would have to be slaughtered and treated in the manner prescribed by religious custom. To the modern observer it might seem as if the feasting was the main purpose of coming together when in actual fact it was only secondary. A Martian dropping in on a company board meeting today may as well conclude that inhabitants of earth observe some strange customs. Whenever they have some serious undertaking they retire to a closed room well protected from intruders where they burn incense in a most peculiar fashion and drink a specially brewed beer mixed with other preparations while they discourse of matters relating to the service of their chief god—Mammon! The point should be obvious. One has only to think of contemporary practice in order to grasp the point we are trying to make. Whenever for any reason a group of people come together, the sharing of food seems to form a part of the proceedings. It may be a committee meeting or it may be a meeting of a more personal and private kind. In order to understand it at all it must be set in its proper context. There seems to be a significant point here too; for in this tendency which is attested in all societies at all times may be seen the basis of the development which led from the primitive institution of sacrifice to the conception of the Eucharist as a sacrifice.

Similarly there was an accepted procedure to be followed when a man wanted a favour from the deity, or wanted to acknowledge the bounty of the deity, or when a man infringed societal regulations and taboos, or when a man was at variance with his fellow. All these were not private but community occasions, and it is necessary to emphasize this in order to point out the difference between ancient Israelite society and modern times. These occasions would in many cases involve acts which the modern observer would describe as a sacrifice. But we would not have penetrated the true nature of the act unless we set it in its total context which both supplies the reason for it and gives it its meaning.

Thus we may seem to be handicapped in our interpretation of ancient Israelite sacrifice because we do not have enough information to set each act within its context. But there are enough indications to suggest that both in organization and constitution ancient Israel was not unlike the nations round about, nor indeed unlike the so-called primitive communities of the modern world. In broad outline therefore the analysis above may be allowed to stand. One has only to look at the laws in Exodus, Numbers, and Leviticus to grasp the point that in sociological constitution Israel was very much like her neighbours. The only difference is that all Israel's laws have now been given a Yahwistic frame of reference. But comparison with the legal enactments of the surrounding nations would suggest that they did not originally have this frame of reference. We cannot stress too strongly the fact that every society, ancient or modern, has its constitutive ideas. Certain things were accepted, others were simply not done. When the latter were perpetrated either in error or deliberately, certain machinery existed for putting things right again. The difference between an ancient society and a modern one is that the gods were always involved in this machinery; the difference between Israel and her neighbours was that only Yahweh was to be involved and that may be the reason why Israelite law developed in a manner not paralleled elsewhere.

If we accept the foregoing as providing a valid principle of interpretation, we may go further and derive yet another from what we know of Israel's life before she settled in Palestine. We may take it as certain that wheaten preparations did not form part of the material of sacrifice before she entered Palestine. Thus, if we find descriptions of sacrifice where cereal offerings are absent, we may be fairly confident that such a description is early. *Ex hypothesi*, descriptions in which cereal offerings form a part would point to a late period.

We turn now to examine a few more passages. In Judg. 6.19–21 Gideon prepares food for a stranger. On his part this was a normal act of hospitality. But the stranger instructs him to dispose of the food in a certain way. When this is done the stranger touches it with his staff and the food is consumed by fire. The stranger vanished and Gideon perceives that his visitor was really Yahweh. A similar instance is recorded in Judg. 13.15–20. Manoah and his wife prepare to entertain a visitor; but the offer of hospitality is declined; instead they are specifically instructed to offer a burnt offering. When this is done their visitor ascended on the flame of the altar while they looked on.

What seems to be important here is the way in which the unwitting sacrifice was treated. It was entirely consumed by fire. There is no suggestion that the divine visitor consumed the food in this way; in fact what is instructive is the absence of any idea that the deity is supposed to consume the food that is offered. They expressly refuse to eat the food that is offered; for they were divine not human. The most that we may infer is that when anything is set apart for a deity this is how it is to be treated. Neither Gideon nor Manoah knew they were speaking to God, otherwise they would have acted differently. This fact makes these passages more significant. If there were any ideas as to the possible or desired effect of sacrifice on the deity, we should expect some mention of them in these two passages at least. Here we can only point to the description of the effect of Utnapishtim's sacrifice on the gods in the Gilgamesh epic in order to prove our point:

> The gods smelled the savour
> The gods smelled the sweet savour
> The gods crowded like flies about the sacrificer.[5]

The absence of any such element from these two passages is surely significant. It would seem then that we cannot safely draw any conclusions as to the conception of the effect of sacrifice upon the deity from these two passages. It is surely in place therefore to suggest that such a conception did not then exist and is to be regarded as a late development. Originally it seems that sacrifice was simply a practical demonstration of homage to the deity.

The other instances of early Israelite sacrifice that we propose to discuss are to be found in the Books of Samuel. In

1 Sam. 1 we have evidence of a yearly sacrifice in Israel; but the details given of the sacrificial act itself are so few that it is not possible to analyse it in the same way as the two accounts in Judges. Certain deductions can however be made. Feasting and drinking were involved, otherwise Eli's rebuke of Hannah would be unintelligible. All the evidence seems to suggest that this was an act of homage which every Israelite paid at the central shrine in Shiloh. There is nothing to suggest that this was communal (cf. 2.13); and it would appear also that this was the occasion when vows were made and fulfilled (1.11, 17, 24). There are many questions raised by the details in this chapter. The materials mentioned in v. 24 are the same as those used in sacrifice (cf. Lev. 1); but the following description in v. 25 does not suggest that it was a sacrifice that Elkanah and Hannah offered. Apart from saying that they slew the bull (*yishḥāṭû* not *yizbᵉḥû*) we are not told what happened to the other materials that they brought with them. If we argue that they offered a sacrifice, it is very puzzling that the passage should omit this very important detail. The details given in 1.4–5 may also supply an important clue to the nature of early Israelite sacrifice. It may be sufficient at this point just to note the quite different atmosphere and emphasis in this description from that which we find in Lev. 1—7.

This same informal and spontaneous atmosphere is found in the description in 1 Sam. 2. 12–17. Perhaps it can be said that the mistake of Eli's sons was that they were stretching this spirit of informality to absurd limits. The informality and the spontaneity which seem to have surrounded these early instances of sacrifice may be a genuine clue as to how they were conceived; and it is a far cry from the stiff and formal priestly regulations in Leviticus.

The next reference to sacrifice in 1 Samuel is in the account of the institution of the monarchy. Although we do not have a description of the sacrificial act itself, there seem to be some important pointers. On inquiring as to the whereabouts of Samuel, Saul and his servants were told to hurry 'because the people have a sacrifice today on the high place'. Samuel could easily be identified by certain signs. Samuel must first come and bless the sacrifice before the people eat of it; until this is done no one touches the food. So Samuel can easily be identified by a

stranger merely by observing the proceedings. It seems that
here we are given a good glimpse of life in an ancient Israelite
village. This particular sacrifice was privately initiated; it
certainly was not a community occasion. If it were there could
be no invited guests (9.13c, 22). It is tempting to make surmises
as to the occasion of the sacrifice and to draw inferences
accordingly, but we shall limit ourselves to what seems obvious
from the available details. The simplest suggestion is that an
individual family had some reason for giving thanks to God
(the modern equivalent would be 'throwing a party') and so
they invite their friends to rejoice with them and to give thanks
to God or to eat bread before God! Everything is done as custom
required at the high place but the rest of the people go about
their business. It seems that sacrifice was communal not in the
sense that it involved the whole community but that it was an
occasion that brought people together. Sacrifice as a purely
private and personal matter to be performed by the individual
in solitude would then be a contradiction in terms; an essential
element in its conception was this bringing together of people.
And when the people are gathered together, the god was surely
among them, so it brought God and men together in a specially
close way. The details in vv. 22–4 appear to be significant as an
indication of the practice on such occasions (cf. vv. 23, 24). That
this detail should be mentioned while nothing is said about how
the portions set apart for God or of how they were treated, may
or may not be significant. It may be that this was simply taken
for granted and therefore the detail was thought unnecessary;
it can also be because no special significance was attached as
yet to the manner in which the god's portion was treated,[6] and
that there was no conception of the effect it was supposed to
have on him. 1 Sam. 10.8 would suggest that great occasions
were marked by sacrifice. Thus Saul's entry upon the kingship
could not be appropriately marked otherwise than by offering
burnt offerings and sacrificing peace offerings. We are tempted
to speculate on the significance of the juxtaposition of these two
types of sacrifice. The frequency with which the two are
mentioned together prompts the question whether they ought
really to be rigidly separated from each other as two distinct
sacrifices.[7] As far as we know there was no sacrifice that did not
involve burning upon the altar. Is it possible then that '*ôlāh*

and *z^ebhaḥ š^elāmîm* were but the two main emphases in one sacrificial occasion which later became elaborated into two separate acts? If the two originally descended from one rite, it may give us an indication of the meaning of the two terms. The *'ôlāh* does not present much difficulty; it is what goes up (in smoke) upon the altar; and on the basis of our earlier analysis *z^ebhaḥ š^elāmîm* would be the sacrifice originating from, expressing, and creating fullness, completeness, welfare, blessing. In other words it was *eucharistic* in character. If this is correct it would provide a reasonable and satisfactory explanation of its close connection with the *tôdhāh, n^edhābhāh,* and *nedher.*

This explanation of the original meaning and significance of *z^ebhaḥ šelāmîm* is confirmed by the references in 1 Sam. 11.15 and 13.9. Saul had just demonstrated his fitness to be king by defeating Nahash and delivering Jabesh-Gilead. It was an occasion of thanksgiving. The later reference presents a little difficulty because it takes place before a battle, not after it. But it is not difficult to see the appropriatenes of the sacrifice if it has the meaning we outlined above. This surely was one occasion when it was necessary to affirm the fullness, the welfare, and the blessing of the community, for it is out of these that victory is to be assured, not their opposite. In other words it is the positive counterpart of the ritual of cursing one's enemies before going to battle.

One further consideration. 1 Sam. 13.10 tells us that as soon as Saul had finished offering the burnt offering Samuel came. In view of what we have seen above about the meaning of the *'ôlāh* which seemed to require a cultic official for its proper performance, is it possible that Saul's error consisted in the usurpation of a priestly prerogative rather than in the fact that he sacrificed as such (1 Sam. 14.31–5)? In other words, if the *'ôlāh* was originally the means of approaching God and of being assured of his good will (i.e. that no one had broken any taboo or was ritually unclean which would make him withdraw his presence), a procedure which in every society is a priestly or cultic function, then Saul was rejected not because he sacrificed (which he did freely later on) but because he played priest; which he was not. If this is correct Saul's rejection can be attributed to the tensions created by the new institution *vis-à-vis* the old, headed by Samuel.

Two more passages remain to be considered. The account of David's encounter with Saul in 1 Sam. 26.17–20 would seem to negate all that we have argued so far about the original nature and meaning of sacrifice: 'Now therefore let my lord the king hear the words of his servant. If it is Yahweh who has stirred you up against me *let him smell a minḥāh*' (v. 19). First it should be observed that, if Yahweh was conceived in grossly materialistic terms, then we should more naturally expect the object of the verb *yāraḥ* to be not *minḥăh* but *'ôlāh*. It can of course be argued that *minḥāh* is used here as a general term for sacrifice and that its use is not significant as indicating what kind of sacrifice was being offered. It would however be quite arbitrary to regard *minḥāh* as a technical term while taking *yāraḥ* literally. Thus the RSV translators would seem to be right in translating 'may he accept an offering'. What this allows us to infer is that the procedure followed in offering sacrifice contained some means of ascertaining whether the sacrificers and therefore their sacrifices were acceptable to the deity (cf. 1 Sam. 14.36–42; Josh. 7). The point we are trying to make is that, if one is unacceptable to a deity for whatever reason, there was no question of offering sacrifice to him. The offence must be removed *before* sacrifice can be offered. This is all that seems implied in David's words except that here the sacrifice was offered with the express purpose of finding out if it was Yahweh who was responsible for the strained relations between him and Saul. It could not therefore be said that the sacrifice was intended to propitiate Yahweh who would thereafter cease to cause mischief between the two men. And it is arguable that if that had been David's meaning he would have expressed himself differently. Rather it seems that precisely because sacrifice had the meaning outlined above it could also be used when there was a manifest breach of welfare. This, we have tried to show, involved as a necessary preliminary a procedure for ascertaining the acceptability of the sacrificers. This would have shown with whom the fault lay. As in the passages cited above, the nature of the fault would have then been discovered and appropriate action taken before resuming the proposed action. It may be significant therefore that Saul quietly ignores David's suggestion but proceeds to accept the blame (v. 21).

The next passage describes the sequel to David's census in 2 Sam. 24. At first sight it would appear that this passage negates all that we have said of sacrifice in the foregoing. Closer examination would, however, seem to suggest otherwise. Although David offers to buy Araunah's threshing floor 'in order to build an altar to the Lord, that the plague may be averted from the people', it is instructive to note that according to the narrative the plague had already been stayed. There could therefore be no question of the sacrifice propitiating Yahweh and expiating David's guilt, and so averting the plague. Yahweh had already 'repented of the evil' and stayed the plague (v. 16); he did not therefore need to be propitiated.

It would seem much more natural to interpret the sacrifice as attesting and confirming Yahweh's good will as evidenced by the staying of the plague (cf. the wish for the king expressed by Araunah after he had offered him his threshing-floor and his oxen *gratis*). What seems more important for our present purpose is that this was obviously a penitential occasion but there is no mention of the sin offering or the guilt offering. If these were early sacrifices, surely this was a most appropriate occasion for them. The additional details given in the parallel account of the Chronicler, 1 Chron. 21, seem to fit very well our present interpretation. When David called upon Yahweh, he *answered* him with fire, thus attesting Yahweh's good will (cf. Job 8.20). But was this the means by which it was discovered whether the sacrificer was acceptable or not?[8] When David had thus been assured of the acceptability of his person, he proceeded to offer sacrifices: *šᵉlāmîm* in 2 Sam. 24.25 but simply *yizbaḥ* in 1 Chron. 21.28. Does this perhaps give us a clue to the frequent juxtaposition of *'ôlāh* and *zᵉbhaḥ šᵉlāmîm*? That is, the former always preceded the latter. And indicated whether one could proceed with the *šᵉlāmîm* or not. If this is correct, then our earlier contention that both were originally parts of a single rite would gain in plausibility. David's building of the altar would have no more significance than that this was the normal way in which the site of a theophany was marked.

At this point we could introduce a further feature in the anatomy of sacrifice. If it began as a single rite that was used on all occasions, joyful as well as sad, then it becomes possible to understand how as a strong sense of sin and penitence developed these would tend to receive greater emphasis in sacrificial practice. Indeed in Israelite religion they eclipsed all other aspects of sacrifice. This was merely one development of sacrificial practice. Others can be observed in the sacrificial practice of surrounding peoples as well as in the Graeco-Roman world, and indeed of contemporary societies in different parts of the world. In every case the prevailing idea of deity influences and determines sacrificial practice; and this would be a sufficient explanation of the fact that certain developments took place in Israel which cannot be paralleled elsewhere. That these developments took place is ample justification of the claim to possess a unique divine revelation. Further confirmation of this may be seen in the fact that when the enhanced and spiritualized view of sacrifice tended to become an end in itself and to constitute a claim upon God, which it never was, further developments did take place which led to the abrogation of sacrifice—a position which paradoxically was not unknown in ancient Israel.

Two insights drawn from contemporary studies in comparative religion would serve to illustrate and substantiate the foregoing claims. The fact has been much commented on, and in Africa much bemoaned, that the High Gods seem to have no cultus and to figure little or not at all in the normal sacrificial cultus. It may be contended that the situation was not much different in ancient Israel. It is scarcely necessary to detail the attributes of the High Gods in order to show that they were much the same as were accorded to Yahweh from earliest times.[9] This would not be adequate substantiation of our argument. But when we find the prophets in devastating criticism of the sacrificial practice of their times, insisting that sacrifice had never been part of Yahweh's original requirement; and when we find scattered notices throughout the Old Testament (not all of which can be late!) making the same point; it would be folly not to see the parallel. At any rate it is increasingly being recognized that there were different levels of religion observed in ancient Israel. (This is still the case even in the Christian Church!) And the story of the Old Testament is the story of how one level, which in all other cases became otiose, subsumed and superseded all the others. Our contention then is that the prophetic attitude to sacrifice should be taken simply at its face value and be regarded as a pointer to the original nature of Yahweh. (As we hope to develop this point more fully in another paper we shall not pursue it further here.)

If the above contention is upheld, it would also involve the conclusion that sacrifices were *not* originally offered to Yahweh in Israel. They were rather part of ethnic tribal religion which did not feature in original Yahwism. The very anxiety of the Elohist and the priestly writers to make Moses offer the first sacrifice exposes not only the artificiality of their scheme but argues a different origin for sacrifice.

If this second contention is also upheld, then we could go on to argue that the story of sacrifice in the Old Testament is the story of how an ethnic religious element came to be baptized into Yahwism with the development that this necessarily brought about in the institution. Thus it seems much can be learned from setting the sacrificial cultus of ancient Israel alongside not only those of their neighbours but of contemporary primitives as well, for they all started at the same level.

We shall not, however, embark upon this undertaking now. This is after all only a preliminary investigation. Even if we have not presented new evidence that would justify a further hearing of the case, it is our hope that enough has been presented to warrant continuation of the inquiry.

NOTES

1 'Sacrifice' in *Biblical Revelation and African Beliefs*, ed. K. A. Dickson and P. Ellingworth (London 1969), p. 58.
2 Ibid., p. 80.
3 The phrase 'to eat bread' occurs quite often in the Old Testament; but 'to eat [bread] before God' occurs only on five other occasions—Deut. 12.7; 14.23, 26; 15.20; 1 Chron. 29.22. The context in each case leaves no doubt that the reference is to sacrifice.
4 See John Bright, *A History of Israel* (London 1972), pp. 88–92.
5 J. B. Pritchard, ed., *Ancient Near East Texts Relating to the Old Testament* (Princeton 1955), p. 95.
6 See p. 28 above.
7 See pp. 22–3 above.
8 See the earlier discussion of 1 Sam. 26.17–20 above.
9 See W. F. Albright, *From Stone Age to Christianity* (Johns Hopkins 1957), p. 170; A. Alt, *Essays on OT History and Religion* (Oxford 1966), pp. 1–67.

The Beginning of the Gospel

A Study of St Mark's Gospel with regard to its First Verse

MARK E. GLASSWELL

The opening verse of St Mark's Gospel has been interpreted in many different ways with regard to its relation in meaning and syntax to the following verses or paragraphs.[1] Broadly speaking, views move between seeing a grammatical connection with the next two or three verses, or a summary of the first paragraph the length of which varies according to different commentators. The first approach is not helped by uncertainty about the construction of vv. 2, 3, and 4 in relation to each other. Decision on these points must inevitably be determined by the sense of each alternative and the content of the verses, in conjunction with a view of the attitude of Mark to what he was writing.

It seems unlikely that καθώς (v. 2) or ἐγένετο (v. 4) should be regarded as connecting links with v. 1 since this would require a conception of the gospel as an entity arising from a prophetic utterance and as a process whose beginning was at a particular time and comprised in a particular event. The words should rather be seen as emphasizing the contents of the verses they introduce but yet in such a way that a relation between prophetic word and actual event is seen between the contents of the verses.

With regard to v. 1 the point would then be, not an identification between the beginning of the gospel and these things, but an assertion that here is where all mention of the gospel must begin, so that basic to it, as its presupposition, there is prophecy and historical event.

This does not mean an identification between the gospel and the account which begins here. So ἀρχή cannot mean 'here begins', nor that the events in the first paragraph (vv. 1–8) can be taken as the beginning of the gospel. We can only accept the sense that here we are at the beginning and the result is the gospel. Thus it is difficult with regard to v. 1 to see a stress here either on the opening verses or the opening section. V. 1 is not a descriptive title for anything but an indication that we are here concerned with the beginning of the gospel, but not in the sense of chronological starting-point but 'basis' or 'origin'. As such the first verse says something relevant to the whole of what follows.

It has been often pointed out since M. Kähler[2] followed by J. Weiss,[3] that Mark's Gospel is a passion-story extended backwards. This was originally a theological judgement about the literary character of the Gospels and Mark in particular. But it has importance for both the literary and theological character of the Gospel's construction and interpretation.

Willi Marxsen[4] has applied this view to the present context and pointed out that since the connection between vv. 2, 3, and 4 must be the work of Mark and not earlier tradition, vv. 2 and 3 were placed prior to vv. 4ff rather than vv. 4ff constructed to follow vv. 2 and 3. This is opposed to Lohmeyer's[5] interpretation that vv. 2 and 3 introduce the event which fulfils the prophecy and comprises the beginning of the gospel. Marxsen sees Mark's Gospel as reading backwards not forwards, with the stress at the end not the beginning. There is not a progression forwards with a causal or chronological connection but a reflection back with each stage dependent on what follows. This implies not that the gospel begins at this point but that the origin of the gospel is traced back. Behind the gospel and the life of Jesus there is John the Baptist and Old Testament prophecy. It means also of course that the beginning goes back to God.[6] As we shall see, however, this should be taken to imply that what we read is not directly the gospel but its presupposition, though Marxsen develops his points differently. Each stage gives way to the next and depends on the next for its significance. After the event of John is the event of Jesus (ἐγένετο—v. 9) or, rather, the event of John precedes that of Jesus. Old Testament prophecy comes alive in the appearance of John and John's message comes alive in the appearance of Jesus (cf. vv. 8, 10). Jesus' role is made plain by God himself (v. 11), but this is not public and is the secret behind the history. This is the gospel of God of which we are now being shown the basis in Jesus himself, in whom it is centred, as Messiah and Son of God.

In 1.14f, John gives way to Jesus, preaching the gospel of God. But this is a gospel preached by Jesus, not about Jesus which is certainly part of the sense of the opening verse of the Gospel. But Mark must have intended some relationship between these two by their proximity and the fact that these, like other original references to the gospel, are the work of Mark himself.[7] The probable ambiguity of the following genitive in 1.1 can also form a link with v. 14. But the fact that here Jesus begins to preach the gospel does not mean that v. 14 represents an historical beginning of the gospel referred to in v. 1 nor, as Marxsen goes on to claim, a sign that the risen Jesus present in the Church is here beginning to proclaim his gospel afresh,[8]—though the fact that the gospel is Jesus' own Word (following Schniewind[9]) implying his presence, and indeed that the gospel of God is Jesus himself[10] can be accepted. The point is how this relates to the book Mark saw himself writing and what he meant by his opening verse in relation to vv. 14 and 15.

J. M. Robinson[11] considers that Mark wrote 'theologically understood history' and asks whether the gospel is to be seen as beginning with John the Baptist or Jesus' preaching of the gospel in vv. 14f. For the two views in the early Church he refers to Acts 1.22 and 10.37. For Mark, according to Robinson, it is John's ministry, which lies between the future tenses of the prophecies of vv. 2f and the perfect tenses of Jesus' proclamation in v. 15.[12]

Against Robinson it is to be doubted whether Mark was emphasizing chronology or an historical 'event of fulfilment', or whether the gospel in v. 1 is to be identified simply as such with that in v. 14. Mark is not progressing from a decisive event to describe the gospel. May he not still be in some way concerned with the 'origin' of the gospel of Jesus Christ rather than the 'Geschehen des Evangeliums'[13] or the preaching and baptism of John as the beginning of the gospel proclaimed in v. 15? John's removal at v. 14 implies theological priority not chronological sequence.[14] There is no emphasis in v. 15 on what went before but a presentation of Jesus' historical preaching in the form of his demand at the time for a response in the present with regard to the future. Jesus alone made that demand and this now stands in the larger context of the gospel of Jesus Christ in v. 1. Mark is less interested in the historical fact of the proclamation itself than that the gospel of Jesus Christ arises out of and depends on this and that Jesus' proclamation is understood only in relation to the gospel of v. 1. That relation is not primarily temporal but christological. The 'origin' of the gospel reveals that the gospel depends on Jesus himself. His relation to the gospel is like his relation to the kingdom of God where it is difficult to say whether Jesus brings the kingdom or the kingdom brings Jesus. Jesus is the origin and fulfilment of the proclamation of the kingdom and of the gospel of which he is both author and content. Neither the kingdom nor the gospel is explicitly present in Jesus' historical preaching but implicit in his person as proclaimed by the gospel.

It is thus that Mark can claim to present the origin of the gospel of and about Jesus Christ and disclose the relevance of Jesus' eschatological gospel to the christological gospel of the Church, and it is thus we can understand the relation between v. 1 and v. 14. The Church's gospel is more than a verbal reiteration of Jesus' historical proclamation although it depends on it. For this reason it is repeated in the context of an exposition of the ἀρχή of that gospel in the Gospel of Mark. Mark is concerned with *both* these things, as different but related in the person of Jesus Christ, so that one is part of the origin of the other.

Here we see that this view differs also from Marxsen's, who does not regard the gospel of v. 1 as being identical with that of v. 14 in the sense that the former starts with the latter in history but in the sense that the latter is reiterated in the former, in a present continuation of Jesus' preaching. Thus Mark's concern would not be historical nor christological, but eschatological. For Marxsen Mark is concerned with the gospel in his own day and the time of Jesus as its starting-point.[15] This gospel is eschatological in that it is to be fulfilled in Mark's own day. There is no interest in this in terms of Jesus' lifetime. Jesus who appears in the Gospel is himself the gospel of God, the one who brought it and will bring it to fulfilment in the near future. What began with Jesus must now find its fulfilment in him.

But this fails to note that it is not the eschatological gospel of Jesus which Mark sees as contemporary but the post-resurrection gospel about Jesus Christ to which Jesus' proclamation is brought to bear witness as achieving its full validity only in that context. There is also more than a verbal reiteration of Jesus' proclamation since the object is now Jesus himself. The previous 'mystery of the kingdom' is now disclosed. Again, ἀρχή means more than chronological beginning. Jesus' historical preaching, eschatological in character, is superseded by something which alone explains it,[16] and this is in the context of the Church's gospel not Jesus' historical preaching. That preaching does itself belong to the ἀρχή of the gospel and is as such reproduced by Mark, but it is as such differentiated from the post-resurrection gospel by the very nature of Mark's writing which relates history to the gospel but does not identify them. Hence the theme of secrecy in Mark.[17]

This should help us understand Mark's narrative of Jesus and his preaching. He wishes to present the relation between Jesus (the historical Jesus) and the gospel. The gospel was not proclaimed by Jesus historically but it is concerned with what Jesus then preached and gives validity to it now in terms of his person.[18] So too there is no 'pre-history' of the gospel given here.[19] Mark presents the earthly life of Jesus as the precondition for the gospel, which includes Jesus' proclamation of the kingdom in v. 15 and the calling of disciples in vv. 16ff. There is in Mark then both 'a believing representation of the divine Master and historical information about the events of Jesus' life'.[20] But it is only true that historical facts (*Tatsachen*) become transparent in face of the majesty of the Master to reveal the might of his divine Word[21] in the gospel of Jesus Christ. Thus was the tradition proclaimed by the Church and thus is it used by Mark in a narrative concerned with the ἀρχή of the gospel.

Thus Mark's narrative is not an historicization of the gospel but is meant to reveal the relation between history and the gospel in the person of Jesus himself.[22] It is no more right to see the kernel of the gospel in the history than to look for an historical kernel in the narrative of which Mark was not conscious.[23] Both history and gospel are in Mark's Gospel but they are kept distinct by the theme of secrecy.[24] Mark is interested in the relation between the historical Jesus and the gospel and Jesus' historical proclamation finds its place here, even though it is not verbally identical with the gospel. The historical Jesus, who has become the subject of the gospel, is defined up to a point by the events of his life and by his preaching, but his full identification is made only by the post-resurrection gospel. This insight explains to a large extent the Gospel of Mark.

Other places in Mark where the evangelist has introduced the word εὐαγγέλιον support this view, such as 8.35 where it parallels a first person pronoun or 14.9 where the future proclamation of the gospel in the whole world will make reference back to historical tradition concerned with Jesus' passion and resurrection. It would remain, having considered the relation of the gospel to its ἀρχή, to consider its relation to τὸ τέλος,[25] which takes into account Mark 13.10. Reference has already been made to Marxsen's view that for Mark the gospel reiterates Jesus' gospel of the End, but there is no space for fuller discussion of this here.[26] Suffice it to say that the time Mark is concerned with here is the time of the gospel over against the future Parousia of the Son of Man, identified with Jesus. Both past and future are understood in terms of Jesus' person. Continuity in the chapter is not found in historical events leading to their consummation but in the identity between Jesus and the Son of Man which is now the subject also of the Church's watching (13.37). In this context the gospel is proclaimed to all the Gentiles, which is still our own context with regard to the gospel and Jesus, in Africa and the whole world. This is in keeping with Harry Sawyerr's christocentric approach in *Creative Evangelism* (London 1968) as well as with that of the author of the Epistle to the Hewbrews who described Jesus as the ἀρχηγὸς καὶ τελειωτὴς τῆς πίστεως. He stands as subject of the gospel at its ἀρχή and its τέλος, though it is the end which will justify the beginning.[27]

NOTES

1   See ten ways in C. E. B. Cranfield, *Gospel according to St. Mark* (Cambridge 1959), p. 34.

2   *The so-called historical Jesus and the historic Biblical Christ* (1964; German reissue 1956), p. 80.

3 *Jesus von Nazareth* (1910), p. 132.

4 *Der evangelist Markus* (Göttingen 1959), pp. 17ff; E.T., *Mark the Evangelist* (New York 1969), pp. 30ff.

5 *Das Evangelium des Markus* (1959), p. 10.

6 Marxsen, op. cit., p. 88; E.T., pp. 132f.

7 This is fairly generally accepted; see P. Stuhlmacher, *Das paulinische Evangelium* 1 Vorgeschichte (Göttingen 1968), p. 235. Cf. also W. Wink, *John the Baptist in the Gospel Tradition* (Cambridge 1968), p. 7.

8 Cf. Marxsen, op. cit., pp. 85ff (E.T., pp. 127ff), accepted by G. Minette de Tillesse, *Le Secret Messianique dans l'Évangile de Marc* (Paris 1968), pp. 408ff.

9 Marxsen, op. cit., p. 87; E.T., p. 131.

10 Ibid., p. 88; E.T., p. 133.

11 *The Problem of History in Mark* (London 1957), pp. 21ff.

12 Robinson's view is supported by J. Schreiber, *Theologie des Vertrauens* (Hamburg 1967), p. 194.

13 Lohmeyer, op. cit., p. 10.

14 Marxsen, op. cit., p. 30; E.T., p. 49.

15 Ibid., pp. 27ff; E.T., pp. 45ff.

16 Cf. G. Gloege, *The day of his coming* (London 1963), p. 128; T. A. Burkill, *Mysterious Revelation* (Cornell U.P. 1963), p. 102. See also Schniewind's view (*Das Evangelium nach Markus* (Göttingen 1936), e.g. pp. 16f, 122, 130) of the messianic secret as the eschatological secret of the presence in the kingdom in Jesus' person, which could be accepted as part of *Mark's* view. Cf. also Schniewind, 'Messiasgeheimnis und Eschatologie', *Nachgelassene Reden und Aufsätze* (Berlin 1952), pp. 1ff.

17 Cf. M. E. Glasswell, 'The Use of Miracles in the Markan Gospel' in *Miracles. Cambridge Studies in their Philosophy and History* (1965), ed. C. F. D. Moule, pp. 154–6, 161. Full discussion of the messianic secret in Mark is the subject of my doctoral thesis which still awaits publication.

18 Cf. H. E. Tödt, *The Son of Man in the Synoptic Tradition* (1963), tr. D. M. Barton, p. 248 (original German e., 1959, p. 227). Mark's 'Gospel understands Christian preaching as concerned not with continuing to teach Jesus' teaching but with the gospel *of* Jesus Christ (Mark 1.1)'.

19 Cf. H. Conzelmann, 'Gegenwart und Zukunft in der synoptischen Tradition', in *Zeitschrift für Theologie und Kirche* 54 (1957), p. 290.

20 Lohmeyer, op. cit., p. 33.

21 Ibid., p. 33.

22 Cf. Glasswell, 'Jesus Christ' in *Theology*, vol. LXVIII (1965), pp. 562f. H. A. E. Sawyerr, 'The Marcan Framework' in *Scottish Journal of Theology* 14, (1961), p. 283, stresses Mark's interest in the person of Jesus.

23 Cf. W. Wrede, *Das Messiasgeheimnis in den Evangelien* (1901), p. 2; E. T., *The Messianic Secret*, tr. J. C. G. Greig (1971), p. 5.

24 Cf. H. Conzelmann, op cit., pp. 294, 295, and E. Schweizer, 'Mark's Contribution to the quest of the historical Jesus', in *New Testament Studies* 10 (1964), p. 423.

25 Cf. Conzelmann, op. cit., pp. 295f.

26 See Marxsen, op. cit., pp. 101ff (E.T., pp. 151ff) and Conzelmann's opposite view, 'Geschichte und Eschaton nach Mark 13' in *Zeitschrift für die neutestamentliche Wissenschaft* 50 (1959), p. 215. Both see Mark 13.10 as Marcan—Marxsen, p. 81 (E.T., p. 122); Conzelmann, p. 219.

27 Cf. O. Michel, *Der Brief an die Hebräer* (6e., 1966), p. 434. All this shows that the definition of 'gospel' for Mark in W. Wink (op. cit., p. 7) is inadequate. The gospel concerns 'God's saving activity in the event of Jesus Christ', and Mark's Gospel looks back to its origin and basis (ἀρχή) in history, as well as to its τέλος, both in terms of the Person of Jesus himself.

The List of Nations in Acts 2

OLOF LINTON

The story of the Pentecost in Acts 2 has caused much trouble among scholars and has given rise to many deliberations and theories. That is not astonishing. For both the account of the talking in tongues and the attached list of nations are in many respects perplexing. What phenomenon is described—glossolalia, speaking in foreign languages, *Sprachwunder*, or *Hörwunder*? And what about the list? Is it a Hellenistic list of historical, geographical, or astronomical origin, a Roman list of provinces, a Jewish list of diaspora, a list of pre-Lucan regions of Christian mission? Anyway it has been a widespread opinion that the story is confused. And in both cases it has been a common supposition that the confusion was due to the fact that 'Luke' has taken over a story (about glossolalia) which he has not understood and a list which originally had another setting. Only in this way did many scholars think it possible to find a reasonable meaning. This attitude had the result that little interest was dedicated to the actual text, but much to speculations concerning the background.

The text was therefore seldom thoroughly analysed and when analysed it was often in order to stress its confusion. One explicit exception is a treatise by my colleague at the University of Copenhagen, Professor Bent Noack, who some years ago published an investigation of Acts 2.1–13, in which he clearly demonstrates that the text, as it stands, is a story about a miraculous speaking of foreign languages.[1] This recognition, he points out, must be fundamental for all further investigations, also for those concerning the background.[2] In a review of Noack's stimulating book I put the question whether the problems of the list might not also be solved along the lines of his thesis, answered it in the affirmative, and added some deliberations in this direction.[3] The present paper carries these considerations further. My thesis is thus that the key to the understanding of the list and its peculiarities lies in the context. Instead of neglecting the context we have to consider it thoroughly.

Why are the attendants there—those Ἰουδαῖοι, ἄνδρες εὐλαβεῖς ἀπὸ παντὸς ἔθνους τῶν ὑπὸ τὸν οὐρανόν? Is it to tell us that there were Jews in most parts of the world or to inform us of the universalism of the Christian faith? Possibly, for surely it would fit into the wider context. The apostles encountered Jews everywhere, and the universal view of the author is accentuated both at the beginning of Acts (1.8) and at the opening of the story of Pentecost (2.5). But the account itself is dominated by another interest: *the assembled Jews are there to attest the miracle.*

Surely it is an odd idea that all these Jews should speak in chorus: 'How is it then that we hear them, each of us in his own native language', but the pattern is well known (cf. the common *Chorschluss*), and must be evaluated as such. And it is evident why the author uses this somewhat clumsy method: he wants to introduce the assembled Jews as witnesses to the miracle. Therefore he not only tells us that they were 'bewildered, because each one heard the apostles talking in his own language' (v. 6) but he also quotes what they say: 'Why, they are all Galileans, are they not, these men who are speaking? How is it then that we hear them, each of us in his own native language?' Thus in vv. 7–8. And in v. 11 likewise: 'we hear them telling in our own tongues the great things God has done'. The attendants are there to attest the miracle. Therefore, they also speak the language of witnesses who have to relate only what they themselves have seen and heard. They do not say: 'they tell' but: 'we hear them telling'.[4]

Many details fit into this predominant idea. The author tells us—or lets the audience tell us—that the apostles were Galileans. The readers of Luke–Acts knew this beforehand, and when it is stressed here, the reason is evidently to emphasize that the apostles spoke in languages that were hitherto unknown to them. Further, the attendants attest that they themselves were acquainted with those foreign languages. They have learnt them already as children (πῶς ἡμεῖς ἀκούομεν ἕκαστος τῇ ἰδίᾳ διαλέκτῳ ἡμῶν ἐν ᾗ ἐγεννήθημεν). There can thus be no mistake, especially as many attest the phenomenon. Surely there are others who think otherwise: they think the apostles are drunk. Many scholars find a contradiction here, because the author first speaks of πάντες then of ἕτεροι: besides 'all' there can be no 'others'. But this objection is out of place here. For certainly the author does not include the mockers among the pious Jewish men whose astonished attestation was just quoted. These all attest the miracle. In many places Luke introduces pious Jews as spokesmen: Zacharias, the father of the Baptist, Simeon (Luke 2.25: ἄνθρωπος δίκαιος καὶ εὐλαβής), Anna, the daughter of Phanuel, the crowds attesting the wonders of Jesus, Joseph of Arimathea (Luke 23.50), Gamaliel, Ananias ('a devout observer of the law and well spoken of by all the Jews of that place': ἀνὴρ εὐλαβὴς κατὰ τὸν νόμον, Acts 22.12). Few of these persons are Christian, but they are pious and open-minded and honest, ready to give honour to God. Besides these pious men, who *all* attested the miracle, there were, so Luke tells us, 'others'. The meaning evidently is that those others missed the subjective qualifications mentioned, perhaps also that they had not even the objective aptitude to attest the miracle: they did not know the languages in question.

This understanding of the text has been too early put aside in order to give place to multifarious deliberations concerning the background: the 'sources' and the possible events before them. The main reason was that scholars found the account, as it stands, fantastical and confused. The starting-point is the conviction that those people who have experienced glossolalia must have had a more 'realistic' view of the phenomenon, and that the story told by Luke is therefore impossible and of a later date. For those who had attended glossolalia must, so it is said, know that glossolalia was nothing but a stammering without any sense or meaning. In fact such an evaluation has always existed and is referred to also in the New Testament. According to Acts some people thought the apostles drunk and according to Paul 'uninstructed persons or unbelievers' (ἰδιῶται ἢ ἄπιστοι) think those speaking in tongues mad (1 Cor. 14.23). Surely there is a difference between Paul and

Acts. Paul acknowledges that no man understands what the πνευματικός says and distinguishes between prophecy and glossolalia and does not identify glossolalia with speaking in foreign languages (although he mentions it as an analogy, 1 Cor. 14.21). But this view does not imply that the glossolalia is a mere stammering without any sense at all. St Paul acknowledges that the πνευματικός is inspired (1 Cor. 14.2) and speaks 'mysteries'—which is not the same as nonsense: God understands him and there are persons who understand it and are able to interpret it. The glossolalia is not *per se* devoid of sense— for how could it be interpreted if it was? Neither Paul nor the Corinthians—who did know glossolalia from experience—have the alleged 'realistic' view that it is a mere stammering without any sense. St Paul—and the Corinthians—surely have not the same idea about glossolalia as Luke, but they have even less in common with the mockers of Acts 2.13. And it is a common conviction in Acts and Corinthians that those speaking in tongues praise God, which does not mean that the Pentecost in Acts is only a specimen of common glossolalia. Luke himself thinks otherwise. He speaks of glossolalia also in 10.46 and 19.6, but it is evident that the Pentecost also according to him is something quite extraordinary.[5] The 'misinterpretation' that we find in Luke is not peculiar to him only and does not *per se* prove that his account would be quite impossible for those knowing glossolalia from experience. For many attendants of ecstatic speaking have, at least sometimes, thought that they heard some words of a foreign language. And also attendants who did not understand anything of what was said—like Paul and others—did yet catch so much that it was a phenomenon of ecstasy and that the inspired 'praised God' (1 Cor. 14.1f). So the account is not quite *so* far from realism as some people think. This does not mean that the account by Luke should be 'realistic' in any modern sense of the word. The monumental scheme and pattern is evident. We must, however, take the version of Luke as it stands. And here there can be no doubt. Luke tells us about a miracle of speaking foreign languages not formerly known to those speaking.

And now to the list. As pointed out above, scholars have often maintained that the list must have been taken from somewhere and have tried to find the prototype. This has so far been a

success that it could be stated that the list belongs to a common
pattern. But it has not been possible to find the actual *Vorlage*.
Above all, however, it has not been possible to find a prototype
that could explain the peculiarities of the list. Many scholars
therefore think that Luke himself has made some additions and
(or) that the list has been mutilated in the course of textual
tradition. Both are possible. For authors, using a traditional
list, have certainly often adapted the list to fit their special
purpose. And the scribal traditions are not unanimous. But
neither supposition helps us much. For why has Luke not
adapted the list better to the context (as generally interpreted),
and why should we not keep to the sound method of *lectio
difficilior* in this case? The lists, which have been adduced, have
not elucidated the obscurities as they were intended to. These
facts motivate the experiment for once to try to explain the list,
not by neglecting the context, but by emphasizing it.

In accordance with the deliberations above we have to start
by acknowledging two facts: (i) the story is about a miracle of
speaking unknown foreign languages; (ii) the listeners are
called upon as witnesses to this miracle.

One of the most striking features of the list is that the purely
Greek regions are missing. The reason can hardly be that there
were few Jews in these parts of the *oikoumene*, nor that these
provinces were untouched by the Christian mission (if we
accept such suppositions). It is more likely that Luke took over a
Greek list of barbaric languages, which could 'explain' why
central Greek regions are missing (but hardly other peculiarities,
see below!). It could also be that a writer such as Luke, who
probably had a Greek education, and who followed an old and
tenacious Greek tradition, would find it difficult to rank Greek
among other foreign languages. If there was an utterance in
Greek, it was already interpreted and was no longer a speech in
the mysterious languages of barbarians or oracles. But there is
perhaps another explanation. As we have seen, the devout men
present are there to attest the miracle, to attest that the apostles
spoke a foreign language not known to them beforehand. That
must obviously be the case with those foreign languages which
are mentioned. With Greek it would be otherwise. For in New
Testament times there were many Jews, not only in the diaspora, but also in Palestine, who could speak Greek, some a

good Greek, some only a little Greek for everyday use. Surely
we hear that the apostles were Galileans and in another
connection that they were uneducated people (ἀγράμματοι
καὶ ἰδιῶται, Acts 4.13), but even in Galilee it certainly happened that humble persons knew a little Greek. And even if the
apostles did not know a word of Greek, the assembled Jews—
many of whom, as former diaspora Jews, understood and
spoke Greek—would hardly be so upset if they heard Greek.
In any case, the fact that the apostles spoke Greek—if they did,
which is neither proposed nor denied—could not be taken as
an undeniable *proof* that the apostles spoke some words in a
language hitherto totally unknown to them. It could be said:
they already know at least some Greek. Luke is clearly aware of
the fact that he tells a very incredible story. Therefore he sum-
mons many witnesses, but omits those who might be disputed.

Another perplexing gap in the list is that Syria is not mentioned. Why? Possibly due to an analogous reason. The
Syrian and the Aramaic languages were very much alike. Of
course it was often difficult for a Syrian to understand an
Aramaic-speaking fellow, but *if* they could understand each
other, nobody would on this account think it a supernatural
miracle. Perhaps Luke himself was a Syrian—as some Gospel-
introductions from the ancient Church tell us. He may have met
some Galileans—either in Galilee, in Antioch, or elsewhere—
and may have observed that he was able to understand them
and they him. If so, he possibly realized that Syrians could not
attest that the apostles spoke a language which was totally
unknown to them beforehand. We cannot know if Luke made
such reflections, but it would explain why he mentions neither
Greeks nor Syrians among those who were perplexed by the
speaking in foreign languages.

Neither the omission of Greece nor that of Syria has, however, caused so much trouble as the appearance of Judea in
the list. It does not seem to fit into the context where otherwise
Jews from foreign countries speak of their familiarity with
different native tongues. Already in old times this was felt as an
alien element and many scholars have tried to improve the
text—sometimes introducing Syria or Armenia into the text
instead of Judea. In modern times the same method has been
used. But nowadays, even here, the idea has been promoted

that we should refer to pre-Lucan factors, i.e. an earlier list which Luke used. If we want to continue this way and yet keep Judea as genuine, there is hardly any other solution than to postulate a Jewish list, which mentioned regions where Jews were living. Such a list would surely not exclude the Jewish homeland. That is Noack's solution, and it is very possible that Luke knew such a list or was otherwise acquainted with such enumerations. For Luke mentions Jews, and he had an interest in referring only to regions in foreign countries where Jews were living. Otherwise he could not use them as witnesses. If Jewish, however, we may wonder why the list does not comprise the genuine Greek boundaries.

It might therefore be appropriate to try the theory proposed above in this case also. What function can the mentioning of Judea have in the present text? Did not Jews in Galilee and Jews in Judea speak the same language? Not exactly. For a Galilean could according to Matt. 26.73 be recognized as such in Jerusalem. But this difference hardly hindered them in understanding each other and is therefore of no consequence in this connection. But Luke might—if a Syrian—have had the experience that Jews from Judaea were more difficult to understand than those from the North. Or he may have heard some rabbis speaking Hebrew or have listened to a lesson from the Hebrew Bible and thereby found that he did not understand it. This language was foreign to him. It is therefore possible that Luke thought that the Jews of Galilee spoke Aramaic—which he could almost accept as a Syrian dialect— and those of Judea spoke Hebrew (cf. Acts 22.2: St Paul speaks to the Jerusalemites τῇ ʻΕβραΐδι διαλέκτῳ). Or he may have thought that the apostles as uneducated Galileans spoke a more popular language, the Jews in Jerusalem the language of the Bible—as some rabbis did or at least were able to do. These deliberations are naturally somewhat hazardous, but if they are only approximately correct, they would substantiate the old traditions of Luke's relations to Syria. One may surely object that Luke was a Greek writer. However, he cannot in fact keep up the high standard he aims at in the beginning of his books. But would one expect more? In any case the ability to write foreign languages is so varying that it is very difficult to prove anything, positively or negatively.

There are other features of the list which have puzzled scholars more or less. The beginning: Parthians, Medes, Elamites, inhabitants of Mesopotamia, is certainly old-fashioned. But Luke was probably aware that there lived Jews in those regions, possibly because he used a Jewish list of diaspora, possibly on account of other information. For otherwise the list would not fit his purpose. The enumeration of regions in Asia Minor has not caused great debates either. Luke seems here to follow tolerably a list of Roman provinces.[6] He need not, however, have used a book for his purpose. It may be reminiscences from his school days, for he probably went to school—a Greek school within the Roman empire. One might wonder why he uses such a list. For the boundaries of the Roman provinces were scarcely identical with the boundaries of language. It is, however, difficult to say anything distinct both as to the actual facts and as to Luke's proficiency. It is hardly probable that Luke was an expert in these things. But he knew that also in these regions there lived Jews, and he had probably some idea that many languages were spoken there. In Lystra Paul and Barnabas encountered natives who ἐπῆραν τὴν φωνὴν αὐτῶν Λυκαονιστὶ λέγοντες (Acts 14.11). Now Lyaconia does not appear in the list. That is not very important, however, but it is an indication that the list is not a list of languages but a list of regions where different languages were spoken.

The mentioning of Αἴγυπτον καὶ τὰ μέρη τῆς Λιβύης τῆς κατὰ Κυρήνην is not astonishing but for its precision. Luke surely knew that there were Jews in Egypt. According to the context, however, he does not here think of those people who speak Greek, but native dialects. As to Libya (which was a Roman province too) he was perhaps reluctant. But he knew perfectly well that there were Jews in Cyrene (Acts 6.9; 11.20; 13.1). That could be the reason for the extraordinary expression.

Also the ending of the list has caused many discussions and theories. Here again there are several features which have amazed many scholars. Surely few have wondered why Luke mentions only the Romans among all western peoples. They are probably right. The world of Luke is that of the eastern Mediterranean. It is enough for him to mention Rome in order to include the Latin language. But why does he not mention proselytes until now? And what about the belated reference to Crete and Arabia?

What language did the Jews in Rome speak? Some of them probably knew Latin, many of them undoubtedly spoke Greek as many or even most of the first Christians in Rome evidently did. Others spoke perhaps—*inter se*—Aramaic. And how much did Luke know about these things? Possibly—I shall not here enter on the great problem of the authorship of Acts—Luke had been to Rome and met Jews who all spoke Greek. So the Jews of Rome, now living in Jerusalem, were no indisputable witnesses to the pentecostal miracle. In this dilemma Luke finds an apt solution. There were among those Jews also proselytes. *They* surely spoke Latin and their testimony was valid.[7] The answer to the question, why Luke does not mention the proselytes till now, is: he had not reflected on them before. They do not appear until Luke needs them.

The mention of Crete and Arabia might be an addition. Going through the list again Luke observes that he had forgotten Crete, examines his memory, and adds Arabia too. This 'explanation' might be sufficient (although one wonders why he missed Cyprus). But it may be that Luke at the end of the list wants to mention some more specimens of the ability of the Spirit. What Luke knew about the language on Crete we cannot know, but he may have heard the rumour that the Cretans spoke a dialect which was difficult to understand. And Arabic was not, as it was later, a lingua franca of wide regions. Some scholars think that Cretans and Arabians just mean something like 'all sorts of people'. Luke probably uses the expression in order to emphasize that the Spirit was able to speak any language, however far-off, small, or foreign it might be.

I would like to end with an analogy, and as this paper is dedicated to an African friend I would like to take it from his own continent. If delegates from all parts of Africa met at a conference somewhere, nobody would be astonished if he heard some words spoken in English (or French). He would simply accept that the person knew the language he spoke. That would correspond to Greek in the world of Acts. And if he met some colleagues from a neighbouring province where the natives spoke a language very like his own, he would perhaps be astonished at the fact that he could understand them and they him, but he would not think it a miracle. That would correspond to Syrian at the Pentecost. But if a little group of countrymen from a hamlet near the conference town began to speak in such a way that they could all hear their own native language, the delegates would surely be utterly surprised. That would correspond to what the ἄνδρες εὐλαβεῖς ἀπὸ παντὸς ἔθνους of Acts experienced. But that would be impossible! Of course it would. But there can be no doubt that Luke thought of the pentecostal miracle in this way.

NOTES

1 Bent Noack, Pinsedagen. *Litterære og historiske problemer i Acta Kap,* 2 og drøftelsen af dem i de sidste årtier, Copenhagen 1968 (Festskrift udgivet af Københavns Universitet i anledning af Hans Majestæt Kongens fødselsdag 11. marts 1968).

2 Cf. especially p. 27.

3 *Dansk teologisk tidsskrift* 32 (1969), pp. 139-41.

4 Cf. Mark 14.58 where almost all Mss. have: ἡμεῖς ἠκούσαμεν αὐτοῦ λέγοντος ὅτι ἐγὼ καταλύσω κτλ while Matthew (26.61) has: εἶπον· οὗτος ἔφη (D: τοῦτον ἠκούσαμεν λέγοντα).

5 Acts 10.46 comes nearest both as to vocabulary, ἤκουον γὰρ αὐτῶν λαλούντων γλώσσαις καὶ μεγαλυνόντων τὸν θεόν, and as to the importance ascribed to the incident. There is, however, no hint at foreign languages. Further it is evident that Luke does not think that glossolalia is a common appearance. That is quite obvious from Acts 11.15, where Peter says: ... ἐπέπεσεν τὸ πνεῦμα τὸ ἅγιον ἐπ’ αὐτοὺς ὥσπερ καὶ ἐφ’ ἡμᾶς ἐν ἀρχῇ.

6 For this hint—as for some others—I am indebted to Dr C. Fabricius, Professor of Greek Language in Gothenburg.

7 Cf. Acts 6.9 ‘certain of the synagogue called the Libertines’, a reading which has also been corrected both in old times (arm) and later (Beza), both substituting Lybiorum.

Nations in the New Testament

NILS A. DAHL

To speak about nations in the New Testament may be an anachronism. Tribes, clans, confederations, kingdoms, and other comprehensive social units have existed throughout history. *Natio* is an old Latin word and has some equivalent in all languages, I assume. Nevertheless, the modern idea of nationality is of fairly recent origin. In several respects it reflects European history during the last centuries a period of conflicts between various national states and cultivation of the national heritage within each one of them. Today we know that we all live in one world, and talk about global perspectives, ecumenical co-operation, and cosmopolitan individuals. But in practice we still tend to give priority to the concept of nations, as evidenced by the existence of the United Nations and innumerable international organizations. The European idea of nationality has become international. Not only the United States of America but ancient empires, kingdoms, groups of tribes, and former colonies around the world struggle to become real nations with a common nationality. Fight against European and North-American imperialism and neo-colonialism is often conducted under the auspices of a nationalism which has been shaped under the impact of the Western nations, as well as in reaction to them.

Another fact is more paradoxical: the modern concept of nationality and modern nationalism have developed in countries in which Christianity has been the dominant religion. Yet there is very little inherent in the essence of Christianity, which should make us identify an individual in terms of his nationality and use 'nation' as a chief category for differentiation within mankind. The development of a number of

European nations, each with its peculiar form of nationalism, is the result of an interplay of a variety of historical factors. Here I would just like to mention one of them: While the Christian Church was in principle one, catholic, world-wide, community, the holy Scriptures provided a paradigmatic model of national existence, that of Israel, the chosen people. The ancient Church read the Old Testament as a Christian book and understood the history of Israel as her own pre-history. But when the Roman empire had disintegrated and when typological and allegorical interpretation receded, the possibility was given that peoples in various countries could draw analogies between ancient Israel and themselves: like David, their kings were kings by the grace of God. Their own nation was the elect one. America was the promised land. The lost ten tribes were, possibly, to be located on the British Isles. The Nazi ideology about the nordic race and the German people, destined to rule on earth, was the worst of caricatures, but not the only one.

The influence of the Old Testament upon the development of European and American ideas of nationality does not make the notion of the chosen people responsible for the growth of nationalism. The nationalistic transformation of biblical ideas was conditioned by given linguistic, historical, and social circumstances. But thoughts and concepts that had been formulated in ancient Israel became tools by means of which concepts of nationality and various national ideologies were shaped. Later on they were secularized. Prophetic words of doom against the chosen but sinful and disobedient people were taken to apply to the Jews. The more specificly religious elements in the Scriptures, ideas about sufferings of the chosen ones, woes against everything big and proud, were taken to belong to the spiritual realm which was the concern of the Church and not of the nations. Modern nationalism was the end product. The complex and paradoxical interrelations of Christianity and nationality deserve to be carefully investigated. The purpose of my sketch has only been to introduce the theme of this essay.

Scholars constantly pay attention to the origin of the New Testament writings at a specific time in history. Less often we have considered that they also originated within a limited geographical area. The scenery of the events reported encompasses only a semi-circle, reaching from Palestine and northernmost Arabia over Syria, Asia Minor, Macedonia, and Greece, to Italy and Rome. The geographical horizon extends further, but is still limited. In the far west we have Spain, naturally enough. In the opposite direction, we hear about countries and peoples east of the Euphrates, but not of anything beyond a line drawn from the Caspian Sea to the Persian Gulf. We hear about Ethiopia, the country south of Egypt: that would correspond more or less to the present Sudan. The home of 'the queen of the South' (Matt. 12.42) may have been even further south; but probably people did not know exactly where to locate it at that time any more than today. Northern countries are not mentioned at all. We hear about the provinces of Pontus, Bithynia, and Gallia, but of no place north of the Alps or the Black Sea. There is not even a reference to the mythical North, known from the Old Testament. The inhabited world, the οἰκουμένη, known to the New Testament writers, is the Mediterranean world with the addition of the Fertile Crescent and some other countries in the Near East. From a political point of view, the world envisaged is the Roman Empire, except for its northern and south-western provinces and with the addition of adjacent kingdoms east and south-east of the borders. We could also say that it is the world in which the Jews were living at that time.

The world of the New Testament was not a world of nations. The most important local units were Roman provinces and within them cities with surrounding areas. There were also rural districts, but in the New Testament we hear little about them, except for the Galilean towns and the Judean wilderness. Local languages continued to be spoken (cf. Acts 14.11). Some of them later re-emerged as national languages. But the public scenery was dominated by world languages: Greek, Latin, and Aramaic.

Geographically, the world of the New Testament coincides more or less with that of the Old. But within this world, nationality had once been more important than it was at the time of the Roman Empire. Not only ancient Israel, but also neighbouring countries such as Edom, Moab, and Ammon, the Aramean kingdom in Damascus, and even Egypt, were more like national states than what later existed in the same areas. The big eastern kingdoms, Assur, Babylonia, Persia, etc. had always been conglomerates of peoples, dominated by one ethnic group. The diminished importance of nationality is reflected in the use of the Hebrew word that comes closest to our term 'nation', *goy*, plural *goyyim*. In New Testament times, *goyyim* and the corresponding Greek term, ἔθνη had become a designation of the big collective of non-Israelites, the Gentiles, with little or no attention paid to the ethnic components of this mass. In Mishnaic Hebrew there is even a secondary singular, *goy*, meaning an individual Gentile, with the feminine form *goyah*, a Gentile woman.

In the New Testament, the term τὰ ἔθνη in most of its occurrences refers to the Gentile world as a whole. Only occasionally the notion that this world is made up of ethnic groups has any significance. When the term πάντα τὰ ἔθνη, 'all nations', is used, ethnic connotations are often somewhat more prominent. But, in general, the contrast between the Jews and the rest of mankind is predominant. The singular form ἔθνος may refer to some unspecified nation, as in Matt. 24.7: 'Nation shall rise against nation'. But when the singular form designates any particular nation, it mostly refers to the Jewish people. That is remarkable, as λαός and not ἔθνος, with its more national connotations, was the preferred word for the people of God. As most New Testament writers may have been born Jews, it is natural enough that 'my nation', 'our nation', or simply 'the nation' means the Jewish nation. But, as a matter of fact, there was hardly any other group within the Roman Empire to which our concept of nation can as easily be applied as to the Jews. Certainly, there was no longer any Jewish state, but the memory of national independence was still alive. Revolutions against the Romans were attempted from time to time. The great wars of liberation (A.D. 66–70 and 132–135) are evidence of a fervent nationalism without full analogy in the rest of the empire.

Yet, measured by our modern standards, the Jews were already then a highly atypical nation. Only a minority of them were living in their own country. Those living in the diaspora did not take part in the national wars of liberation, although they occasionally made local revolts of their own. There was no common Jewish language. In some areas, probably mainly within the local population of Judea, Hebrew was still a spoken language, not a language of liturgy and learned studies only. The discoveries in the Judean desert have made us realize how much literature was still written in the national language, again a fact without real analogy. But the vast majority of Jews spoke an international world language, either Aramaic or Greek.

In theory, the Jews had a common ancestry and were all descendants of Abraham, Isaac, and Jacob. In practice, there had been a great deal of racial mixture from the conquest of Canaan onwards. The enforced circumcision of the population in territories conquered by the Hasmonean princes added new elements to the mixture. Scholars disagree about how many people voluntarily joined Judaism and became proselytes. In any case, it was possible to become a Jew by acceptance of the Jewish religion, and to cease to be a Jew by abandoning it. Jewishness could without difficulty be combined with citizenship in a Hellenistic city. In the New Testament we hear about Jews who are Alexandrians, Tarsians, Egyptians, Cyreneans, Cypriots, etc. In fact, a high percentage of designations of nationality refers to Jews from various cities and countries.

New Testament attitudes to Judaism would be a topic of its own. Here it may suffice to say that the Jews are not treated as representatives of one nation among many. The list of privileges in Rom. 9.4–5 is a good illustration of that. Negative statements about the Jews are occasionally reminiscent of anti-Jewish attitudes in the ancient world (cf. 1 Thess. 2.15f). But when the Jews are said to have blind eyes, hardened hearts, and so on, this is not meant as a description of Jewish national character. Most of these statements go back to inner-Jewish controversies, from the prophets of doom onwards. To the first disciples of Jesus, it must have been a shocking experience that Jews handed their Master over to Gentiles. What is reflected in the New Testament is not a conflict between Jews and people of other nations but a controversy between those who rejected the crucified Messiah and those who believed in him.

Next to the Jews, the Greeks are most frequently mentioned in the New Testament writings. But our concept of nationality fits the Greeks of that age even less than it fits the Jews. For many centuries Greeks had not only been living on the Greek mainland and on the many islands but also in Asia Minor, in Sicily and Southern Italy, and even elsewhere. The Greeks had joined forces in fighting the Persians, but a unified Greek state did not exist in Antiquity. Only Philip of Macedonia brought about some kind of political unification. Not the country or the nation but the city state, the *polis*, was the socio-political unit in which the Greek way of life was developed and cultivated. The basic unity was linguistic. Greeks were persons who spoke an understandable, civilized language, in contrast to Barbarians who said: 'Bar-bar-bar-ba'. As time passed the contrast between Greeks and Barbarians became an opposition of culture as much as of language. Education and culture (παιδεία) made a man Greek. A Greek national literature did exist, with Homer as the great classic. Even the Greek historians, Herodotus, Thucydides, and others may deserve special mention. But Greek culture did also include elements which were not to the same extent related to a common history: philosophy, drama, sport, etc. It was possible to become Greek by adopting the Greek language, Greek culture, and Greek way of living. Normally, this had to include citizenship of a Greek city. But since the time of Alexander there were Greek cities almost all over the Near East. In many of them only a tiny minority, if anybody, was Greek by ethnic origin. In Mark 7.26 we are told about a Greek woman who was of Syrophenician descent.

In New Testament usage the word Ἕλλην means a person who is not a Jew but a Gentile. In the majority of cases, the Greeks are mentioned together with the Jews. The expression 'Jews and Greeks' means all men, just like 'Jews and Gentiles', or 'Greeks and Barbarians'. Two opposing terms are used to circumscribe the totality, which encompasses both the 'in-group' and the 'out-group'. The peculiar use of 'Greeks', meaning non-Jews, has its historical background in the conflicts of the second century B.C., especially during the reign of Antiochus IV Epiphanes. At that time the Jews who remained faithful to their own religious tradition opposed the Hellenizers in Jerusalem and had to fight the Greeks, i.e. the Seleucid king and his armies.

There is one famous statement about the Greeks in the New

Testament: 'The Jews demand signs, and the Greeks seek after wisdom' (1 Cor. 1.22). One can use this as a starting-point for reflections upon the differences of Hebrew and Greek mentality. But within the context of 1 Corinthians, the similarity between the two groups is more important than the contrast: the crucified Christ is an offensive foolishness to all men, Jews and Greeks alike, whereas he is the power of God and the wisdom of God to those who are called. The aside in Acts 17.21 is therefore a better example of demographic description: 'For all the Athenians and the visiting foreigners spent their time in nothing else, but to tell or to hear news'. But this piece of learned information applies to the city of Athens with its peculiar style.

The Romans were a nation of yet another type. To my knowledge, 'Roman' is not used as one of two opposite terms, as Jew and Gentile or Greek and Barbarian. One might, however, compare the contrast between the city of Rome and the rest of the world, the *orbis terrarum*. Whatever happened happened either *in urbe* or *in orbe*. To a real Roman such as Cicero, life in Rome was the life worth living. In principle, Romans are citizens of the city of Rome. This remained so even after Rome had become an empire and Roman citizenship had been given not only to inhabitants of Rome and Roman colonies, but also to people in all Italy. It was granted as a privilege to individuals, some of whom had paid for it (cf. Acts 22.28). Freedmen of a Roman citizen acquired citizenship themselves. In the New Testament the term Roman mostly occurs with reference to Paul's status as a Roman citizen. We also hear that Paul was handed over to the Romans as a prisoner (Acts 28.17). A statement about Roman practice is attributed to Festus: 'It is not Roman practice to grant the delivery of any man before the accused has been confronted with his accusers and had an opportunity to defend himself against the charge' (Acts 25.16). According to the Fourth Gospel, a council of chief priests and Pharisees engaged in deliberations about what to do with Jesus, lest the Romans should come and capture both the holy place and the nation (John 11.48). Latin is called the Roman language (John 19.20). But Roman citizenship, Roman law, and Roman military power are the chief features mentioned in the New Testament.

It is not easy to say whether or not the Jews, the Greeks, and the Romans of New Testament times can appropriately be described as nations. In fact, it is difficult to give any precise definition of the term nation. When we speak of a nation, we think of a comprehensive social unit, constituted by several of the following factors: racial features; ethnic descent or widespread intermarriage; a common country, language, government; political organization; laws and customs; culture and/or religion. We should add: common enemies (few things unite better than that); common history; and some common aspirations, say, the aspiration of maintaining or forming an independent state. All of these factors are seldom, if ever, combined. The problem is that it is impossible to tell exactly how many and which of them have to be held in common before we should apply the concept of nation. The matter is even further complicated because a subjective factor comes in. One might almost say that a nation is made up of persons who consider themselves, and who are considered by others to be a nation.

Consideration of the 'nations' in Antiquity, as reflected in the New Testament, draws our attention to the lack of precision inherent in the concept 'nation' itself. We find not only various nations but different types of nationality. In short, Jewish nationality is most of all religious, Greek nationality is linguistic and cultural, and Roman is political. For this reason it was possible to be a Jew by descent and religion, a Greek by language, culture, and residence, and a Roman by virtue of Roman citizenship. As an example one might mention Paul, a Jew who according to Acts was from Tarsus, and a Roman citizen. Yet the contrast between the Jewish and the Greek way of life was felt strongly; most of those who might have spoken of themselves as being both Jews and Greeks would hesitate to do so. It should also be observed that one could be Jewish, Greek, or Roman in various ways and to various degrees. Members of the Qumran community, and other groups too, tended to think of themselves as the true Israel. The Athenians, I would guess, may have considered most inhabitants of 'Greek cities' in Syria as only slightly veiled Barbarians. The members of the ancient Roman families would certainly not have regarded all who enjoyed the privilege of

Roman citizenship to be genuine Romans. But this just adds to the fluidity of the concept 'nation'.

A glance at the main nations mentioned in the New Testament reveals the time-conditioned nature of the modern concept of nationality. Taking into consideration the conditions in the Roman Empire, it is not surprising that New Testament writers do not often stress the overcoming of racial and national differences in the Church of Christ. The universal nature of the gospel is chiefly seen in terms of its destination for the non-Jewish part of mankind as well as for the people of the covenant. In the great commission it is said: μαθητεύσατε πάντα τὰ ἔθνη (Matt. 28.19). But it is not certain that the comprehensive collective 'all nations' is really thought of in terms of a number of distinguishable nations, like those who nowadays have a seat in the United Nations.

Luke speaks of the universal destination of the gospel in geographical, not in national, terms (Acts 1.8). The story about Pentecost in Jerusalem in Acts 2 may be read as a prefiguration of churches in all nations, in each of which the great acts of God are to be proclaimed in the mother tongue. But that was hardly Luke's intention. In the context, the catalogue of 'Parthians, and Medes, and Elamites', etc. refers to Jews, proselytes, and godfearers who had come to Jerusalem from a great number of peoples and provinces. They represent the whole house of Israel, gathered from among all nations (Acts 2.5, 36). The divided reaction to the pentecostal event (Acts 2.11, 13) is symbolic of the split within Israel that will result from the apostolic preaching.

The Ethiopian baptized by Philip is the only individual from outside the Roman Empire whose conversion is reported (Acts 8.26–40). What made his conversion to be remembered and told as a legend was neither his African provenance nor his black skin. (It is quite possible that he was black, but that is never said.) The occurrence was remarkable because he was a eunuch, and thus, according to the rules in Deut. 23, did not have access to the assembly of the Lord. The Ethiopian represents persons at the fringe of Judaism. In the Lucan composition his story has been placed between the evangelization among the Samaritans and the vocation of Paul, preparing for the mission to the Gentiles. Thus we get a picture of a progressive widening of the circle reached by the gospel; but the question of nationality has no special importance.

To Paul, as to Luke, the city of Rome was of special importance; the letter to the Romans is evidence of that. But the unity in Christ is primarily conceived as a unity of circumcised Jews and uncircumcised Gentiles (e.g. Gal. 6.15). The most famous formula of unity reads: 'There is neither Jew nor Greek, there is neither slave nor free, there is no longer male and female, for you are all one in Christ Jesus' (Gal. 3.28). Having been brought up to think in terms of nationality and race, we would like to add other pairs, say, 'neither German nor Englishman, neither American nor African, neither black nor white'. But for Paul the abolition of distinctions caused by the Mosaic law was the one dominant aspect of unity in Christ. In contrast to the Gentile, the slave, and the woman, the free Jewish male was obliged—and privileged—to observe all the commandments and religious rites. For Paul the abolition of those special duties and privileges is the main social implication of the unity and freedom in Christ. But it may be added that in his day the distinction between slave and free had little, if anything, to do with differences between ethnic groups; there were Greek and Jewish, as well as Germanic, Asian, or African slaves.

Apart from the three years spent in Arabia, i.e. in the Nabatean kingdom, Paul's work concentrated upon Hellenistic cities. But even Barbarians are within his horizon: 'I am a debtor both to Greeks and to Barbarians, both to wise and to uneducated' (Rom. 1.14). The two contrasting pairs, ῞Ελληνες/ βάρβαροι and σοφοί/ἀνόητοι are virtually synonymous. Paul owes the gospel of Christ both to highly cultivated Greeks and to uneducated, 'foolish' Barbarians. In Colossians the Barbarians are included in the formula of unification: 'Here there is no longer Greek and Jew, circumcised and uncircumcised, Barbarian, Scythian, slave, free man, but Christ is all, and in all' (Col. 3.11). The formula 'male and female' (cf. Gen. 1.27) has been dropped, as it was open to misunderstanding (cf. 1 Cor. 7 and 11.2ff). Almost as a substitute, the Barbarian and the Scythian have been added. We should have expected another pair of contrasts like 'Greek and Barbarian'. But the Greek had already been mentioned in pair with the Jew. Thus, the Scythian is inserted, not as a contrast to the

Barbarian, but as a typical, even extreme, example of a Barbarian.

Once Paul adds an attributive adjective to an ethnic name: 'O foolish Galatians!' (ʾΩ ἀνόητοι Γαλάται, Gal. 3.1). Paul thinks that the Galatians are foolish because they are turning away from the gospel which he preached; they observe days and months and are on the verge of accepting circumcision. But, as we have seen, the adjective ἀνόητος means 'uneducated', 'barbarian', as well as 'foolish' (Rom. 1.14). The Galatians were a Celtic tribe that had settled in Asia Minor in the third century B.C. They had been known as simpleminded Barbarians. Later on, they had been hellenized; but it is always hard to get rid of a stereotype once it has been fixed. Paul must have been aware of the possibility that he could be understood to say: 'You uneducated, barbarian Galatians!' Yet Paul cannot have intended to insult his readers, whose confidence and loyalty he seeks to regain. I would guess that Paul was not the first to use the phrase ἀνόητοι Γαλάται; he picks it up from his opponents and gives it an ironical twist and a double meaning.

There are several elements of irony and even sarcasm in Galatians (e.g. 1.6, 10; 2.6; 5.12). I do not think that Paul had been subject to a frontal attack. The Judaizers rather presented themselves as fulfillers of the work begun by him. Elsewhere he himself 'preached circumcision' (5.11). His good reputation in the churches of Judea and among the leaders in Jerusalem was adduced as a proof of that (cf. 1.22–4 and 2.1ff). In Galatia Paul had preached the gospel without any reference to matters of the Mosaic law, but this was explained as missionary adaptation (cf. 1.10). Paul had changed his voice and told less than the full truth (cf. 4.16, 20). Understood as a response to charges like this, Paul's apologetic 'autobiography' in Gal. 1—2 makes good sense. Paul claims that he received his gospel and was sent to the Gentiles by a revelation of the risen Christ (1.11–16). He was never commissioned by the authorities in Jerusalem (1.16b–20). In his dealings with them he never concealed anything; on his second visit to Jerusalem he was even accompanied by Titus, an uncircumcised Greek (2.1ff). The agreement reached in Jerusalem implied a full recognition of Paul's mission to the Gentiles, and thus of the gospel that he had preached in Galatia (2.6–10). In Antioch Paul had even opposed Cephas face to face (2.11ff).

If this reconstruction is basically correct, the irony in Gal. 3.1 becomes meaningful. Paul was said to have been submissive to the 'men of repute', 'the reputed pillars' in Jerusalem (cf. 2.2, 6, 9. The designation οἱ δοκοῦντες was probably coined by the opponents). Towards the Galatians he had been condescending, treating them as unsophisticated Barbarians who should not be bothered by matters of calendar and legal questions; a simplified gospel might be good enough for them, and thus it would be easier to persuade them. This explains the element of irony in Paul's remarks about the 'men of repute': 'Whatsoever they were, makes no difference to me; God shows no partiality' (2.6). We should supply what is not said in plain words: 'Nor do I'. Paul asserts that he has always been the same person and upheld the same gospel, whether he preached to 'uneducated Galatians' or stood face to face with the 'men of repute' in Jerusalem. He did not treat the Galatians as Barbarians and would never have thought that they were *that* foolish as they turn out to be when they, who began 'in the Spirit', are now seeking perfection 'in the flesh', by circumcising their foreskin (3.3).

The Galatian controversy has to do with the doctrine of justification, but missionary practice was also at stake. Paul was accused of false adaptation because he had preached the gospel in isolation from the Mosaic law and the Jewish way of life. He, on the contrary, holds that the gospel is falsified if specific matters of legal observation and patterns of behaviour are added to the gospel of God's free grace in Jesus Christ for all men without distinction. This, and no other gospel, is what the Christian Church owes to Jews, to Greeks, to 'foolish Galatians' and other Barbarians, to all nations.

Almost by accident the Galatians became a New Testament prototype for peoples who are neither Jewish, Greek, nor Roman. The Cretans had the bad luck that a saying about them was quoted in Titus 1.12. But they were Greeks. In our context it is of greater interest to take notice of the remarks about the friendliness (φιλανθρωπία) of the Barbarians of Malta (Acts 28.2ff). In general, Jews, Greeks, and Romans are the predominant 'nations' in the New Testament writings. The

Samaritans might also have been mentioned, but a treatment of this peculiar group would contribute little to our general theme. There is one book, however, that treats the nations in a way that differs from what we find in the rest of the New Testament: the Revelation of John.

In the Book of Revelation we find what we may miss elsewhere, the image of people from all nations gathered into the Church of Christ. We are made to listen to the heavenly praise of the Lamb: 'Worthy art thou to take the scroll and break its seals; for thou wast slain, and by thy blood didst purchase for God men of every tribe and tongue and people and nation' (5.9f). We get the vision of the great multitude from every nation and all tribes, peoples, and tongues, standing in white clothes before the throne and before the Lamb (7.9). At the same time we are told that power over every tribe and tongue and nation was given to the beast (13.7). The great harlot is sitting upon many waters, which symbolizes peoples, multitudes, nations, and tongues (17.1,15). She has the name 'Babylon the Great' (17.5), but her features are those of the imperial city, Rome: big business and shipping, slave trade, luxury, licentiousness, imperialism, and exploitation. All the nations were deceived by her sorceries and given of 'the wine of the wrath of her fornication' (18.23; 14.8 and 18.3).

A number of ethnic terms are used more or less synonymously: φυλή, γλῶσσα, λαός, ἔθνος, and even ὄχλος (17.5; cf. 10.11; 11.9; 14.6). No one of the words is to be given a precise definition; what is important is the inclusion of all mankind and all possible ethnic, tribal, or national units of which it is made up. Even when it stands by itself, the term τὰ ἔθνη in the Apocalypse designates a plurality of nations, not the Gentiles as a collective unit. The only possible exception is the prophecy in 11.2, that the outside temple court will be handed over to the Gentile nations who are to tread the holy city under foot. In spite of the Old Testament language, the nations are envisaged in their relationship to the world city and the empire as much as to the people of God. It is also remarkable how often the Apocalypticist speaks in plural about the kings of the earth. The seven kings of Rev. 17.9 would seem to be Roman emperors. In other contexts 'the kings' are either all sovereigns on earth or just the non-Roman kings. The relations of these kings to the world power are ambiguous. They act as allies of the beast (19.19; cf. 17.12–14). They have committed fornication with the harlot, enjoying her pleasures (17.2; 18.3,9). They will lament for her, when they see her burning (18.9). And yet, invasion of the kings from east of the Euphrates is a threatening danger (16.12–19). Ten kings, represented by the ten horns of the scarlet beast, do hate the harlot; they shall make her desolate and naked, and eat her flesh, and burn her with fire (17.3,16).

The whole imagery is grotesque. The seer has even succeeded in making barbarian Greek a magnificent artistic medium. His specific theme is the victory of the crucified Jesus, who conquers all powers and all rulers opposed to God and vindicates his chosen and suffering slaves. In order to depict this, the seer uses not only the language of psalms and prophets but also ancient myths about the beasts of original chaos. But at the same time the visions reflect the contemporaneous world situation. Not only the kings of the earth but also apocalyptic riders, infernal locusts, and devastating armies have attributes which make one think of the Parthians and other nations and tribes outside the borders of the empire (cf. 6.1–8; 9.1–11, 13–19). Invasion, war and bloodshed, pestilence, hunger, and inflation did not belong to the world of apocalyptic visions only. All of this represented actual or potential realities. Treaties and alliances provided only uncertain safety in the more or less permanent East–West conflict of the age. In the visions of John we sense some of the mixture of fear and fascination which the danger from the East evoked among oppressed minorities within the empire.

In the Apocalypse the world of nations, ethnic, tribal, and linguistic groups is seen under a twofold perspective. The nations are engaged on both sides in the final, cosmic conflict. They are associated and allied with the powers of anti-Christ; but they are also suppressed and exploited, and they will take their revenge. Christ shall conquer the beasts and all their allies; he shall rule the nations with a rod of iron (12.5; 19.15; cf. Ps. 2.9 and Isa. 11.4). But the conqueror is none other than the Lamb that was slaughtered in order to purchase men from all nations, tribes, and tongues. Opposed to the harlot 'Babylon' is the heavenly city, the new Jerusalem, the bride of

Christ. The seer seems to envisage a plurality of peoples even there; in variation of the old formula he writes that God shall dwell among men and they shall be his peoples (λαοὶ αὐτοῦ ἔσονται, 21.3). In any case, there is room for the nations even in the vision of the eternal city: they shall walk in her light, and the kings of the earth shall—voluntarily—bring their glory, the glory and honour of the nations, into her (21.24, 26; cf. Isa. 60; Ps. 72.10–15). Leaves from the tree of life will be for the healing of the nations (22.2).

No doubt John conceives of the cosmic conflict in religious terms: God, 'the king of the nations' (15.3), and Christ, 'King of Kings and Lord of Lords' (19.16) are contrasted with the beasts and the worship paid to them, deification of emperors and glorification of the Roman city and empire. John writes to persecuted Christians, comforting them and pleading their cause. And yet, in doing so, he has also given voice and words to the spiritual resistance against Rome, not to say to the hatred against Roman imperialism, big business, exploitation, and luxury, the hatred latent in many minority groups in the empire. He opens up a vision of hope, not only for the salvation of individuals of all nations and tribes but also for a new future for the nations themselves.

Paul's Speech on the Areopagus

C. K. BARRETT

Few parts of the New Testament have been so fully and so frequently discussed as Luke's account of Paul's visit to Athens in Acts 17.15–34, and on few has so great a wealth of scholarship been expended. The story has been repeatedly analysed, and its historical value assessed, with results varying from complete acceptance to complete denial of its trustworthiness; the speech itself has been compared with Greek philosophical and Hellenistic Jewish literature, and a mass of parallel material collected. The results are to be found not only in commentaries, but in long essays such as Dibelius's,[1] and books such as Gärtner's,[2] which not only collect parallels to the thoughts contained in the speech but also compare its form and purpose with those of speeches found in Greek historical writing in general. In comparison with such studies the present essay moves within very narrow limits. Except in one direction it makes no attempt to add to the wealth of illustrative quotation; its aim is rather to interpret that which others have collected in the light of Luke's general purpose in Acts. Most students of Acts would agree that it is at least one of Luke's major motives to show the victorious progress of the gospel from Jerusalem to Rome.[3] The last words of the book are a triumphant conclusion: '[Paul] spent a full two years in his own hired lodging and received all those who visited him, preaching the kingdom of God and teaching the things concerning the Lord Jesus Christ with all freedom and without restraint' (28.30f). These words not only express the victory of the gospel, but do so in a way characteristic of Luke.[4] Not for him the theological exposition of the gospel as the power of God unto salvation (Rom. 1.16) that Paul writes; his was the kind of mind that sees truth always in concrete events, and in relation to persons. It is this that explains his concentration upon a few outstanding preachers of the gospel, notably Peter and Paul. It is partly responsible for the judgement of his work as a *theologia gloriae*.[5] Luke does not represent his heroes as almost uniformly successful and as delivered from their enemies—Peter from the Council and from Herod, Paul from the Jews and from imprisonment at Philippi, and so on—because he believes that the gospel is an infallible charm that brings security to those who accept and practise it. His heroes do in fact suffer a good deal (though indeed they are as a rule speedily delivered from their suffering), and one of them lays down the principle that it is through many afflictions that we are to enter the kingdom of God (14.22). Luke's conviction is that the word of God is not bound (cf. 2 Tim. 2.9); no power on earth can hinder the spread of the gospel. But his way of expressing this conviction is to tell the story of successful preachers; the power of the gospel becomes visible in the power of the preacher, and the Lord's love for his people in their deliverance from peril. This may lack the profundity of Pauline theology, but it is hardly a betrayal of it.

Paul's whole career is represented in this light, from his deliverance from the threat to his life at Damascus (9.25) and the successful preaching in Paphos (13.6–12) to the last words of the book, quoted above. Does Luke intend the visit to Athens, carefully written up as something of a 'set piece',[6] to be an exception to this record? It seems unlikely. 17.34 has always been a problem to commentators. Are the men, including Dionysius the Areopagite, who believed, and Damaris, represented as no more than a meagre harvest, or does Luke mean to say, Even in Athens there were converts? In view of the drift of the book as a whole, the latter is the more likely possibility. The names are probably traditional: it is unlikely that Luke simply invented them. It is probable that the hazy impression given by the concluding sentences of the paragraph is due to the fact that Luke was trying to compress several different thoughts into small compass. On the one hand, he wished to indicate that Athens, the citadel where pagan religion and philosophy were entrenched, offered to Paul serious opposition and a real threat. On the other hand, Paul not only escaped the threat, but won converts. The lack of clarity is found in verse 32 as well

as in verse 34. Two groups (οἱ μέν ... οἱ δέ ...) are distinguished. There is no doubt that the first group consisted of
mockers (ἐχλεύαζον). But does ἀκουσόμεθά σου περὶ τούτου
καὶ πάλιν mean, We are so impressed by your message that
we should like to hear it again, or, We are not really interested—
let us adjourn the question *sine die*? The μέν–δέ construction
suggests that Luke saw a real contrast between the two groups,
and he would be writing with unusual carelessness if he said,
Some mocked; but others mocked by proposing an indefinite
postponement.[7]

Moreover, Luke adds, οὕτως ὁ Παῦλος ἐξῆλθεν ἐκ μέσου
αὐτῶν. Cf. Luke 4.30, αὐτὸς δὲ διελθὼν διὰ μέσου αὐτῶν
ἐπορεύετο, where Jesus escapes attack at Nazareth; also Acts
23.10, ἐκέλευσεν τὸ στράτευμα καταβὰν ἁρπάσαι αὐτὸν ἐκ
μέσου αὐτῶν, where the Roman force rescues Paul from being
torn in pieces by the Jewish Council. The evidence is hardly
adequate for us to describe the expression as a Lucan formula
for escape from danger, but it adds at least some weight to the
view that Paul caused serious dissension among the Greek
philosophers as he was later to do among the Jewish members
of the Sanhedrin, and that in the end he came safely out of an
ugly situation.

It looks then as if Luke's final view of the outcome of the visit
to Athens was that Paul encountered a stiff obstacle, provoked
dissension, escaped attack, and made at least some converts. As
elsewhere, the Lord's hand was with him. We turn to the beginning of the passage to find out how the opposition was made up.
Elsewhere the resistance to Paul was usually located in the
synagogue. Jews might at first receive him favourably and
invite him to speak in the synagogue (e.g. 13.15), but after he
had spoken and attracted a good deal of attention they turned
against him (e.g. 13.45). There is no comment on the attitude
of the Athenian synagogue, which is dismissed in half a verse
(17.17a): there were synagogues everywhere, but there was
only one Athens, and Luke proceeds to deal with it as a special
case.[8] He notes the following points.

(a) The city was overrun with idols (κατείδωλον, 17.16); that
is, it was a seat not of Judaism but of popular Greek
religion. This is taken up in the opening words of the

speech: κατὰ πάντα ὡς δεισιδαιμονεστέρους ὑμᾶς θεωρῶ
(17.22). The reference to the altar dedicated ἀγνώστῳ θεῷ
(17.23) is the beginning of Paul's comment on his environment rather than a description; see further below (p. 75).

(b) It was characteristic of the Athenians to desire to hear or
say some new thing (17.21); that is, Paul had to deal with
the Greek love of novelty,[9] an unstable society, more
interested in entertainment than religion.

(c) Paul found himself engaged in argument[10] with philosophers, and brought by them to appear before, or on, the
Areopagus.[11]

The philosophers are specifically described as Epicureans and
Stoics (17.18). Why are these two schools mentioned? Many
commentaries simply pass this question by, as if it were the most
natural thing in the world that only Epicureans and Stoics
should be mentioned, and as if Pythagoreans, Cynics, Peri-
patetics, Sceptics, and the rest did not exist. Others[12] suggest
that the Epicureans and Stoics were the most important, or
popular, schools. Whether this was in fact so is difficult to
determine. The popularity of the Stoics is clear,[13] and there is
no doubt that the Epicureans too made a considerable impact
on the Hellenistic age. Each had its seat—the Porch and the
Garden—in Athens. But Luke's own careful description is
sufficient to remind us[14] that Zeno and Epicurus were not the
only, or indeed the greatest, philosophers who had worked in
Athens. It is suggested here that the two schools are named
because Luke had their tenets in mind, and alluded to them in
the speech he puts in Paul's mouth.

That Paul's speech is closely related to Stoicism has very
frequently been observed, and there is no need to repeat the
evidence in detail here.[15] The unity of mankind (v. 26), the
divine appointment of seasons and natural boundaries (26),[16]
the divine environment in which men live and move—often
enough conceived pantheistically by Stoics (28), the natural
kinship of men with God, summed up in the words of Aratus
(τοῦ γὰρ καὶ γένος ἐσμέν, 28): all of these are familiar points
of contact between the speech and well-known Stoic doctrines.
To speak of such points of contact is not to say that Luke
abandons the Christian faith for Stoicism, meaning by his words

exactly what Stoics meant by them, nor is it to deny that the Stoicism may have reached Luke by way of Hellenistic Judaism. The question whether Paul himself would have used Stoic material in this way is not considered in this paper. In view however of this relation between the Areopagus address and Stoicism it is not unreasonable to think that Luke mentioned the Stoics in v. 18 in order to prepare for the allusions, and to suggest that he mentioned the Epicureans for the same reason.

This suggestion would no more make Paul an Epicurean than the familiar observation of Stoic parallels makes him a Stoic. Before we look at the speech from the point of view suggested it may be well to consider the kind of argument that forms the basis of the speeches, especially the Pauline speeches, in Acts. As a rule the operative factor is Judaism, to which Luke's attitude is a double one. On the one hand, the Jews are an elect race (13.17), chosen by God to exercise a special function and to receive a special promise which was not given to mankind as a whole: 'Brothers, sons of the race of Abraham, and the God-fearers among you, to you has been sent the message of this salvation' (13.26). In virtue of this the Jews are a standing rebuke to their heathen neighbours, especially in respect of idolatry. On the other hand, the Jews have so abused their privileges that they can in the end only be rejected: 'It was necessary that the word of God should be spoken first of all to you; but since you thrust it away, and judge yourselves unworthy of eternal life, behold! we turn to the Gentiles' (13.46). The Jews can be used against heathen religion, but in the end must themselves be reproved and rejected as themselves in error.

In Acts 17.15-34, as was noted above, the Jews are scarcely mentioned, and play no significant role; the Stoics however are used in a similar way, for some of their insights are used to make major points in Paul's argument. The human race *is* one, it *was* made for a special relation with God, and it *is* man's business to discern this relation and to live in accordance with it. So far the Stoics are right, and they can be used against Athenian scepticism, atheism, and flippancy. They know that life is real and earnest, and that men must feel after God. But they worship God in ignorance, and what lies ahead of the human race is *not* (as they think) an ἐκπύρωσις and a new

beginning of the age-old cycle, but the judgement of the world
through Jesus Christ.

Do the Epicureans, and Epicureanism, play a similar role?
It seems that they do; but to demonstrate it it is necessary to go
back to what is recorded of Paul's first impression of Athens:
it is idol-ridden, and more than a little superstitious
(κατείδωλος, δεισιδαιμονέστερος). Now it is well known
that, though he conformed to the public rituals, Epicurus
vehemently resisted superstition—the religion of fear and dread
of the gods.

> So fear of the gods, fear of their anger towards the living and
> of their vengeance on the dead, played a great part in Greek
> religion. Perhaps Epicurus had experienced it himself.
> Perhaps he had undergone a crisis of conscience from which
> he had emerged victorious. If that is so we can understand
> better his unfailing certitude. He was convinced, at any rate,
> that *deisidaimonia* prevailed all about him, and as he had
> reached the haven of safety and, in a sentiment of universal
> benevolence, wished to lead others into it, he felt it to be his
> first care to banish this fear which utterly prevents peace of
> mind (*ataraxia*).[17]

This attitude appears in the work of Epicurus himself,[18] and
very notably in his greatest follower, Lucretius, especially in the
famous passage where the latter celebrates the achievement of
the former, *De Rerum Natura* i. 63–80.[19] Epicurus was not an
atheist, though the charge was often brought against him; but
he was a determined opponent of the kind of religion that was
still current in Athens in the first century A.D., and he opposed
to false opinions about the deity the true opinion which he
himself held. He could therefore be called in as Paul's ally in
the sort of argument that is used in Acts 17.22–5. Nothing
man could do by religious manoeuvring could affect the gods;
the thought that the gods could need anything was particularly shocking—the gods were perfectly blessed and happy
beings.[20]

That Epicurus and popular religion could thus be played off,
the one against the other, is neatly demonstrated by Plutarch's
tract *De Superstitione* (Περὶ Δεισιδαιμονίας). It is true that in
this tract Plutarch does not mention Epicurus by name, and

sets over against the superstition—religiosity—that he attacks, atheism (ἀθεότης). In this however Plutarch is joining in the false—though common and understandable—charge referred to in the last paragraph; that he had Epicureanism in mind is shown by his reference to Epicurus's atomic theory. For it is part of his atheist's belief that the universe originated in atoms (1: ἀτόμοις τίς οἴεται καὶ κενὸν ἀρχὰς εἶναι τῶν ὅλων;)—a view that points clearly to Epicurus. And Plutarch, though himself no atheist, sees in Epicurean 'atheism' a valuable check to the even greater evil of superstition, the δεισιδαιμονία that Paul encountered in Athens. For 'atheism is complete insensibility (ἀπάθεια) to the divine, since it fails to perceive the good (τὸ ἀγαθόν); but superstition is an excess of feeling (πολυπάθεια), as it supposes the good to be evil' (6). The context connects the errors of δεισιδαιμονία, as Paul does, with idolatry: 'They are persuaded by the coppersmiths and the sculptors and the wax-modellers that the bodies of the gods have human form, and such things they form, and spend their time on (κατασχολάζουσι), and worship' (ibid.). Plutarch uses Epicureanism to rebuke superstition, and at the same time makes it clear that for Epicurean 'atheism' he has no sympathy.

It seems reasonable to understand the Areopagus speech on similar lines. Paul finds Athens in the grip of popular, superstitious religion. This bears witness to both elements in the truth contained in the altar dedication, ἀγνώστῳ θεῷ: there is a God, and men do not know him. Paul enlists the aid of the philosophers, using in the first place the rational criticism of the Epicureans to attack the folly and especially the idolatry of popular religion, and then the theism of the Stoics to establish (against the Epicureans) the immediate and intimate nearness of God, and man's obligation to follow the path of duty and of (true) religion, rather than that of pleasure. But all these propaedeutics come in the end under judgement: men must repent, for God has appointed a day in which he means to judge the world in righteousness, by a Man whom he has appointed, and raised from the dead (17.31).

Whether this kind of argument was used by the historical Paul, and how far and in what ways it may be applicable to the present missionary situation of the Church, are questions too

wide for discussion in this short essay: but they are nevertheless
worthy of attention.

NOTES

1 M. Dibelius, 'Paul on the Areopagus', in *Studies in the Acts of the
   Apostles* (London 1956), pp. 26–77; also 'Paul in Athens', op. cit.,
   pp. 78–83.

2 B. Gärtner, *The Areopagus Speech and Natural Revelation* (Uppsala 1955).

3 For example, F. V. Filson, *Three Crucial Decades* (London 1964), p. 13,
   '... the church, inspired and directed by the Holy Spirit, had the
   power to persist in its Christian witness and make steady progress in
   spite of continual opposition and persecution'. See the context.

4 I have briefly discussed this characteristic in an essay in a collected
   volume of *New Testament Essays* (London 1972), pp. 77f.

5 See references and discussion in I. H. Marshall, *Luke: Historian and
   Theologian* (Exeter 1970), pp. 209ff.

6 See M. Dibelius, op. cit., pp. 78–83; E. Haenchen, *Die Apostelgeschichte*
   (Göttingen 1965), p. 465 (quoting A. D. Nock's important review of
   Dibelius in *Gnomon* 25 (1953), pp. 497–506).

7 Haenchen (ad loc.) interprets similarly, adding that Luke will have
   taken the open mockers to be Epicureans.

8 To some extent the speech at Lystra (14.15ff) is parallel to that at
   Athens, but it lacks the explicit philosophical background.

9 The commentaries supply ample confirmatory evidence; see especially
   H. Conzelmann, *Die Apostelgeschichte* (Tübingen 1963), ad loc.

10 As Haenchen (ad loc.) notes, Luke's word at verse 18 (συμβάλλειν)
   is ambiguous. It may mean simply 'to converse', or 'to dispute'. It is
   not clear that Luke means that Paul conversed with the Stoics and
   disputed with the Epicureans.

11 It is disputed whether the term Areopagus denotes a court or a locality.
   It may be that Luke himself was not entirely clear about this. The
   question does not affect the argument of this essay.

12 For example, Conzelmann (ad loc.): 'Stoiker und Epikuräer sind als
   Vertreter der beiden Schulen genannt, die man in der breiten Öffent-
   lichkeit am besten kennt.'

13 'The philosophy of the Hellenistic world was the Stoa; all else was
   secondary' (W. W. Tarn, *Hellenistic Civilisation* (London 1930), p. 290).

14 It is hard to think that Luke did not have in mind, if not the accounts
   by Plato and Xenophon, at least popular material about Socrates; see
   17.17 (the Agora), 18 (ξένων δαιμονίων), 22 ("Ανδρες 'Αθηναῖοι).

15 In addition to commentaries, M. Pohlenz, 'Paulus und die Stoa',
   ZNW 42 (1949), pp. 69–104; W. Eltester, 'Gott und die Natur in der
   Areopagrede', *Neutestamentliche Studien für Rudolf Bultmann* (Berlin
   1954), pp. 202–27; cf. 'Schöpfungsoffenbarung und natürliche
   Theologie im frühen Christentum', *NTS* 3 (1957), pp. 93–114.

16 The meaning of προστεταγμένους καιροὺς καὶ τὰς ὁροθεσίας τῆς κατοικίας αὐτῶν is much disputed, but the dispute does not affect the present argument.

17 A. J. Festugière, *Epicurus and his Gods* (Oxford 1955), pp. 56f. The character of the δεισιδαίμων is described by Theophrastus (*Characters* 16).

18 *Epistle to Menoeceus* 123: Gods there are, since the knowledge of them is by clear vision. But they are not such as the many believe them to be: for indeed they do not consistently represent them as they believe them to be. And the impious man (ἀσεβής) is not he who denies the gods of the many, but he who attaches to the gods the beliefs of the many (translation from C. Bailey, *Epicurus: the extant Remains* (Oxford 1926), pp. 83, 85). Cf. *Epistle to Herodotus* 81.

19 The passage may be quoted in the translation of R. E. Latham (in the Penguin *Lucretius* (Harmondsworth 1955), p. 29): When human life lay grovelling in all men's sight, crushed to the earth under the dead weight of superstition (*oppressa gravi sub relligione*) whose grim features lowered menacingly upon mortals from the four quarters of the sky, a man of Greece was first to raise mortal eyes in defiance, first to stand erect and brave the challenge. Fables of the gods did not crush him, nor the lightning flash and the growling menace of the sky. Rather, they quickened his manhood, so that he, first of all men, longed to smash the constraining locks of nature's doors. The vital vigour of his mind prevailed. He ventured far out beyond the flaming ramparts of the world and voyaged in mind throughout infinity. Returning victorious, he proclaimed to us what can be and what cannot; how a limit is fixed to the power of everything and an immovable frontier post. Therefore superstition (*relligio*) in its turn lies crushed beneath his feet, and we by his triumph are lifted level with the skies.

20 See note 18. In *Epistle to Menoeceus* 134 it is a *reductio ad absurdum* of deterministic natural philosophy to say that 'it were better to follow the myths about the gods than to become a slave to the destiny of the natural philosophers: for the former suggests a hope of placating the gods by worship, whereas the latter involves a necessity which knows no placation' (Bailey, p. 91). A belief that is inferior to the myths is quite intolerable. Fragment LXV (Vatican Collection): It is vain, to ask of the gods what a man is capable of supplying for himself (Bailey, p. 117). Fragment 58: If God listened to the prayers of men, all men would quickly have perished; for they are for ever praying for evil against one another (Bailey, p. 135). Cf. Lucretius v. 147–56.

Interpreting Paul by Paul
An Essay in the Comparative Study of Pauline Thought

―――――◆◆◆◆―――――

C. F. D. MOULE

It is a well-known principle of interpretation that a writer is his own best commentator; but it certainly does not follow that the best commentary is the one that goes no further than the pages of its text; and New Testament interpretation has been so vastly enriched since the days of Wettstein—to go no further back—by the researches of scholars into the world of thought in which the New Testament was born, that it would be sheer obscurantism to retreat again within the narrow confines of the canonical Scriptures.

Nevertheless, I want to suggest that the very success of the normal techniques of New Testament study, bringing in, as they do, parallels from outside, has tended to obscure the importance of a comparative study of an author within himself; and I offer a few examples of comparative studies within the Pauline writings, by way of hinting, at least, at the possibilities of this method. I am glad to dedicate this essay to the honour of a valued colleague in *Studiorum Novi Testamenti Societas*, while, at the same time, gratefully acknowledging the hospitality of the University of Uppsala, at which some of this material (in a different form) was delivered as a lecture in September 1964.

1. My first example, from Phil. 2, presupposes a previous essay of mine;[1] and, in the light of it, my first step has to be the negative one of rejecting what has sometimes been claimed as a parallel. In that essay I attempted to make a case for construing the famous phrase in v. 6 to mean that Jesus did not interpret God-likeness in terms of getting but of giving—not of 'snatching' (ἁρπαγμός) but of self-emptying (ἑαυτὸν ἐκένωσεν). This is only a tentative conclusion, and I am well aware that

(although it is not new, but a revival of an earlier exegesis) there are arguments—perhaps decisive arguments—against it. But supposing it is allowed to stand, then what has sometimes been seen² as a parallel (as well as a contrast) between Phil. 2.5–11 and 3.7–11 is, after all, less close a parallel than it appeared to be; or, rather, what has been interpreted as both likeness and contrast becomes, on this showing, mainly contrast. In Phil. 3 Paul says that he had learnt to regard as sheer loss, as worthless, what he had once regarded as gain (κέρδη—a collective plural), whereas in Phil. 2 (on this showing) Jesus is not, after all, described as regarding God-likeness as something not to be treated as gain (ἁρπαγμός in the sense usually attributed to it in this passage). If that were the sense, it would, indeed, be a close parallel. But, instead, he is described as refusing to regard God-likeness as a matter of 'getting' or 'snatching'. If so, then Phil. 2 and 3 run in rather different directions of thought. So much for the rejection of alleged parallels.

But there are other passages within the Pauline corpus which do, perhaps, offer valid and significant parallels to other parts of Phil. 2. In the essay referred to, I have already tried to adduce parallels for the phrase in v. 5, τοῦτο φρονεῖτε ἐν ὑμῖν ὃ καὶ ἐν Χριστῷ Ἰησοῦ, to support the (unfashionable) interpretation 'adopt the same attitude, in your mutual relations, as was found in Christ Jesus'. Here, without repeating what is said there, I want simply to develop the point a little further by noting that the more generally accepted interpretation—'adopt, in your mutual relations, the same attitude as you adopt in union with Christ Jesus'—runs contrary to the Pauline attitude as evidenced elsewhere. The last thing Paul is likely to have done is to conceive that life 'in Christ' could be distinguished from life in the community. We know well enough that when he is using ἐν in this incorporative (mystical–ecclesiastical) sense, the resulting phrase is sometimes virtually synonymous with 'in the Church'; and we should need extremely strong evidence before conceding that Paul could possibly have allowed that life 'in the Lord' could be lived in any different way from life 'in the community'.

The characteristic Pauline contrast is between what Christians actually *are* by baptism and what they must *become* by implementing it—not between what they are in their *private* relations with Christ and what they are in their relations with one another in the *community*. In an article on the 'become what you are' theme in 1 Corinthians, G. Friedrich[3] brings this out clearly. For instance, on 1 Cor. 6.1–11 he shows that Paul is exhorting the Christians to implement in their everyday life what is given them in baptism, and adds: 'the actual relations between Christians is conditioned by their belonging to Christ' ('durch die Zugehörigkeit zu Christus wird das konkrete Verhalten der Christen bestimmt', p. 246). But at no point (this is my own comment, not Friedrich's) is there any such phrase as 'be as respectful towards one another as you are towards Christ'. Perhaps the nearest thing in 1 Corinthians to a parallel to the false interpretation (as I take it to be) of Phil. 2.5 might be in the latter part of that same ch. 6 of 1 Corinthians, where to be κολλώμενος τῷ κυρίῳ is shown to be flat contradictory to and incompatible with being κολλώμενος τῇ πόρνῃ: adherence to the Lord is incompatible with adherence to a harlot. But the true parallel to that would be if Paul had said in Philippians 'you cannot be both ἐν Χριστῷ 'Ιησοῦ and ἐν τῷ κόσμῳ and so not ἐν ἀλλήλοις'; but this he does not say.

I believe that most commentators who do take Phil. 2.5 in the way I am opposing, unconsciously supply, mentally, some word of obligation or fittingness, as though it has been τοῦτο φρονεῖτε ἐν ὑμῖν ὃ καὶ ἀνῆκον ἐν Χριστῷ 'Ιησοῦ—'adopt that attitude in your mutual relations which *is proper for those who are* in Christ'. It may be added that, as M. Bouttier has shown,[4] the normal Pauline usage for the sense which these commentators try to defend would probably have made him write ἐν κυρίῳ rather than ἐν Χριστῷ 'Ιησοῦ. Κύριος on the whole (though, of course, not uniformly) tends to be used in ethical exhortations relating to the present, Χριστός in historical, kerygmatic statements relating to what God has actually done in Jesus Christ. But, finally, there is another Pauline passage that may be relevant, namely, the opening phrase of Phil. 2 itself—the much-debated εἴ τις οὖν παράκλησις ἐν Χριστῷ. This could be (and has been) interpreted to mean something like 'If I may appeal to you as incorporate in Christ . . .' (as members, that is, of the one Body). But it seems to me to make better and more natural sense if we take it to mean 'If I may appeal to Christ's example . . .'. It is noteworthy that the triple form of this verse (continuing with ἀγάπη and κοινωνία πνεύματος) is strikingly similar to 'the grace' in 2 Cor. 13.13; and there the χάρις of the Lord Jesus Christ is surely (again), in the first instance at least, a reference to the gracious life and character of Jesus. If this line of interpretation is sound, it strengthens the case for interpreting the phrase τοῦτο φρονεῖτε κ.τ.λ. in the way I would advocate—as an appeal to the known character of Jesus.

2. Next, a notorious *crux commentatorum*, 2 Cor. 5.21, which, I believe, gains some clarification by being laid alongside of 1 Cor. 1.30. This was pointed out to me by a pupil, but I have not discussed it with him: I merely accept the reference and attempt to use it in my own way.

The problem is the difficult question of the precise meaning of ἁμαρτίαν ἐποίησεν—made more difficult if (as seems to me not impossible) it is not *intended* to be precise. If one had to decide upon a quite precise meaning, it would probably have to be 'made a sin offering'. Although ἁμαρτία much less often means 'sin offering' in the LXX than *ḥaṭṭ'ath* means 'sin offering' in the MT,[5] yet the τὸν μὴ γνόντα ἁμαρτίαν (which could be much the same as ἄμωμον, etc.) might encourage us to adopt this interpretation. But I suspect we ought to look for a less precise and more evocative, a broader and more widely applicable sense, and this is where the parallel from 1 Corinthians perhaps applies. Ignoring, for the moment, the ἁμαρτία-phrase in 2 Cor. 5.21, and attending, instead, to the other half of the sentence, we find a close parallel to the 1 Corinthians phrase. 2 Cor. 5.21b has ἵνα ἡμεῖς γενώμεθα δικαιοσύνη θεοῦ ἐν αὐτῷ. In 1 Cor. 1.30 we read: ἐξ αὐτοῦ δὲ ὑμεῖς ἐστε ἐν Χριστῷ Ἰησοῦ ('by virtue of incorporation in Christ Jesus you exist, by God's creative act') ὃς ἐγενήθη σοφία ἡμῖν ἀπὸ θεοῦ, δικαιοσύνη τε καὶ ἁγιασμὸς καὶ ἀπολύτρωσις . . . ('for Christ has become for us—by God's appointment—righteousness and sanctification and redemption'). In 2 Cor. 5.21b we, by incorporation in Christ, *become* '*righteousness*'; here, because we are incorporate in Christ, he has *become* '*righteousness*' for us. In both passages alike, the ἐν Χριστῷ results in a kind of *communicatio idiomatum* (if one may

presume to put it so)—though, thus far, only in *one* direction—
the identification, by virtue of our union with Christ, of *his*
qualities as *ours*. Now, it is nowhere in 1 Cor. 1, but, if anywhere at all, only in 2 Cor. 5.21a that *reciprocal communicatio* is
suggested. It is one thing to say that we may 'become' Christ's
righteousness (or that his righteousness may become ours)—
quite another to suggest that he may 'become' our sin (or that
our sin may become his). Yet, the communication in the one
direction is, perhaps, an encouragement to an exegesis which
dares to make it a *reciprocal* communication. If this is a tolerable
interpretation, it can only mean that our sinful *environment* and
circumstances were communicated to Christ—that he involved
himself in all the disabilities of the human situation. Paul
certainly would not attribute actual sin to Christ—indeed, he
explicitly rules it out. But his very ruling of it out may, after all,
be in order to describe Christ, not as the sin offering without
blemish, but as the one who 'took' our sinful 'conditions'—
though without actual sin.

3.   Finally, turning back though only a few verses, from 2 Cor.
5.21, consider one more among the most controverted of all
the passages in the epistles—2 Cor. 4.5—5.10—side by side with
Rom. 8.20ff. This particular parallel has often been drawn
before—indeed, no commentator could fail to note it; but I
believe that certain implications in it have yet to be given their
full weight.

First, I must once again presuppose an already published
article,[6] in which I have argued for an interpretation of 2 Cor.
4.7—5.4 in some such way as the following.

2 Cor. 4.7ff starts by emphasizing the weakness and frailty of
the apostle (and his colleagues?) in contrast to the divine
glory of Christ of which, paradoxically, they are the revealers.

vv. 10f They always carry about with them in their bodies
the νέκρωσις of Jesus. This means, I take it, that, whereas
all men (of necessity) carry about mortality with them, the
apostles are constantly incurring the special risks attaching
to their dangerous martyr-lives; and, further, that, whereas
all men, as mortal, have to come to terms with νέκρωσις,
the Christian accepts it as the νέκρωσις of *Jesus*—that is, as

something already affirmed and reckoned with triumphantly by Jesus. It is because the Christian apostle can accept his mortality *as that of Jesus* that the life also of Jesus may be manifested in the same sphere. The secret of Jesus' resurrection-life is precisely his whole-hearted acceptance of the principle of letting go—of accepting mortality in obedience to God's plan.

v. 12 In so far as the apostle is an evangelist, what he suffers and achieves is suffered and achieved on behalf of his converts: in this sense, his acceptance of death means life for them.

vv. 13ff This principle of resurrection and life *via* the acceptance of mortality (as the mortality of Jesus) is then further elaborated. Buoyed up by his vision of the unseen, eternal glory, the apostle is able to accept, as only temporary and as purposeful and educative, the decay and suffering to which this life is now subjected.

5.1ff For, he continues, we know that if this earthly house—this tent—is despatched, we have a house provided by God, an eternal, heavenly one, not made by human hands.

Then follow two parallel καὶ γάρ-clauses, in quick succession, both with much the same meaning, followed, in turn, by a clause starting ὁ δέ . . .

I take this καὶ γάρ and ὁ δέ to be an example of concessive clauses in parataxis, so that, when turned into more idiomatic syntaxis, they would mean: 'for *although* it is true that we groan, etc., *nevertheless* God knows what he is doing'.

The sense, on this showing, comes out thus:

For although it is true that we groan in this body, because we long to *add* the heavenly dwelling on top of it, instead of having to endure the painful process of beginning to part with the one before we can begin to get the other in exchange . . .

[then, repeating much the same sense in a second, parallel clause:]

For although (I say) we who are in this 'tent' groan and are depressed because we do not want to *strip*, but rather to *add* more clothes, in such a way that the mortal might be absorbed into life . . ., yet, in fact, it is God himself who has made us and adapted us for [and here I conjecture the meaning of αὐτὸ τοῦτο] precisely this process of stripping off the mortal in exchange for the immortal. This physical–spiritual metabolism is part of God's plan; and, to reassure us, he has given us the Spirit as a pledge.

[This is mentioned to meet that horrific, shuddering dread that passes, like a cloud, over the apostle's mind: v. 3 if, that is (εἴ γε καί), when thus clothed we shall not be found (after all) to be left naked.]

The weakest point in this exegesis is, perhaps, the taking ὁ κατεργασάμενος as = 'he who made and adapted', 'designed' (as though the sense were 'that is what we are *for*'). Commentators generally do accept this sense. Héring, in loc., renders 'celui qui nous a *formés par cette destinée*'; Leitzmann-Kümmel, 'dafür zubereitet hat'; NEB 'shaped us for this very end'. But Bauer, s.v. 3, *jmdn. zu etw. instand setzen*, can quote no parallels except Hdt. 7.6.1,[7] Xen. *Mem.* 2.3.11,[8] in both of which, however, it seems clearly to mean 'prevail upon'.[9] If, however, this special sense of κατεργάσασθαι be allowed (and, in the context, it seems difficult to give it any other), and if this exegesis as a whole proves possible, then we have a consistent theme—there is pain in 'detachment'; there is anxiety in 'steering blind'; nevertheless, it is part of God's design, and was accepted by Christ; and the presence of the Spirit is the guarantee of this.

Rom. 8.18–25 runs as follows (NEB.):
For I reckon that the sufferings we now endure bear no comparison with the splendour, as yet unrevealed, which is in store for us. For the created universe waits with eager expectation for God's sons to be revealed. It was made the victim of frustration, not by its own choice, but because of him who made it so; yet always there was hope, because the universe itself is to be freed from the shackles of mortality and enter upon the liberty and splendour of the children of God. Up to the present, we know, the whole created universe groans in all its parts as if in the pangs of childbirth. Not only so but even we, to whom the Spirit is given as firstfruits

of the harvest to come, are groaning inwardly while we wait
for God to make us his sons and set our whole body free. For
we have been saved, though only in hope. Now to see is no
longer to hope: why should a man endure and wait for what
he already sees? But if we hope for something we do not yet
see, then, in waiting for it, we show our endurance.

Now, it is obvious that there are parallels here, as well as
contrasts, between the 2 Corinthians and the Romans passages.
J. Dupont characterized these very ably in *Gnosis*,[10] where he
stresses the similarity of theme, through decided differences of
expression, in the two passages. 2 Corinthians he calls more
Greek in 'provenance'.

One of the reasons, I suspect, contributing to the difference
of expression as between the two passages is, even more than a
difference in 'provenance', the difference between the collective
and cosmic vision of Rom. 8 and the individual scale of 2 Cor.
4–5. Dupont is right that the basic theme is the same in both
cases; not only the 'provenance', but the aspects of it treated
in the two passages are, nevertheless, distinctly different. And,
although it is quite true that, in other parts of the Corinthian
correspondence also, Paul uses Hellenistic terms for Jewish
themes (as F. Schweizer puts it, 'Paulus redet also sachlich
jüdisch, terminologisch hellenistisch', TWNT vi, 419), it may
be, I think, aspect of subject, even more than context of thought,
that has determined the respective choices of language. It is
worth while to note, for instance, that in what I believe[11] is so
different a context as Phil. 1.23 Paul is working with the same
pattern as in 2 Cor. 5—that of departure from one sphere of
life into another: τὴν ἐπιθυμίαν ἔχων εἰς τὸ ἀναλῦσαι καὶ
σὺν Χριστῷ εἶναι. This implies, exactly as 2 Cor. 5.6ff does,
that to depart from this life is, in some sense, to be nearer to
Christ, and thus, sounds like a concession to Hellenism. But I
suggest that this disconcertingly dualistic mode of thought is due
not so much to a Hellenistic context as to the fact that, concerning an individual, when he is not being considered primarily
in the light of the collective and corporate purposes of God,
this is Paul's quite normal way of thinking. For an *individual*,
the end of this life may well be viewed as a kind of consummation, followed at once by a fulfilment of the presence of God; but

when it is the *collective* purpose of God that comes into view, then some notion of waiting and of incompleteness needs to be brought into play, to emphasize that the consummation of the individual, in a sense, cannot be dissociated from that of the whole people of God.[12]

In Rom. 8, as in 2 Cor. 5, there is groaning. But in Rom. 8, it is cosmic. In Rom. 8 non-human nature as well as human, non-Christians as well as Christians, share the groaning. It is occasioned (apparently) by φθορά—or, in other words, mortality. The necessity of change and decay is what seems so universally sad, such cause for groaning. Freedom—glorious freedom—from annihilation (from 'servitude to decay'[13]) is what all creation yearns for. And this, Paul says, is, in fact, going to be achieved—but only by the Spirit of God in man which—paradoxically—enables him to *accept* (to embrace) mortality, and to accept it in Christ's way, by affirming, with Christ's filial obedience, 'Abba! Father! thy will be done!' This, and this alone, is the formula for release into life and freedom. (It is just like the apostle, in 2 Cor. 4.10, accepting νέκρωσις as the νέκρωσις of *Jesus*.) It is man alone, in all creation, who is capable of this conscious act of affirmation: he alone can say 'Father!'; to him alone is sonship given, through Jesus Christ. It is thus man who articulates creation's obedience. *That* (perhaps Paul is saying) is what God has made him for. *That* is why the rest of creation strains its eyes to see the glorious liberty of God's sons.

Here, then, is a characteristically biblical answer to the distress of transience. The gnostic answer was in very different terms—in terms of the *escape* from mortality of something inherently immortal. The Jewish–Christian answer to the sighing and groaning of insecurity and transience is in terms not of escape from matter but of the utterly dedicated, obedient use of matter. Paradoxically, it is the obedient acceptance of the situation, it is coming to terms with decay and transitoriness, which is the way beyond it.

Now, in 2 Cor. 4—5 exactly the same principle, I believe—that of obedient use—is brought to bear on the problem of decay in the individual human. I doubt whether the focal point is death, so much as the total process of detachment from the transient, of which death is only the completion. Any person is bound, sooner or later, to notice in his own physique, the signs of decay: he becomes aware of ageing, of failing powers, of being—however gradually—'used up' physically. If the person in question happens to be a missionary apostle, living dangerously, daily taking his life in his hands,[14] this is the more evident. He will be particularly aware of always carrying νέκρωσις about wherever he goes (2 Cor. 4.10), of the continual wearing away of his external self (2 Cor. 4.16, ὁ ἔξω ἡμῶν ἄνθρωπος διαφθείρεται).

Thus, when it comes to the groaning (2 Cor. 5.2,4), it is for the same reason as in Rom. 8: it is because of φθορά, because of the burden and sorrow of having to 'let go'—of having to watch the 'clothing' we have got used to, the body we are so intimate with, being worn out and 'taken off'. It is essentially the same distress over φθορά as in Rom. 8, but it is here scaled down from all creation to the human and from collective humanity to the individual human.

And the answer that is given is essentially the same also: the Christian answer is neither hope for the escape of an indestructible soul from decaying matter, nor a convulsive effort to cling to the perishable, but the affirmative and obedient use—and using up—of matter—the taking of transitory matter into the service of the eternal purposes of God. The νέκρωσις that is always being carried about with us is the νέκρωσις of *Jesus*:[15] he has himself already set his stamp of filial obedience on this process; and it is for this very process that God himself has designed us: ὁ δὲ κατεργασάμενος ἡμᾶς εἰς αὐτὸ τοῦτο θεός; and, as a guarantee of it, he has given us the Spirit: δοὺς ἡμῖν τὸν ἀρραβῶνα τοῦ πνεύματος.

The parallel with Rom. 8 is extraordinarily close: it is the Spirit which enables man not to escape from but to use the transitory, material world with such affirmative obedience, with such creative filial dedication, that, in using up and wearing out his body, he is actually achieving a better, an immortal existence: glorious freedom in exchange for servitude to decay, an eternal dwelling in heaven in exchange for the temporary tent.

It is the presence of the Spirit, too, which supports us through the pain. For detachment is a painful process. We do not like using up what is visible: what guarantee have we that anything better is being achieved in exchange for this risk? Therefore we groan. In Rom. 8 we groan, despite our possession of the firstfruits of the Spirit, because it is only in hope, only in prospect, that we have been saved. We are eagerly hoping for something we do not yet actually see. In 2 Cor. 5 we groan, because we do not like taking off the familiar clothes we wear: what guarantee is there that we shall not, in the end, find ourselves stark naked?[16] It is only by the 'radar' of faith that we walk, not by optical direction.

Thus, in the two passages, the work of the Spirit is introduced differently, but basically with the same intention. In Rom. 8, after saying that despite the presence of the Spirit we groan, Paul goes on to say that the Spirit does come to the rescue of our infirmities. In 2 Cor. 5, he says that despite the groaning, despite the besetting doubts, nevertheless, there is the reassurance brought by the Spirit. The main difference here is only a difference in the pattern of clauses. But that is a detail of style. On the whole, the pattern of thought in the two passages is strikingly similar—the more strikingly in that (as I have said) the *aspect* of the theme differs in the two passages, and the language and phrasing are by no means identical.

The constructive and creative character of self-surrender, when it is in obedience to the will of God, has taken firm hold of the very springs of St Paul's thinking. It is the gospel of the cross, working itself out in a way of life that is affirmative and positive in proportion as it offers up all that is transitory for God's service instead of either trying to escape from it or clinging possessively on to it.

And here, Phil. 2 and 3 together may be brought in again as relevant. In Phil. 2 (if the interpretation I have been adopting is correct) Paul is affirming the basic principle that it is divine to 'let go'—that divinity is the opposite of possessiveness. Similarly, in Phil. 3 (despite the lack, as I have suggested, of exact parallel) Paul is describing how, in Christ, he himself found the way to 'let go': what had been gain he had come to reckon loss. Conformity to death—the death of Christ—is his hope of life. But now it can be seen that the phrase in Phil. 3.10, συμμορφιζόμενος τῷ θανάτῳ αὐτοῦ, is really very close to the phrase in 2 Cor. 4.10, πάντοτε τὴν νέκρωσιν τοῦ Ἰησοῦ ἐν τῷ σώματι περιφέροντες. And the uncertainty-clauses in all three are also significantly comparable. The εἴ πως καταντήσω εἰς τὴν ἐξανάστασιν τὴν ἐκ νεκρῶν of Phil. 3.11 is in the same tone of hope (but not absolute certainty) as sounds, more or less clearly, in Rom. 8.24 (τῇ γὰρ ἐλπίδι ἐσώθημεν). So, in 2 Cor. 5.3, if I am right in interpreting εἴ γε καὶ ἐνδυσάμενοι οὐ γυμνοὶ εὑρεθησόμεθα as a cloud of uncertainty passing over the apostle's confidence, we have the same motif at its least assured. Finally, the whole miraculous process by which God creates something glorious and permanent out of the humiliated and transitory, as described both in Rom. 8 and in 2 Cor. 4—5, is clinched and summed up in Phil. 3.21 with the ὃς μετασχηματίσει τὸ σῶμα τῆς ταπεινώσεως ἡμῶν σύμμορφον τῷ σώματι τῆς δόξης αὐτοῦ, κατὰ τὴν ἐνέργειαν[17] τοῦ δύνασθαι αὐτὸν καὶ ὑποτάξαι αὐτῷ τὰ πάντα.

Only a few select parallels have been adduced. But in the light of them, and of many others which could have been discussed, there is a question that may profitably be asked: How far was Paul a coherent theological thinker? It seems likely that Paul sometimes gave considerable freedom to an amanuensis to express things in his own way. It seems certain that, in each epistle, Paul himself was meeting a specific situation and adapting his language and his thought-forms and his emphasis to that particular need, with no attempt to reconcile what he said then with what he had said in the past, or might say in the future, in the face of a different set of circumstances. Further, it is clear enough that, in certain passages, as in 2 Cor. 4—5, he makes concessions to ways of thought which, logically, are incompatible with the general thought-forms within which he moves (see Dupont already cited). This being so, it is the more remarkable that, when one looks at the skeleton of thought and the bones of the argument, they are so consistently the same. The more I weigh Paul's words and the more I try to puzzle out their meaning, the more I am impressed by the tenacity of thought with which he holds on to a mainly consistent body of doctrines. Perhaps part of the secret of the immeasurably powerful influence exerted by this prince of thinkers over so many generations is, in fact, the simple coherence of his basic convictions—a coherence which is derived, I think, from the fact that all this thoughts are ἐν Χριστῷ.

NOTES

1 'Further Reflexions on Philippians 2.5–11' in *Apostolic History and the Gospel: Biblical and Historical Essays Presented to F. F. Bruce* (London 1970), pp. 264ff.

2 See, for example, F. C. Porter, *The Mind of Christ in Paul* (New York/London 1932), pp. 215ff; M. Bouttier, *La Condition Chrétienne Selon S. Paul* (Geneva 1964), pp. 9ff: E.T. *Christianity according to Paul* (London 1966), pp. 15ff.

3 'Christus, Einheit und Norm der Christen', *Kerygma und Dogma* 4 (1963), pp. 235ff.

4 *En Christ* (Paris 1962), p. 57.

5 LXX much more often uses περὶ ἁμαρτίας; but see Lev. 4.21, 24; 5.12; Num. 6.14.

6 'St Paul and Dualism: the Pauline Conception of Resurrection', *NTS* 12.2 (Jan. 1966), pp. 106ff. To literature there quoted, add, now, C.-H. Hunzinger, 'Die Hoffnung angesichts des Todes im Wandel der paulinischen Aussagen', in *Leben angesichts des Todes: Beiträge zum theologischen Problem des Todes* (für H. Thielicke) (Tübingen 1968), pp. 69ff (pp. 76ff).

7 χρόνῳ δὲ κατεργάσατό τε καὶ ἀνέπεισε [Μαρδόνιος] Ξέρξην ὥστε ποιέειν ταῦτα.

8 εἴ τινα τῶν γνωρίμων βούλοιτο κατεργάσασθαι, ὁπότε θύοι, καλεῖν σε ἐπὶ δεῖπνον . . .

9 See Liddell and Scott. Where κατεργάσασθαι = 'make',' produce', in the N.T., it is with impersonal objects.

10 *Gnosis: la Connaissance Religieuse dans les Épîtres de Saint Paul* (Paris/Louvain 1949), p. 110, n. 3.

11 Though see Dupont, as in n. 12.

12 See J. Dupont, Σὺν Χριστῷ, *L'union avec le Christ suivant St Paul* 1 (Paris/Louvain 1952), pp. 115–91, for comparison between 2 Cor. 4.7—5.10 and Phil. 1.20–4 (esp. pp. 172f).

13 G. Harder, in TWNT *s.v.* φθείρειν, argues for construing ἡ δουλεία τῆς φθορᾶς as though τῆς φθορᾶς were a gen. of quality, parallel to τῆς δόξης which qualifies ἐλευθερία. Surely obj. gen. is more natural, for φθορᾶς?

14 Cf. 1 Cor. 15.30–2; 2 Cor. 4.11.

15 See J. Dupont, Σὺν Χριστῷ, pp. 124ff.

16 Cf. Col. 1.24. (So J. Dupont, Σὺν Χριστῷ, p. 125.)

17 Perhaps cf. ὁ κατεργασάμενος in 2 Cor. 5.5.

BIBLIOGRAPHICAL NOTE
If this essay had not been finished before their publication, I would have referred to J. Carmignac, L'importance de la place d'une negation (Phil.2.6)', *NTS* 18(1972), pp. 131 ff, which constitutes a serious challenge to my interpretation of ἁρπαγμός, and to M. D. Hooker, 'Interchange in Christ', *JTS*, n.s.22 (1971), pp. 349ff, which has important things to say about what I discuss on pp. 81f.   C.F.D.M.

The Freedom of the Christian according to Romans 8.2

C. E. B. CRANFIELD

Rom. 8.1 connects not with 7.25a or 7.25b but with 7.6,[1] 7.7–25 being a needful explanation. It draws out the significance (ἄρα, RV: 'therefore') of the paragraph 7.1–6, in which Paul took up and elucidated the statement 'for ye are not under law' which he had made in 6.14 (that this was meant in the strictly limited sense that you are not under the-law-as-condemning-you or under the law's condemnation is confirmed by the content of 8.1). Since this is so, and since 8.2, with which we are concerned, is connected with 8.1 by 'for', it would not be at all surprising if 8.2 picked up or repeated or was in some way parallel to something already said in 7.1–6. In fact it spells out the truth which was hinted at in the last part of the concluding sentence of 7.1–6. The last clause of 7.6 spoke of a service 'in newness of the spirit' (so the RV, but 'spirit' should have an initial capital letter) as the result of liberation from the-law-as-condemning-us. Now 8.2 expresses this result in a different way, describing it as a further liberation. To say that we have been set free from the law of sin and of death by 'the law of the Spirit of life' is another way of saying that we now serve in newness of the Spirit.

This verse speaks of a liberation which has taken place.[2] But, before we can determine at all precisely what it has to tell us about the nature of the Christian's freedom, it is necessary to answer three preliminary questions:

(i)   What is the significance of the first 'the law'?
(ii) Is 'of life' dependent on 'the Spirit', or is it, as well as 'of the Spirit', dependent on 'the law'?
(iii) Is 'in Christ Jesus' to be taken closely with 'life' or with

'made . . . free', or could the Greek possibly mean either 'the law which in Christ Jesus is the law of the Spirit of life' or 'the law in Christ Jesus which is also the law of the Spirit of life?'

It will be convenient to take (iii) first. Of the four alternatives mentioned above, the last two should surely be rejected as being forced.[3] A good many interpreters have favoured the first,[4] and the latter part of 6.23 has been claimed as support for it. But the second alternative seems a more natural way of understanding the Greek, and the fact that it is indicated in the following sentence (joined as it is with this verse by 'for') that it is through the mission of his Son that God has accomplished what is there described as the condemnation of sin in the flesh argues strongly in its favour. We conclude that 'in Christ Jesus' should be connected with the verb and understood as indicating the basis of the action accomplished by 'the law of the Spirit of life'.

With regard to (i), the first 'the law' of this verse has been variously explained as signifying the Holy Spirit himself[5] or faith[6] or the gospel[7] or the authority exercised by the Holy Spirit[8] or—more vaguely—the spiritual life resulting from union with Christ[9] or the religion which is possible in Christ.[10] But, in view of the fact that 'the law of sin and of death' mentioned later in the verse is most naturally understood to be identical with 'the law of sin' referred to in 7.23 and 25, which is also referred to as 'a different law' in 7.23, it seems natural to ask whether we should not also identify 'the law of the Spirit of life' with 'the law of God' mentioned in 7.22 and 25 and also 'the law of my mind' mentioned in 7.23, to which 'the law of sin' is opposed (7.23 and 25). This explanation has the advantage of economy; for by accepting it we should avoid the necessity of attributing to Paul a reference to yet another law. Moreover, it may also be said in its support that such an association of God's law with 'Spirit' and 'life' might be explained as intended to recall 'For we know that the law is spiritual' in 7.14 and 'the commandment, which was unto life' in 7.10. But this explanation is not free from objection. A statement to the effect that God's law has set the Christian free from the law of sin and of death seems hardly to be in accord with the thought of this paragraph, the theme of which is God's establishment of his law by his gift of his Spirit to men, and which speaks of 'what the law could not do, in that it was weak through the flesh' (v. 3). The subject which, in the light of the context, seems appropriate to this predicate is not God's law but the new factor in the human situation, namely, the Holy Spirit's presence and effective authority and pressure. We conclude that the most probable interpretation of the first 'the law' in this verse is that which understands it to refer to the authority and constraint brought to bear on believers by the Spirit of God.

If what has just been said is correct, then both the occurrences of the word 'law' in this verse are metaphorical, since it is scarcely to be doubted that in its second occurrence here it is a metaphor.[11] It would seem that Paul first used 'law' metaphorically to denote the power, the authority, the control exercised over us by sin (7.21, 23, 25), because he saw this as a terrible travesty, a grotesque parody, of that authority over us which belongs by right to God's holy law, and then by analogy used it to denote the authority exercised over us, the powerful pressure exerted upon our lives, by the Holy Spirit.

Question (ii) may be dealt with more briefly. While it is possible that both the genitives 'of the Spirit' and 'of life' should be understood as dependent on 'the law' (the sense would then be that the law referred to is both the law of the Spirit and also the law of life—we might then translate the phrase 'the Spirit's life-giving law'), it is perhaps on the whole more likely that 'of life' was meant to depend on 'of the Spirit', and that the sense intended is 'the law of the life-giving Spirit'.[12]

We are now in a position to try to draw out the significance of this verse, which is a statement to the effect that the authority exercised over the Christian by the Holy Spirit, the Giver of life, has, in Christ, liberated him from the authority of sin and of its inevitable concomitant, death.

In the first place, this verse makes it clear that, in Paul's view, the freedom of the Christian about which he is speaking in this chapter is something which has been brought about by the Holy Spirit, and not something which has been—or ever can be—engineered by human ingenuity or won by human courage or resolution. The liberation has been effected by the Holy

Spirit's assertion of his authority over a man's life, his taking hold of it and exerting his pressure upon it. The freedom of the Christian's existence, in so far as it really is the freedom Paul means, both has its origin in, and is continually sustained by, the miraculous activity of him, of whom Paul says elsewhere: 'where the Spirit of the Lord is, there is liberty' (2 Cor. 3.17).

In the second place, this verse—if we were right in what we said above about the words 'in Christ Jesus'—indicates that the basis, the necessary prior condition, of the liberation effected in the lives of particular men and women by the Holy Spirit is what God has done in Jesus Christ, that altogether final, decisive, once-for-all condemnation of sin accomplished by God in the life, death, resurrection, and ascension of his incarnate Son, to which the next verse refers. The fact that the Christian's freedom is miraculous does not mean that it has been achieved without cost: its cost has been borne by God himself. We may compare the declaration of the Fourth Evangelist that 'the Spirit was not yet given; because Jesus was not yet glorified' (John 7.39: the RV supplement 'given' no doubt expresses correctly the intended meaning of what is probably the original reading). Before the pressure of the Spirit of God could be applied to the lives of men in the way in which it is applied to the life of the Christian believer, it was necessary that Christ should complete his work.

In the third place, what the law of the Spirit of life is here said to have brought about is the liberation of particular men from the law (that is, the authority, the power, the constraint) of sin and of death. Here the question immediately arises: How is this confident assertion to be understood alongside 7.14b ('but I am carnal, sold under sin'), 7.23 ('but I see a different law in my members, warring against the law of my mind, and bringing me into captivity under the law of sin which is in my members') and 7.25b ('So then I myself . . . serve . . . with the flesh the law of sin') ?

It is true, of course, that a good many interpreters of Paul down the centuries have insisted, and a good many interpreters of him today still insist, that 7.14–24 cannot refer to the Christian life, and, even among those who recognize that these verses do not fit the pre-conversion life, there are some who argue that what is depicted in them belongs to a stage of the

Christian life which can be left behind, a stage in which the Christian is still trying to fight the battle in his own strength, and see 8.1ff as describing a subsequent deliverance. We cannot argue this issue here,[13] but can only state our conviction that it is only by accepting that in 7.14–24 Paul 'is depicting in his own person the character and extent of the weakness of believers'[14] that we do justice to the text of Romans. Understood in isolation from chapters 6 and 8 and from 12.1—15.13, 7.14–24 would certainly give a thoroughly wrong impression of the Christian life; but, taken closely together with them, it brings out forcefully an aspect of Christian existence which we ignore or gloss over at our peril. In this mortal life the Christian never escapes entirely from the hold of sin, and the more seriously he strives to live from grace and to submit to the discipline of the gospel, the more sensitive he becomes to his continuing sinfulness. Even his very best activities are marred by the egotism which is still powerful within him. To take an obvious example—though the Christian preacher has no need to apologize to God or to man for the fact that he preaches the gospel, God alone fully knows how much he needs to be ashamed of the manner and the motivation of his preaching; for how big and how subtly all-pervasive is the part played by human egotism in all that goes on in Christian pulpits! Nor is it otherwise with the Christian biblical scholar and his studying and teaching and writing!

But how then can it be true to say that the law of the Spirit of life has set the believer free from the law of sin and of death? The correct answer to this question is surely that the difference between the Christian's slavery to sin and the non-Christian's is so great as to warrant Paul's ἠλευθέρωσεν (RV: 'made ... free'). The Christian is no longer a willing, unresisting, or only ineffectually resisting, slave. (Much less, of course, is he one who stupidly imagines that slavery to sin is itself the great emancipation!) He is in a position to resist—and to resist to real purpose. For the Holy Spirit has laid hold on him and is exerting his pressure upon him, both giving him an inner freedom (cf. the words 'So then I myself with the mind serve the law of God' in 7.25 and 'the law of my mind' (i.e. the law which my mind acknowledges) in 7.23) and also enabling him to resist sin, to fight back manfully. The Christian's life (as Paul understands

it) is one unceasing rebellion against the usurping tyranny of
sin in the name of man's rightful Lord. Its hall-mark is the fact
that in it the battle is seriously joined. The latter part of
Rom. 7 is altogether misunderstood if it is taken to be describing
the anguish of the unresisting or but ineffectually resisting
slave: what it describes is the no less real, but very different,
anguish of strenuous and relentless conflict, which never ceases
till the battle is finally won.

Moreover, it is not just that the Spirit has given the believer
the freedom to resist the power of sin, to fight back. There is
the further fact that the power of the Spirit which is at work in
the believer is infinitely stronger than the power of sin, so that
there is no question of any sort of equilibrium between them.
The Christian knows that, powerful though sin indeed is and
capable of worsting him again and again, the Spirit's power
must triumph in the end and the power of sin and death pass
away.

The freedom to resist sin is not, of course, merely negative.
It is—positively—freedom for obedience to God, freedom for
God's law, as v. 4 makes clear ('that the ordinance of the law
might be fulfilled in us . . .'), not indeed freedom perfectly to
fulfil it, but freedom to make a beginning, to be turned in the
direction of obedience, to begin to love God with all one's
heart and soul and mind and strength and to love one's
neighbour as oneself.

One other point remains to be noticed. In both the AV and
the RV the object of the verb is 'me'; but the ancient witnesses
to the text present an interesting variety of readings: με ('me'),
ἡμᾶς ('us'), σε ('thee') and, finally, no expressed object at all.
The first and second of these readings should almost certainly
be set aside, since they are easily explicable as assimilations to
the first person singular used in 7.7–25 and to the first person
plural used in 8.4, respectively. The possibility that originally
the object of the verb was unexpressed (the reader being left to
supply it from v. 1) cannot be ruled out altogether—there is
some slight textual evidence in support of it, and the σε could
be explained as an accidental reduplication of the final syllable
of the verb. But, as far as the possibility of accidental error is
concerned, the word σε could just as easily have been omitted
by haplography as inserted by reduplication; and σε is too

unexpected here to be a deliberate attempt at improvement on the part of a copyist. In these circumstances the reading σε, which is the best-attested reading (B א G 1739 it syᵖ), must surely be accepted.[15]

Instances of the singling out of the individual as representative of the group for the sake of greater vividness (a feature which is characteristic of, but of course in no way peculiar to, the style of the Hellenistic diatribe) are not uncommon in Romans (cf. 2.1,3–5,17–27; 9.19f; 10.9; 11.17–24; 13.3f; 14.4,10,15,20–2). But the present instance of the use of the second person singular is especially interesting because it is so unexpected and is confined to the one word. It would seem that Paul, being fully aware of the momentousness and amazingness of the truth he was stating (with its highly significant past tense), wanted to make sure that each individual Christian in the Church in Rome realized that what was being said in this sentence was not merely something which might be true for some Christians but applied to him personally and particularly.[16] He was, in effect, saying to each individual member of the Church: 'The gates of the prison have been thrown open for thee, and the door of thine own particular prison cell stands open too. Wilt thou not dare to take the opportunity that is thine and be free?'

NOTES

1 Cf., for example, J. A. Bengel, *Gnomon Novi Testamenti* (3 e., reprinted London 1862), p. 527; C. K. Barrett, *The Epistle to the Romans* (London 1957), p. 154.

2 The tense of ἠλευθέρωσεν is surely not to be explained as 'a kind of gnomic aorist' to be represented 'by an English present', as Barrett, op. cit., p. 153, n. 1, suggests, but rather as indicating that the reference is to the gift of the Spirit to the Christian as an event in the past—the Christians in Rome *have received* the Holy Spirit (cf. especially 8.9–11, 15–16, 23).

3 Barrett's translation (op. cit., p. 153), 'the religion which is made possible in Christ Jesus, namely, that of the life-giving Spirit', would seem to be on the lines of the last alternative.

4 e.g. J. Denney, in *The Expositor's Greek Testament* 2 (3 e., London 1904), p. 644; C. H. Dodd, *The Epistle to the Romans* (London 1932), pp. 118f; O. Michel, *Der Brief an die Römer* (4 e., Göttingen 1966), p. 189.

5 By, for example, John Chrysostom, in J. P. Migne, *Patrologia Graeca* 60, col. 513; Thomas Aquinas, *Opera* (e. altera Veneta) 6 (Venice

1775), p. 91; John Calvin, *The Epistles of Paul the Apostle to the Romans and to the Thessalonians*, tr. R. Mackenzie (Edinburgh 1961), p. 156.

6 Cf. Thomas Aquinas, ibid. ('Alio modo lex spiritus potest dici proprius effectus Spiritus sancti, scilicet fides per dilectionem operans: quae quidem et docet interius de agendis, . . .').

7 So Bengel, op. cit., p. 528, explains 'law of the Spirit' as 'evangelium cordi inscriptum'.

8 Cf., for example, W. Sanday and A. C. Headlam, *The Epistle to the Romans* (5 e., Edinburgh 1902), p. 190.

9 Cf., for example, M. J. Lagrange, *Saint Paul: Épître aux Romains* (reprinted, Paris 1950), p. 192, and J. Huby, *Saint Paul: Épître aux Romains* (new e. by S. Lyonnet, Paris 1957), p. 277. Neither Lagrange nor Huby understands πνεῦμα here to refer to the Holy Spirit.

10 Cf. Barrett, op. cit., p. 153.

11 I am here withdrawing something which I said in 'St Paul and the Law', in *Scottish Journal of Theology* 17 (1964), pp. 56f. I said there with reference to this verse: 'by "the law of sin and of death" . . . we understand . . . either the law as perverted by man's sin and turned into a law of sin and death or the inner necessity of our fallen nature'. I am now convinced that the former of these alternatives is not a possible interpretation.

12 For the connection between the Spirit and life cf., for example, vv. 6, 10f, and 13.

13 It is discussed at length in my forthcoming I.C.C. Commentary on Romans.

14 Calvin, op. cit., p. 149, commenting on v. 15.

15 As it is by Nestle, Merk, and the 1958 edition of the British and Foreign Bible Society's text. The United Bible Societies' text (1966) surprisingly reads με.

16 It is to be noted that such recent English versions as the New English Bible and the Jerusalem Bible, having jettisoned the second person singular in favour of the plural of politeness (the latter altogether and the former except in prayer), are unable to bring out here the full significance of the Greek.

Justification by Faith
in Modern Theology

H. E. W. TURNER

The tribute of a *Festschrift* to Professor Sawyerr is richly deserved in view of his long and distinguished career as a theological teacher and University administrator in Sierra Leone. There can be few clergy in the diocese in whose training he has not played a large part, and many from other parts of West Africa have also had the benefit of his scholarship and teaching. Not only the Department of Theology at Fourah Bay but also the University of Sierra Leone as a whole have owed much to his administrative care and skill, often lavished at the expense of his own time for leisure and research. His association with Fourah Bay has extended from the time when it was a small and struggling missionary institution to the present time when as a fully independent University it is taking further steps to serve the academic future of his country which will mean for him retirement from the Chair of Theology, not indeed for a well-earned retirement, but for the even harder and more exacting task of integrating into a single University structure institutions of different origin and function but with an identical aim to serve their country in the things of the mind and the spirit.

The long connection between the University of Durham and Fourah Bay College and our personal association for close on twenty years made the opportunity of making a contribution to this book particularly welcome. But here a serious difficulty arose. The general themes of the book, Pauline Theology in its technical sense and the study of West African Religion are hardly promising fields for a worker in the fields of Patristic and Dogmatic Theology. I have therefore tried to make the best (or the worst) of both worlds by selecting the topic of

Justification by Faith only in modern theology. Although I can hardly expect that Professor Sawyerr will agree with all the opinions that will be expressed, I know that he will accept it as a small token of the writer's warm friendship and regard.

For some years I was reluctant to handle this subject even in lectures to our students because of a theological encounter which occurred at the Anglican–Scandinavian Conference held at Helsinki in 1952, which convinced me that I did not really know anything about the doctrine at all. Inevitably the question arose, as it usually does in conversations with Lutherans. I described the form of the doctrine which I had been taught at Wycliffe Hall, Oxford as a 'theology of the threshold'. Another Anglican delegate who had been at Wycliffe slightly before my time confirmed that this might be the impression of the doctrine left on me by the teaching which we had both received. The Lutherans were, however, unanimous in condemning it as too subjective, too pietistic. In most Lutheran circles Pietism is a term of theological abuse! The present Bishop of Lincoln who had just left the post of Principal of Cuddesdon College, a rather different type of Anglican theological college, offered an interpretation of the doctrine which the Lutherans gladly accepted. This was based on an essay by Fr Congreve, s.s.j.e. on the Christian Life considered as a Response. To have Wycliffe Hall rejected and the Cowley Fathers accepted by Lutherans, whose communion can be described as the Church of Justification by Faith *par excellence*, threw me into a muddle from which I have been slowly extricating myself ever since.

This process has not been helped by the relative neglect of the study of the doctrine in Anglican theology in recent years. Luther certainly regarded it as the acid test of being a church, the *articulus stantis aut cadentis ecclesiae*, and the importance which the English Reformers attached to it is proved by the explicit reference to the Homilies (probably the Homily on the Salvation of Mankind) in Article XI of the Thirty-nine Articles. It was regarded as 'the grand question which hangeth yet in controversy between us and the Church of Rome'. Yet the publication of Newman's *Lectures on Justification* in 1838 hardly created the same stir as his *Tract XC*, still less, his *Essay on the Development of Doctrine* in 1845. Connop Thirlwall, Bishop of St David's, who held moderate and even liberal views, pronounced the dispute to be 'one of words involving no difference of opinion'. As to Rome, many today would regard Papal Infallibility, Anglican Orders, and Mariology to be more important matters of dispute. Hans Küng's book on Justification reaches a fairly close understanding with Karl Barth.

Yet I am not so sure that more than a mere cross-purpose is at stake here. Certainly differences of terminology made a certain contribution to misunderstanding which goes far behind the period of the Reformation itself. It is familiar ground, at least for those brought up on Sanday and Headlam's *Commentary on the Epistle to the Romans*, that δικαιοῦν has a putative significance (to deem righteous) but the Latin translation *justificare* clearly has a factitative significance (to make righteous). This by itself led to a difference of coverage in the term. The Greek would support Luther who discovered in the term and the experience to which it led the answer to his agonizing question 'How can I find a gracious God?' whereas the Council of Trent included in the term both Justification and Sanctification. It is instructive to read side by side the two commentaries of Sanday and Headlam and of Fr F. Prat, s.j. with this difference in mind. Fr Prat always seems to me to get on too far and too fast in the early chapters of Romans because for him the term has a wider 'pack' than either Sanday and Headlam allow or probably than St Paul intended. The Reformed insistence upon *sola fide* (which St Paul never actually says) and the Tridentine Definition *fides formata caritate* (which St Paul never says either!) are really defining different things which are not incompatible in themselves. The *sola fide*, which of course directly excludes merit or good works as a ground of salvation, also serves the important function of a floodlighting device, while the *caritas* of which the Roman Catholic formula speaks is not ignored in the Reformed view but inserted theologically in a different place. As usual in theological controversy there is more common ground between the contestants than they were prepared to admit. The Reformed is concerned to deny the proposition that good works or merit contribute to our salvation. This rests upon the finished work of Christ, and that alone. The Tridentine formula only regards good works as the final cause of our justification. Dom Gregory Dix used to say that the medieval alternative was a theory of Justification by 'dodges', and against that he was as adamant as the Reformers themselves.

Where the shoe would pinch for some would neither be with Justification nor with Justification by Faith but with the further description 'justification by Faith only' and here I am inclined to think that more is at stake than it is sometimes fashionable to imagine. The *sola fide* is not merely concerned with the exclusion of merit as a ground of salvation; it also leads to a reorientation of theology. This is at least the view that I want to explore in this contribution.

Or am I wrong at the start in believing that Justification itself is a commonly accepted concept? Certainly Luther's tormenting question does not frame itself in everybody's mind and the need for justification is not obvious to everyone. The situation in which Luther found himself is more common than many imagine in the pressures of modern life but in my experience help is needed before people are ready to phrase the question in this way. Justification is concerned with God's acceptance of unacceptable man into fellowship with himself for the sake of Christ. This is the full Pauline doctrine but reductionist-sounding simplifications are offered by some modern theologians. Justification is sometimes rendered simply as a mere acceptance of the unacceptable almost as a thing in itself or as a self-acceptance on the part of the unacceptable. No doubt both these are parts of the story. To be accepted through Christ is more than merely to be accepted and to be accepted by God more than simply to accept oneself. The forensic background of the term is clear enough, but this does not exhaust either the content or the implications of the term. Vindication might serve as a translation provided that the idea of one who has no personal *locus standi* is included within it. But restoration to fellowship is at least the target of Justification and may even be included more or less directly in the word itself.

Faith is no less crucial to the formula than Justification and has of course a more positive filling than simply 'not by merit or good works'. The linguistic situation is not of the order 'A equals not B'. Even in the New Testament faith has more than one meaning. For St Paul it is normally commitment, surrender, or engagement—the *fides qua creditur*. In some later New Testament writings it is rather the content of faith, the *credenda* or the *fides quae creditur*. The concept of faith in the Epistle to the Hebrews comes somewhere between the two. Perhaps with the Platonist or Philonic background of the writer it could best be paraphrased as 'insight leading to action'. It is with the first nuance that we are particularly concerned in the formula under discussion, though it can readily be seen that neither of the other two is irrelevant; it is certainly not primary. The faith which the formula finds as the only necessary ground on our part for restoration to fellowship with God through Christ is faith in the Pauline sense. Without commitment, surrender, or engagement, the restoration of fellowship with God is impossible, and this must be further interpreted not as an act of private enterprise on our part but strictly as a response to what God has already done through Christ to make this restoration possible. *Fides* (in this sense) has a certain relationship to *fiducia* (confidence or assurance) but this is better understood not as the essence of faith but as a corollary or by-product. Neither Luther (at least in some moments) nor Kierkegaard was notable for his assurance. Both were emphatically men of faith.

Justification by faith has been accused of subjectivism, and the charge can fairly be made against some forms of the doctrine. Here Père Bouyer, a convert from Lutheranism to Roman Catholicism, offers a useful distinction. The doctrine indeed marks the re-enthronement of subjectivity in religion, the insistence that no more uniformity of practice, no community of rites, no body of beliefs accepted *en bloc* can by themselves avail for salvation. Subjectivity as a reciprocal to objectivity is a necessary dimension in religion. The massive objectivity of the medieval Church displayed alike in an ecclesiastical machine of juggernaut proportions and in theological systems of increasing elaboration and complexity made such a protest necessary and overdue. Subjectivity can equally run to seed and become subjectivism when the corresponding need for the opposite polarity of objectivity passes out of account. Examples can easily be found in Pietism and in the theology of Schleiermacher where Pietism confronts the Enlightenment. But the transition from the one to the other is neither as automatic or inevitable as Père Bouyer seems to think.

The faith which alone is saving faith, the sole way in which salvation is applied to the roots of man's being is engagement, commitment, or surrender in response to God's prior act of acceptance in Christ. And the floodlighting here is indispensable and irreducible.

But many will still find the adjective *sola* a stumbling-block. While not actually used by St Paul in this context, it is implicit in his whole discussion of Justification. Even so its character as a floodlighting and not merely an exclusive technique must be borne in mind. The Reformers were much given to its use. Besides *sola fide* we can set *sola gratia* and *sola scriptura*. It would be a complete misunderstanding of the Reformation to set the *sola fide* and the *sola gratia* at loggerheads with each other. Justification is always *propter Christum* and therefore by grace as well as by faith. It would never have occurred to Luther or to those who stand with him that Justification was other than centred in Christ and grounded in grace. The Epistle to the Romans which is the source-book and title-deeds for Justification by faith and which brought peace to Luther is thoroughly christocentric and speaks plainly of grace.

Nor again is the *sola* concerned to dispense with Church or sacraments. Both the article on the Church in the Augsburg Confession and the Anglican Article XIX, which is closely related to it, speaks of the visible Church of Christ as a congregation of faithful men in which the pure word of God is preached, and the sacraments duly ministered according to Christ's ordinance. It is not the case that a man is justified first and then (let us hope) joins a church. As to the sacraments, we can recall that in moments of doubt Luther used to recall, not 'I am converted' but 'I am baptized'. In line with this, at the Helsinki discussion a Swedish friend said that if he was asked by a Swedish Nonconformist 'Are you justified?' he would reply with the counter-question 'Are you baptized?'. It may be recalled that in the Epistle to the Romans St Paul immediately follows his discussion of Justification with a high doctrine of Baptism in the opening verses of chapter 6. Luther's doctrine of the Eucharistic Presence will concern us later in this paper; it is certainly a high one.

Nor again despite the exclusion of merit or good works as a ground of salvation is the necessity for good works or right conduct neglected by the doctrine. St Paul in the Epistle to the

Romans has to answer the question, 'Shall we continue in sin that grace may abound?', with an emphatic No, and one of the purposes of the Epistle of James seems to be a correction of a misunderstanding of St Paul of this type. 2 Peter also complains of unlearned and unstable men who wrest the teaching of our beloved brother Paul to their own destruction. Luther too had to fight back to back with himself against Rome on the one hand and the Antinomians on the other. A book like James Hogg's *Confessions of a Justified Sinner* is melancholy evidence for the continuance of this tendency at a later period. It can be a recurrent danger for those whose spiritual aspirations are not matched by an equal moral earnestness.

Luther's point here is wholly different. Justification and Sanctification belong inextricably together but they cannot be identified with each other or (against Trent) included in a single composite formula. The former is primary, the latter a necessary corollary. Justification is the antecedent cause of Sanctification, its grounds or source. To include the one in the other, or to attach the same linguistic label to both, whether on the ground of the etymology of the Latin (though not the Greek) equivalent of Justification or for some more theological reason was for him a serious error of method. While both are in Christ, the inclusion of cause and effect under the same head is a theological confusion. The Tridentine formula *fides caritate formata* is not in error in linking faith and love together but (for Luther) in including the antecedent cause and the final end of the process in a common description. Evangelical spirituality is certainly not lacking in moral earnestness; rather it sees it as the fruit of gratitude, dependence, and responsive love. It is not, however, the ground of justification but its consequence. Both Sanctification and Justification cannot be built into a single verbal structure.

If, then, the exclusive function of the principle of Justification by Faith alone is far more restricted than might be supposed, it has important consequences in Christian Spirituality which led particularly in Luther to a reorientation of the Christian life, what we may describe as his breakthrough to Christ. One way of summarizing this is to draw a contrast between Imputation and Impartation in the life of grace. We need not delay too much on the appropriateness of the words themselves, although they played their part in the controversy as it was classically understood; we are concerned less with words than with meanings. For the Evangelical real life is Encounter with God. The importance of *coram Deo* (in the presence of God), which runs like a motif through the writings of Luther, cannot be overemphasized. The crucial point is a change of relationship. For the Catholic, however, real life is being and the crucial point is a change of nature. For an Evangelical Grace is relational, for the Catholic it is ontological. The Pauline understanding, especially in Galatians and Romans, supports the former while the latter appeals to 2 Peter 1, 4, 'that we might become partakers of the divine nature', and the traditional language of divinization built upon it in the early Church.

Here the evidence of Luther again gives us our clue and that in two ways. Luther always insisted that man is a *viator* (traveller) and therefore every Christian reality comes to him under the form of the cross. He is always *in via* and not yet *in gloria* and therefore any attempt to understand either grace or the theology of the Christian life ontologically represents an illicit anticipation of glory and a forgetfulness of the fact that we are still *in via*. I have described the doctrine of Grace to which it leads as relational; it could as easily be described as eschatological.

The second hint given by Luther is equally revealing. It is the catchword *simul peccator et justus* which many find surprising or unintelligible. But for Luther man is both, inescapably both, and must remain so during the whole of his pilgrimage. That was one reason why my description of Justification by Faith as a 'theology of the threshold' at Helsinki seemed so inadequate to my Lutheran critics. It isolated one moment at which man was a sinner from his whole existence in which he was both. This adds force to the contention that in Luther we have an eschatology of Grace, for eschatology is the one dimension of discourse in which we are compelled to use the language of paradox, 'It is' and 'It is not'. We may perhaps recall the baptismal paradox of the New Testament. Christians become by Baptism transferred to the New Age, while remaining nevertheless in the Old. The Old (if we may so describe it) is dead but it won't lie down. Two very different Anglican voices, Dom Gregory Dix and Bishop J. E. Fison, unite in describing the paradox as requiring Christians to 'become what they are'. The alternative Catholic ontology seems to smooth out the paradox into a kind of quantitative progress. To Luther it might reply that the more a man was '*justus*' the less he was '*peccator*'. But it is doubtful whether the paradox can be ironed out in so simple a manner.

Both sides are exposed to criticism from the other which may be more or less relevant. The Evangelical wishes to say two things, 'Our salvation is all of God' and 'It is wrought in ourselves but not by ourselves'. It is always of faith and never by sight and therefore any quantitative or measurable progress is excluded. To the Catholic this seems to lead either to a purely extrinsic or external righteousness or else to a righteousness which is fictional and therefore unreal. On the other hand, the Catholic will always appear to make too much our own what is continually and not merely initially the work of God's grace in ourselves.

The charge against the Evangelical at this point is not justified. His classical preference for the language of imputation does not reduce the work of grace to the level of a mere fiction. For him the work of grace just because it is God's work is a reality, but its context is always a life of faith. It is nothing in us, it is the work of God arising from an operation of the Holy Spirit upon us and within us in so far as we are in Christ. Imputed righteousness is neither unreal nor fictional; it is, as it were, righteousness on 'lease-lend', a righteousness which is neither initially nor at any subsequent stage while we remain *in via* our own righteousness. The difference between the two types of spirituality broadly corresponds to the distinction which N. P. Williams found between the two approaches to Grace which he labelled Monergism and Synergism respectively.

Theology and Spirituality are certainly interconnected. How directly may, however, be a matter of opinion, for objective truth or reliable statements in theology and our different but inevitably present subjective 'lead-in' are not identical. In some cases spirituality follows theology and the *fides quae creditur* determines the shape taken by the *fides qua creditur*. In other cases spirituality provides the principle by which the selection of a number of possible options is made. To some (like myself) extreme radical hypotheses about the Gospels evoke the 'spirituality response' 'They have taken away my Lord and I know not where they have laid him'; for others the whole question is a matter of indifference, whether for them faith rests in an existential moment of decision as with Bultmann or in some form of Catholic Modernism of the Loisy type. Yet if I say to myself as a Christian 'This cannot be right', I cannot be exempted as a theologian from the task of evaluating the evidence and following the argument where it leads me. Again (to use a different example) are the Mariological Definitions of the Roman Catholic Church during the last century the theological registration of Marian devotion or are they attempts to round off the theology of the Incarnation? Perhaps something of both. Some relation between theology and spirituality exists but it cannot be applied either automatically or in one direction alone.

Certainly the principle of Justification by faith alone, if it primarily defines a spiritual attitude, has theological repercussions, particularly in those areas in which we have defended it against the charge of being exclusive. We have seen its place in the recovery of subjectivity as an important polarity in Christian existence against the seemingly monolithic emphasis upon objectivity in the medieval Church. If it excludes merit or good works as a ground of salvation, it insists upon their place as the fruit of obedience and love which is involved in a restored relationship to God. Right doing is impossible apart from right being understood in this sense. In the sphere of the theology of Grace it stands for a relational or an eschatological rather than ontological context in which it can be best understood. It is perhaps more arguable whether the adoption of an existentialist rather than an ontological stance towards the doctrine of God in some Continental Lutheran theologians owes more to the doctrine of Justification by Faith or to the philosophical opinions of Heidegger and the attempt to clothe Christianity in contemporary dress. It is, however, in the fields of the doctrine of the Church, the Ministry, and the Sacraments that we should finally turn our attention for the influence of the spirituality of Justification by Faith upon theology. Perhaps in view of the use of Lutheran examples it may not be out of place to point out that the writer is and remains an Anglican!

1. With regard to the doctrine of the Church exception is normally taken to what Roger Mehl calls *Ecclesia quoad substantiam* (the Church considered as a substance). Ontological treatments of the Church such as are presupposed in E. Mersch *The Whole Church* and even in Dr Mascall's *Christ, the Christian and the Church* are excluded not only because they are too static in their implications but also because they are in danger of forgetting that the Church as we know it is *in via* and not yet *in gloria*. It is not that any Evangelical is blind to the importance of the Pauline image of the Body of Christ; it is simply that he is allergic to some implications drawn from it. The rediscovery of the idea of the pilgrim Church by Vatican II seems a hopeful sign of theological cross-fertilization here.

2. On Church Order the Lutheran Churches have a distinctive view which is bound up with the doctrine of Justification by Faith. While firm in their insistence upon a regular and stable Ministry of the Word and Sacraments they display a considerable degree of indifference as to the precise form which it takes. The Church of Sweden retained the Historic Episcopate at the Reformation and the Church of Finland has restored it in recent years. The Churches of Denmark and Norway have an episcopate without the element of the Apostolic Succession, while other Lutheran Churches have adopted what is fundamentally a Presbyterian Church order. All Lutheran Churches are naturally in full communion with each other. A German Lutheran bishop at the Lund Conference who remarked that his regional Church (*Landeskirche*) had no fixed pattern of ministry but that he could accept the Anglican form provided that it was not made a matter of salvation, had not stepped out of his Lutheran framework of reference. While not every Swedish churchman would accept this approach I have heard an eminent Swedish theologian adapt a Pauline phrase, that they possessed the Apostolic Succession 'as though they had it not'. For Lutheranism the form of the ministry has been classically one of the *adiaphora* (things indifferent). They would have the agreement of many Anglican Evangelicals who, while loyal to their own Church order, refuse to regard the Historic Episcopate as of the *esse* of the Church, and on grounds certainly not unconnected with the principle of Justification by

Faith alone. Clearly the so-called 'pipe-line theory of grace', once more popular in Anglican circles than it has recently become, would be rejected by the champions of doctrine which we are considering.

3. The doctrine does not imply a 'low view' of the sacraments. Luther's words of personal reassurance, '*baptizatus sum*', have already been quoted. His doctrine of the Real Presence as 'in, with and under' the bread and wine implies a high view of the Eucharist. It is, however, qualified to some extent by the Lutheran distinction between *in usu* and *extra usum* with its direct exclusion of Reservation and an attitude to what is left over of the consecrated elements which, however logical on this theory, would come strangely to any Anglican. Here the category of Action is strongly asserted against the terminology of substances but combined with a strongly realistic doctrine of the Presence in use. Luther's strong protest against the doctrine of the Mass militated historically against any doctrine of eucharistic sacrifice. What a modern Swedish theologian can make of it can be found in Bishop Aulen's ecumenically minded book *Eucharist and Sacrifice*. This may well fall within Lutheran limits; it is unlikely that Luther could ever have written it himself, any more than Calvin would have assented to the opinions of Max Thurian in every particular.

Certainly the principle of *ex opere operato* is excluded by the doctrine of Justification by Faith alone, though not the element of givenness for which it essentially stood. This does not imply the acceptance of the counter-principle *ex opere operantis*, the Donatist theory designed to cover the supposed effect of the unworthiness of the minister on the efficacy of the sacrament. This is expressly rejected by the Augsburg Confession as well as the Thirty-nine Articles, no less than by the more tradition-ally minded Churches of Christendom. An Evangelical who wished to be loyal to the principle of Justification by Faith only would probably warm to what might be called 'the grace–faith reciprocal'—the assertion of a sacramental givenness to be taken and received by faith.

Happily much of the heat has gone out of the Reformation controversies in which the principle of Justification by Faith only was classically formulated, as the approval given by

Lutherans to the essay by Fr Congreve in the anecdote with which this contribution opened plainly shows. Some of the values embodied by the principle, though characteristic of it, are not peculiar to it. Yet 'Justification by Faith only' affirms spiritual approaches to God and doctrinal attitudes which are still relevant today. Positively these include a relationship to God which includes commitment and surrender as an indispensable ingredient, the understanding of the Christian Life (which includes Christian conduct) as a response to God's saving initiative in Christ, with the marks of gratitude, dependence, and responsive love. Negatively it stands as a beacon light against any attempt by the Church to absolutize itself, to turn itself from a penultimate into an ultimate, to forget that it is still *in via* and not yet *in gloria*, the pilgrim people of God. It offers a radical challenge to the Church's engrossment with secondary aims at the expense of ultimate targets. The danger of Pharisaism, against which St Paul reacted so strongly and which was the springboard for his breakthrough to Christ, still besets the Christian Church. St Paul (as well as Luther) has much to say to twentieth-century Christians whether in Durham or Sierra Leone.

Erasmus and the Bishops of Durham

S. L. GREENSLADE

Soon after the University of Durham had been founded (1832), the impressive Norman castle from which the 'Prince-Bishops' had administered the County Palatine became the home of University College, but it serves also as a general headquarters. Harry Sawyerr must sometimes have sat in the medieval Hall, eating meals cooked in the old kitchen whose buttery hatch bears the date 1499 and the Pelican badge of Bishop Foxe; he must often have passed through Tunstall's doors into the Castle Courtyard and walked along Tunstall's Gallery to his Chapel, its stalls carved with the arms of Ruthall.

Erasmus saw none of this but he knew Foxe and Ruthall and Tunstall, and Wolsey too, all appointed to the great northern see for reasons of policy, ecclesiastical and secular, but all of them humanists willing to stand patron to the eminent scholar. Tunstall was an intimate friend. Erasmus' contacts with them, while not always coincident with their Durham episcopates,[1] illuminate some aspects of the Henrician Reformation, especially its relation to the New Learning and the problem of heresy.

Erasmus would have enjoyed knowing the book-loving John Shirwood, Foxe's predecessor (1484–94), but there is no sign of any acquaintance. Richard Foxe became Bishop of Durham in 1494 and was translated to Winchester in 1501. When Erasmus first visited England in 1499 he came to know friends of Foxe in London and Oxford, but probably not Foxe in person. Next time, however, late in 1505, he addressed two letters 'London, from the bishop's house', apparently Foxe's Winchester House, Southwark (*Epp.* 185–6),[2] and friendship is the theme when he dedicated his translation of Lucian's

Toxaris to Foxe (*tantus patronus, tam potens amicus*) as a New Year gift. 'Please go on loving and helping Erasmus as you have been (187)'. Correspondence in 1511 with his friend Ammonius, Latin Secretary to Henry VIII, shows how eagerly Erasmus courted Foxe's patronage. He sends letters for Ammonius to present to Foxe and Ruthall, waiting anxiously to hear how they have been received. 'Winchester is friendly', Ammonius replies, 'but complains that you don't visit him. I said you were shy.' Another time, 'I chose a wrong moment. Better come yourself (239, 243, 247, 249).' Later, Ruthall told Ammonius that the decision (some appointment for Erasmus?) rested with Foxe; it was eventually Archbishop Warham who gave him an English benefice. Still later, More reported how highly Foxe praised Erasmus' Latin version of the Greek Testament—so enlightening, better than ten commentaries (502).

In 1519–20 Erasmus consulted Foxe about his English opponent Lee (whom we shall meet again). Don't believe his calumnies, he pleads. Could the wise bishop not advise him to restrain his fury (973, 1099)? Above all, Erasmus rejoiced in Foxe's founding of Corpus Christi, Oxford. 'How I love Winchester who, at his own expense, has dedicated his most magnificent College to good letters (965).' 'This is truly acting like a bishop', he wrote in glowing terms to the first President of Corpus, John Claymond, commended to him by More and Tunstall (990; cf. 1661).

Nothing is known of any contact between Erasmus and Bishop Senhouse (1502–5) who was succeeded after a vacancy by Christopher Bainbridge. A scholar, an old-fashioned one, he was mainly a diplomat. Translated to York in 1508, he became a Cardinal and represented England at the Court of Rome. One of Erasmus' close friends, Richard Pace, was his secretary and later Wolsey's.

Thomas Ruthall has cropped up in Foxe's company. Secretary to Henry VII since 1499, he shared the chief business of State with Foxe in Henry VIII's early years, was Bishop of Durham 1509–23, and succeeded Foxe as Lord Privy Seal in 1516, 'singing treble to Wolsey's bass'. The contemporary historian Polydore Vergil testifies to his learning, wide experience, honesty, and vigilance in affairs. Pairing him with Foxe,

Erasmus dedicated to him a version of Lucian's *Timon* in 1506, belauding his courtesy, scholarship, and authority at Court. These Lucian pieces formed part of a joint production with More, who dedicated the whole to Ruthall, whose wisdom, honesty, and dignity (he says) are linked with unusual modesty.

Ruthall helped Erasmus: once he sent him ten gold crowns from the spoils of victory over the French, another time six nobles (280–1, 295). Perhaps he seemed importunate, for Ruthall procured him no grand position in England (282). So Erasmus tried again in 1515 with the dedication of his *Seneca*, spoils of scholarly warfare with manuscripts (325). Ruthall, he now tells Cardinal Riario, is his special patron in England; and More reports that the dedication was most acceptable (333, 388).

But sad trouble arose. Knowing that his *Seneca* had been carelessly produced, Erasmus prepared a second edition, and, Ruthall long dead, dedicated it to the Bishop of Cracow. He was not responsible, he claimed, for the faults in its predecessor which by this change he wants to disclaim. He has to confess that, visiting England in 1516, he had found his old friend surprisingly frigid. He fished out the reason. A bookseller had failed him: Ruthall had never received his dedication copy and thought Erasmus was laughing at him by allusions to it in several letters. Besides, someone pointed out the mistakes. 'So I lost credit—and no ordinary friend (2091).' Erasmus tried to break the silence in 1519 by sending a copy of his *Paraphrase of Galatians*. The reply, if there was one, has not survived (974).

To Erasmus, Wolsey—who never set foot in his Durham diocese (1523–29, while also York)—is usually Lincoln, York, Cardinal. For a scholar to seek patronage was no disgrace. He hankered after a place in England and wooed Wolsey with dedications. A few days after he had congratulated Ammonius on pleasing the rising Dean of York, Thomas Wolsey was named Bishop of Lincoln. Erasmus jumped in with the dedication of a piece he had translated from Plutarch in 1512, still unpublished. It came, like Foxe's, a tiny New Year present to a big man: please count Erasmus among your humblest clients (284, 287). More Plutarch was dedicated to King Henry (272), and Erasmus told friends that the King and Wolsey, now all-powerful with him, 'are making me magnificent promises

(295–6)'. When the Plutarch was printed, the compliments were elaborated: Wolsey is an incomparable hero, ready to help everyone (297). Soon Erasmus' anchor of fortune is fixed upon Wolsey whose generosity will perhaps prepare him some refreshment in England (348; cf. 350). One result was that Wolsey, then nominally Bishop of Tournai, offered him a canonry there; but Erasmus hesitated and it went to another man. More was sure Wolsey would find him something better, probably in England. Two years later More is still confident (601), and indeed in 1517 Erasmus was handsomely received by the King and Wolsey (*Rex alter*), who offered him a splendid house and a good income (649, 658, 694). Unsettled by other prospects, he declined what he had eagerly sought. But in 1519 he was again hoping for an invitation to England (961–7) and confessed his foolishness. 'If I'd accepted your, and the King's, kind offer, I could have enjoyed a dignified life in England among scholarly friends instead of calumnious theologians in Louvain (1060).'

Were these solicitations just flattery? No, Erasmus genuinely admired the Cardinal's gifts to Oxford which culminated in the founding of Christ Church (965, 967), and it was not always money or place that he desired, but Wolsey's approval of his New Testament and protection against his (and its) enemies, particularly the Englishmen, Lee and Standish (967, 1132). Dedicating his *Paraphrases* on Peter and Jude—Peter a fitting gift for so great a prelate—he asked only that Wolsey's favour should encourage promising young scholars in England. His influence could do so much to revive Peter's gospel philosophy (1112 of A.D. 1520; cf. 1369).

But could one trust Wolsey to understand the gospel according to Erasmus, his *philosophia Christiana*? To keep in favour, Erasmus must disclaim Luther, although he perceived how greatly the Reformer might promote the true gospel and was long reluctant to take sides.[3] He temporized. A famous letter tells Wolsey how his enemies confuse humanism and Lutheranism, how unfairly they attack Erasmus, who has read only a few pages of Luther (967). He wants time to read him right through. Proudly, but mistakenly, he informs Melanchthon and Oecolampadius that his influence with Wolsey has saved Luther's books from a public burning in England (1102, 1113).

When Henry published the *Assertio Septem Sacramentorum* (1521) that earned him the title *Defender of the Faith*, the inscribed copy which he sent to Erasmus went astray, though he saw Wolsey's at Bruges, a happy occasion when he sat, 'a welcome guest, I believe', among such grandees as the King of Denmark and the Cardinal. Some suspected him of a hand in Henry's book, and when Luther replied to it, others saw Erasmus' work in that too! Hence indignant denials, which Henry and Wolsey accepted: Erasmus disclaimed any pact with the Lutherans (1227–8, 1263, 1342, 1367, 1383, 1386; cf. 1875).

Now everybody pressed Erasmus to attack Luther: Pope, Emperor, kings, bishops, scholars. After genuine efforts at reconciliation he yielded, the optimistic educator and moralist offended by Luther's pessimistic view of man's fallen will. Hence *De Libero Arbitrio*, 1524, which Erasmus would have dedicated to Wolsey, or the Pope, had he not feared the repute of a hireling or a toady (1486). When Luther replied with *De Servo Arbitrio*, Erasmus rejoined with *Hyperaspistes*. He had broken completely with the Reformers. He could not safely disregard the authority of Emperor, Pope, Henry, Wolsey (*Ep.* 1538 to Oecolampadius in 1525). Luther had met his moderation with utter hostility, he tells Wolsey. The cause of good letters must be finally distinguished from Lutheranism. Wolsey seems to have invited him back to England, possibly for his Oxford college.

Erasmus was now substantially conservative, though not with Wolsey's conservatism. When the Cardinal fell, Erasmus moralized, quoted classical tags, told stories of his pride, and rejoiced that England would have More for Chancellor, agreeing perhaps with those English humanists who now saw in Wolsey an obstacle to their kind of reform (2241, 2253, 2750, 2758).[4]

Wolsey was a great patron. Cuthbert Tunstall was patron and friend, even an ideal to Erasmus who described him to Budé as 'besides the two literatures [Latin and Greek] in which he surpasses all his countrymen, a man of tried judgement and refined taste, almost unheard-of modesty, cheerful and pleasant manners without loss to dignity'. Praises ring through thirty years: highest of all, he is very like Thomas More. Admiring his erudition, Erasmus reveres his character, his wisdom, his generosity, indeed his sanctity. 'You cannot believe what a wide world of excellencies I embrace when I name him.' 'This age has no man more learned, none better, none more humane, antiquity records few peers. There is no better man in England. What an example for bishops!'[5] When his friend Tunstall became *Londoniensis, Dunelmensis*, eminent in Church and State, the scholar had at times to cultivate the magnate, boasted a little of his friendship and patronage, a delicate balance to keep. But admiration and friendship were true and reciprocal.

Tunstall was studying Greek and Law in Padua when Erasmus visited England in 1499. Presumably they met in London in 1506, for he was one of four friends to whom Erasmus submitted his Latin version of two plays of Euripides which (he tells the publisher Aldus) they greatly approved. Tunstall was soon a leading ecclesiastical lawyer, Chancellor to the Archbishop of Canterbury, member of the circle at Doctors' Commons which included Colet, Grocyn, and More, Master of the Rolls in 1516; Erasmus knew of his annotations on the Civil Law. Then politics: Henry sent him as ambassador to the Emperor in Flanders, 1515-17, and later to Germany and Spain. He rose in the Church: Dean of Salisbury 1521, Bishop of London 1522, of Durham 1530—an unprecedented translation suggesting that the King needed his political experience and diplomatic sagacity, as well as his ecclesiastical support, in the North. We will briefly trace Erasmus' contacts with him, and then consider Tunstall's interest in Erasmus as scholar and churchman.

There is no evidence that they met in London during 1508, but friendship quickened through Erasmus' prolonged stay in Cambridge and London 1511-14, since in May 1515 he could say 'the two most learned men in England are at Bruges, Cuthbert Tunstall and Thomas More, my close friends (332)'. Erasmus was absent in Basel during the early part of Tunstall's embassy, but dined with him in Brussels on 3 June 1516, and took a room near him for the winter. They were much together (475) and later Erasmus was proud to recall their living together (2443). It was now that Erasmus tried so hard to make Budé and Tunstall pen-friends (480, 571-2) and that Tunstall dissuaded him from seeking a career in Paris. Now, too, they worked together on the New Testament, and More sought Tunstall's opinion of *Utopia* (481). But, Erasmus sadly admits, the ambassador was often too busy to see him. By now Tunstall was helping with money, as some anxious letters indicate.

During an embassy in 1521 the friends met at Bruges, and there is occasional correspondence from 1518–19 and 1523–4, when Tunstall showed interest in Erasmus' patristic work and concern about his attitude to Luther. Then a break in extant letters (some are lost) until 1529–30, with scholarship and heresy still under discussion; and in 1531 Tunstall was restraining Erasmus' sharp tongue. He, however, was now less in touch with his English friends, certainly with remote Durham (2831). He died in 1536, ignorant of the troubles which awaited his friend and patron.

Though Tunstall had no share in Erasmus' first New Testament (A.D. 1516), revision, quickly begun, reveals H. M. Ambassador to the Imperial Court poring over Greek manuscripts with Erasmus. 'We have collated the whole New Testament', Erasmus told More (597). Tunstall also supplied a good manuscript, much advice, and fifty French crowns—'truly faithful and friendly assistance'. Tunstall approved of Erasmus' annotations which 'open up the Greek sources to our age so thoroughly that they leave nothing for anyone else to do'. Still, everyone eagerly awaits the polished revision (663). In April 1518 Erasmus informs Tunstall that he is putting everything aside to get the New Testament out, with Pope Leo's support, he hopes. This letter (832) shows that Tunstall had questioned Erasmus' choice of words in places, wanting him to be more classical than the Vulgate. But Erasmus produces good warrant for *hyemare* in Caesar and *exaltare* in Columella. In October Erasmus reported progress (886). William Latimer's notes arrived too late, for he had finished Matthew and part of Mark. He has just sent copy to Basel, including the *Arguments* to the Epistles, added at Tunstall's suggestion. All should be complete by January, and Tunstall shall have one of three copies printed on vellum.[6] Erasmus will then continue his popular commentaries, the *Paraphrases*. In October 1519 Tunstall is told, optimistically, 'I shall finish the *Paraphrases* this winter.' It took till 1524.

Obviously we do not know all Tunstall's help to Erasmus' New Testament work. For instance, it emerges quite accidentally from letters to Sepulveda in 1534 (2905, 2951) that Erasmus had relied on Tunstall's inspection of papal bulls concerning the relative merits of Greek and Latin texts—and Tunstall got it wrong!

The perpetual onslaughts upon Erasmus' biblical publications make too intricate a story to tell here; enough that Tunstall was his friend and confidant throughout. Faber Stapulensis, a good scholar and friendly to reform, admired Erasmus. Alas, they fell out over the interpretation of *Hebrews* 2, as Erasmus complains to More (597) and Tunstall (607, 642–3) who replied that, while he approved Faber's Pauline commentaries in general, it was malicious and arrogant of him to attack Erasmus. Now it is Erasmus who is sorry to find Tunstall so hard on Faber, who is really a man in a thousand (663, 675).

Conflict with Edward Lee was longer and sharper. The young scholar had wished to help Erasmus with notes on the New Testament and for a time they got on well together. But Lee was ambitious (he was to become Archbishop of York), thought that Erasmus sometimes ignored his suggestions and sometimes used them without giving him his due credit, and so grew jealous. Everything went wrong, however hard their common friends in England laboured to end the quarrel. 'I know you don't like my *Apologiae*',[7] Erasmus wrote to Tunstall, 'and that you are trying to mediate. I think I'm being lenient— but I don't want to fight with you (1029).'

Patristic and biblical study went hand in hand for Erasmus since, in his judgement, the Fathers had acknowledged the final authority of Scripture and had rightly shaped their doctrine by exegesis rather than by syllogistic reasoning. So in expounding the New Testament he drew abundantly upon them: they were sources to which the Church should return for refreshment. Some of them he published, several for the first time. As humanist, Tunstall welcomed this Christian counterpart to the revival of pagan classics; as bishop and theologian, he was cautious. Excellent that Erasmus should popularize John Chrysostom. How better spend his time than in finishing his translation of Chrysostom on Acts (2226). And now that

Froben proposes a complete edition, Erasmus must ensure that he does not include any of Oecolampadius' editions: the margins stuffed with Lutheran notes, the versions bad, as English scholars report (unjustly; Erasmus commends his knowledge of Greek, 1835). Erasmus replied that he'd taken up the Acts manuscript again—and he'd never read anything less learned! 'I could do better drunk or snoring.' It cannot be genuine. (Erasmus was wrong, but there is a problem about these commentaries.) Then he gave Tunstall much information on available versions of Chrysostom (2263).

John of Damascus was safe reading. Perhaps Tunstall had asked Erasmus to find him a copy, which he could not do, some indication of the handicaps under which scholars then laboured (1487).

The real trouble was Erasmus' devotion to Origen. Had he not said in 1518, 'One page of Origen teaches me more about Christian philosophy than ten of Augustine (844)'? Later, amidst acute Lutheran controversy, he published part of a Latin version of Origen on Matthew which contained eucharistic statements offensive both to Christian antiquity and to contemporary scholars according to Tunstall, who doubted their authenticity. Anyhow, he says, Origen often displeased the ancients; Erasmus should demonstrate his loyalty to the Church (2226).

Erasmus admitted Origen's occasional doctrinal errors, in days before orthodoxy had been defined, but pointed to his superiority as exegete. He must be read. Tunstall continued anxious. Years before he had told his friend that the Fathers were never better than when defending Christianity or attacking heresy. Where does Origen's learning shine more brightly than against Celsus? The true service of a Christian knight (an allusion to Erasmus' *Enchiridion Militis Christiani*) is defeating heresies (1367). Now he warns, 'I'd rather that work stayed hidden than that you should be thought to approve it by translating it (2226).'

The scholar was touchy, defending Origen's words. As for himself, 'Why should I have to defend myself more than anyone else? My writings are all catholic (2263).' He went on pertinaciously with his Origen until, as a friend wrote, death snatched it from his hands. The two volumes were published posthumously in 1536, superseding Merlin's edition of 1512, to which Erasmus was greatly indebted.

Tunstall joined in the pressure put upon Erasmus to attack Luther, as already described, and we have seen how he turned Erasmus' love of the Fathers to that end: they were at their best against heresy. 'Put your loyalty beyond question, accept the Pope's invitation to take the field against the Lutherans who smirch your reputation by counting you of their party. The Church begs you to slay the Hydra. Only be bold, and the world pledges you victory (1367).' Erasmus still mediates and differentiates. He most fears the Anabaptists who make Luther seem almost orthodox (1369). Next year, however, 'The die is cast, my *De Libero Arbitrio* is out; I expect to be stoned (1487).' Even so his scorn for ultra-conservative theologians and monks kept him under suspicion; Tunstall still worried. In 1527 he and More were again demanding books against Luther, though Erasmus believed this would merely stoke the furnace and thought Tunstall, under a King whose word settled everything, could not comprehend his difficulties in Basel (1804). Two years later Tunstall grieves to learn of Basel's fall into heresy. Erasmus, who so rashly prints Origen when eucharistic controversy is rife, *must* protect himself. 'Anchor yourself to the orthodox Church, correct anything in your writings which it disapproves.' He particularly disliked the satirical *Colloquies* (2226). Though (as we saw) Erasmus is rather prickly, he reassures his old friend, now Bishop of Durham: 'I shall never leave the unity of the Church (2263).'

One part of Tunstall's episcopal duties may have offended Erasmus' deeply-felt principle of toleration. He had to suppress heresy, was even, Erasmus had heard, something like the Spanish Grand Inquisitor (2033, 2133). Though this was incorrect, since Tunstall's authority was limited to his diocese, London was the chief publishing centre, and he several times had Lutheran books burned and urged More to suppress English translations of them. Tyndale's New Testament was also burned, and Tunstall imprisoned men who circulated it. Once his Vicar-General summoned the printer Berthelet for publishing books without approval, including some translations from Erasmus himself! Generally, however, he displayed moderation, certainly during his long Durham episcopate.

Since Tunstall had welcomed Erasmus' Greek Testament with its new (non-Vulgate) Latin version, it may seem strange that he should oppose his desire, echoed by Tyndale, to have every peasant reading Scripture in his own tongue. But it was not inconsistent. He backed Erasmus' scholarship, but not Tyndale's Lutheranism. Later he approved vernacular versions.

More's last extant letter to Erasmus (2831 of A.D. 1533) mentions 'our heretic Tyndale', wandering in exile, and Erasmus must have known of More's long controversy with him. It may be chance that no reference occurs in his letters. Or was it tact? But once he had taken his own stand against Luther, he would hardly have wished to hold More back. A startling gloss on the change in Erasmus is his commendation of Cochlaeus (Dobneck) to James VI of Scotland when that king was asking whether laymen should have vernacular bibles (2886). Cochlaeus was the very man who stopped the printing of Tyndale's first Testament.[8] But Cochlaeus had ties with several of Erasmus' English friends, including More, Fisher, and Tunstall, and Erasmus wrote an amicable letter to him in 1527 (1863).

Erasmus bequeathed to Tunstall a set of his forthcoming *Opera Omnia* and died in 1536, just before heavy trouble began to fall on his true friend and patron, whose learning and character were universally respected.

That so many bishops of Durham were the sort of men in whom Erasmus could find friends and patrons has historical significance for the humanist element in the English Reformation. Are there lessons for today? Historical situations do not recur exactly. Relations between Church and State have changed; so have the circumstances of professional scholars. But two threads running through this story greatly concern us today: biblical study and Christian unity.

The battle for vernacular scriptures is won, but the problems of revelation, orthodoxy, and authority remain. We can return neither to the biblicism which used proof-texts to settle every issue, to a simple 'The Bible says . . .', nor to mere obedience to ecclesiastics arranging dogmas in catechisms. Erasmus' recourse to patristic biblical exegesis as a method of learning or teaching theology, implying that the early centuries escaped corruption by scholasticism, sounds quite Anglican and contains sense, but must stand criticism from less traditional theologians. Here his hatred of schism comes in. Men of good will, seeking truth in unity and charity, *can* find it. But unnecessary definition *de fide* is harmful. Fundamentals necessary to salvation are plain enough; with agreement on these, secondary differences are allowable within unity. Again characteristically (not exclusively!) Anglican, and sensible.

Yet to many Erasmus' outlook seems shallow and moralistic, lacking Luther's boldness and depth. Where charity (unity) and truth conflict, as at the Reformation, ecumenism has to be an uneasy blend of patience and impatience, with trust in God's action transcending sweet reason, and faith that grace transforms the unruly wills and affections of sinful men. Erasmus agreed, but without Luther's passion. Was he also too cosmopolitan, where Luther was too German? Can Africans contribute their own response to Scripture? We are heirs of both in some measure if, while facing new knowledge, we confidently expose ourselves to the creative power of God's Word.

NOTES

1 I hope my little subterfuge will be condoned.

2 Erasmus' correspondence is cited by the numbers in P. S. Allen's edition. All students of Erasmus are immeasurably indebted to Allen. See his note here for Foxe's house.

3 For Erasmus' attitude to Luther see Preserved Smith, *Erasmus*, ch. xii (1923) or, in full detail, R. H. Murray, *Erasmus and Luther* (1920). I can only touch on points which concern Wolsey and Tunstall.

4 On this point see J. K. McConica, *English Humanists and Reformation Politics* (2e., 1968), pp. 107–11, perhaps getting a little too much out of Erasmus' statements.

5 This last phrase comes from *Ep.* 1629, when Erasmus was sending Tunstall's book on arithmetic, *De Arte Supputandi*, to the Bishop of Przemysl.

6 This copy passed to Toby Matthew, Bishop of Durham and Archbishop of York. It was in York Minster library till 1932.

7 Erasmus' *Defences* were as often *Attacks*. The one most relevant here is the *Apologia qua respondet duabus invectivis Edvardi Lei*, ed. W. K. Ferguson in *Erasmi Opuscula* (1933), with an instructive introduction.

8 See J. F. Mozley, *William Tyndale*, pp. 57–61, and Allen's note on *Ep.* 1863.

The Missionary Expansion of
Ecclesia Anglicana

MAX WARREN

In the Gospel according to St Luke the incident is recorded
when the impetuous disciples of our Lord, James and John,
angered by the discourtesy of some Samaritan villagers, wanted
to emulate the prophet Elijah and call down fire upon them.
Jesus turned and rebuked them (Luke 9.55). At this point the
Jerusalem Bible adds, in a marginal note, 'You do not know
what spirit you are made of. The Son of Man came not to
destroy souls but to save them.' That marginal note has some
Ms. support. It is quoted here for two reasons which do not
depend upon manuscript support but upon Christian experience.

First of those reasons is the uniting truth which binds in one
all Christians, whatever their ecclesiastical allegiance, that
Jesus, our Lord, came not to destroy souls but to save them.
The second reason rests upon the hint implicit in the words 'You
do not know what spirit you are made of'. The hint is that
spiritual heredity may be as important as, indeed more important than, any other kind of descent. St John Baptist (Luke 3.8)
and St Paul (Rom. 2.29) would seem to establish the point.

For the purpose of this essay this scriptural introduction is
the ground of the affirmation that the missionary expansion
of Ecclesia Anglicana, as surely as the missionary expansion of
any other Christian tradition, derives from the very heart of
the Faith itself. For ourselves then, we claim direct descent
from that dawn of Christianity in our island when, as seems
almost certain, Christian legionaries in the Roman army built
a church in the Roman fort at Dover, some time in the second
century A.D. Of that early Romano-British Church we know
very little. That it was firmly rooted in Britain can be estab-

lished beyond contradiction by two facts. At the Council of
Arles in A.D. 314 there were present three British bishops, those
of York, London, and Lincoln, from whom the contemporary
holders of those sees claim an unbroken succession. A more
comprehensive claim can be based upon the astonishing vitality
and missionary enthusiasm of the Celtic Church of St Patrick,
St Ninian, St Columba, and St Aidan, something of whose
missionary zeal penetrated throughout western Europe through
the dynamic ministry of such different men as Columbanus and
Gall, whose example, in turn, must have influenced Willibrod
and Boniface.

Important as were St Augustine and Theodore of Tarsus,
they entered a succession. They did not create it. What they did
do was to prepare the way for the historic decision of the Synod
of Whitby in A.D. 664 by which the Ecclesia Anglicana became
indisputably linked in custom and tradition with the Church
of the European continent and in an intimate, if not always easy,
relationship with the see of Rome. Whatever the overtures and
undertones of the phrase in Magna Carta—'Ecclesia Anglicana
libera sit'—a proposition was thereby advanced which, in
more ways than one, has received a lively interpretation in
subsequent history.

This is no place to pursue the fascinating story of the expansion of the Christian Faith in the Dark Ages, or its flowering
in the Middle Ages. What is interesting is to note that the
missionary pattern of those times in which monasteries were
the centres of culture, of agricultural experiment, of education,
healing, and social welfare, these together with the activities
of the preaching orders set a pattern, which, whatever the
differences in outward form, has been an enduring feature of the
missionary enterprise ever since. The Mission complex of the
nineteenth and early twentieth century of Church, School,
Hospital, and itinerating Missionary was a close adaptation
of the same principle which once led to the conversion of
Europe.

With that brief excursion into the remoter past we can turn
to some descriptions of the process by which the Ecclesia
Anglicana, which achieved autonomy in the sixteenth century,
became a world-wide communion.

The story of this process is a complicated one. If Professor

Seeley, one time Regius Professor of History at Cambridge, was right in saying that the British Empire was founded in a fit of absence of mind, he could with justice have added, had he thought of it, that the growth of the Anglican Communion owed nothing whatever to any kind of co-ordinated planning.

We can best begin by recognizing that the sixteenth and seventeenth centuries saw the shattering of the medieval synthesis of Church and State, the fragmentation of the ideal of the *Corpus Christianum*. It remains, nevertheless, true that most Christian thinkers in those centuries refused to accept this fragmentation as final: insisted, indeed, on believing that the synthesis was still alive. The doctrine of the Divine Right of Kings was the sixteenth and seventeenth-century version of the medieval doctrine of the 'two swords'. This can be seen in the strict Lutheran doctrine of the two realms, and in English history it is encapsulated in James the First's dictum 'No Bishop, No King'. In the great missionary expansion of the Roman Church the intimate alliance of the Papal See with the kingdoms of Spain and Portugal ensured that the concept of the integral relationship of Church and State would be exported wherever the fleets of Spain and Portugal might sail. Diaz and da Gama, Cortez and Pizarro saw themselves as crusaders. Their expeditions were at once a conquest for commerce and the cross.

This basic assumption of European man in the sixteenth and seventeenth centuries determined the shape taken by the Church of England. The Elizabethan establishment was conceived both politically and religiously as an assertion in local terms of the medieval synthesis. But those were stormy centuries. And, in England, energy was for the time being concentrated by the Ecclesia Anglicana in defining its position doctrinally, and also in defining its relationship with the State. It is at least interesting to reflect that this redefinition, for that is what it was, took liturgical form. The Book of Common Prayer of 1552 proved to be the real cement of the body politic, as it proved to be the real bond of union which held together men of very different theological persuasions. And the Book of Common Prayer has had a determining influence on the growth of the Anglican Communion. It is not altogether an accident that virtually the first sign of expansion on the part of the English Church was the

Celebration of the Holy Communion according to the Book of Common Prayer, by the Chaplain of Sir Francis Drake's ship, when the crew landed in 1570 a few miles north of where San Francisco stands today. A monument to that liturgical occasion will be found between the Twin Peaks of that fascinating city.

Again there is a faint, very faint, hint of things to come in a resolution of the English East India Company in 1614 to educate an Indian youth who had been brought to England so that 'he might upon occasion be sent unto his country where God may be pleased to make him an instrument in converting some of his nation'[1]—a somewhat modest beginning for Anglican Missions!

The Charter of 1698 of that same East India Company made provisions for a Christian minister in each garrison and main factory centre, and ordered all its ministers to learn Portuguese (the *lingua franca* of these posts) 'the better to instruct the servants and slaves of the Company and its agents in the Protestant religion'.[2] It is on record that the Book of Common Prayer was in regular use in these centres of the East India Company.

Coincident in time with that charter of 1698 was the activity of one of the most remarkable figures in Anglican history, Thomas Bray. As much as any single man could do he pioneered the missionary outreach of the Church of England. It is a remarkable story of a parish priest who first dedicated his energies to making the Book of Common Prayer come alive for his small village church congregation. From his experience of reviving religious observances in that village he proceeded to produce in 1696 *Catechetical Lectures on the Preliminary Questions and Answers of the Church Catechism, in four volumes*. This captured attention, for in the previous year Archbishop Tenison had issued injunctions, under the authority of the Crown, one of which required obedience to the 59th canon, calling for regular catechizing of the young on Sundays.[3]

Thomas Bray might well have remained a quiet parish priest, known for his learning and devotion, but not otherwise remarked in history but for an unusual combination of circumstances. In 1634 all the activities of the Church outside the British Isles had been put under the Bishop of London's care. In 1675 one of the most vigorous and far-seeing Bishops of

London was appointed in the person of Henry Compton. He soon discovered that the Colonies of America and the West Indies were in a grave state of spiritual neglect and decay. Directly his jurisdiction was confirmed by the Government he set to work to find a remedy. He persuaded King Charles II to offer a bounty of £20 to any minister or schoolmaster who would go to the colonies and £1200 to supply prayer books and Bibles for the churches there. In 1694 a zealous Anglican was appointed Governor of Maryland and he asked Bishop Compton to appoint a Commissary who would exercise ecclesiastical discipline and give leadership to the clergy. Bishop Compton decided that Thomas Bray was the man for this responsibility.

Bray realistically reckoned that only the poorer clergy would be willing to volunteer to leave England for North America, their prospects in their own country being so bleak. But just because of their poverty they would be unable to afford books. This other piece of realism launched Bray on his most constructive achievement, the provision of libraries for the parishes overseas, a provision which he was to extend to all the rural-deaneries, and many market towns of England itself. He was in fact the pioneer of the Public Library as we know it today. He first set out in print in 1695 his *Proposals for encouraging Learning and Religion in the Foreign Plantations*, and so with the encouragement of archbishop and bishops made his plea for public support. In 1697 he expanded his vision in *An Essay towards promoting all Necessary and Useful knowledge, both Divine and Human, in all parts of His Majesty's Dominions both at home and abroad.*

On 19 December 1697 Bishop Compton held an Ordination of Missionaries in St Paul's Cathedral—Bray preached the sermon. Only that autumn had the choir of Wren's great new building been completed, so it is almost certain that this was the first ordination service held in the new cathedral, a significant fact in itself, for during the next two centuries a very high percentage of Anglican missionary priests were ordained in St Paul's Cathedral, being first examined by the Bishop of London as to their fitness for this ministry.

Bray was soon clear that this undertaking of providing libraries for clergy and parish churches at home and abroad could not continue as the voluntary effort of one man. With four friends on 8 March 1699, he formed the first Missionary Society of the Church of England, the Society for Promoting Christian Knowledge, with the primary purpose of making available the Book of Common Prayer and other Christian literature and, what was equally important, the payment of schoolmasters and the erection of school buildings. From this start the missionary enterprise was again seen as being as much concerned with England itself as with the plantations and colonies overseas.

Bray, however, in his capacity as Commissary for Maryland, had to secure men who would go out to be pastors in the parishes overseas. Nor did he limit his purview to Maryland. He was as concerned for the other colonies and not least for Newfoundland. To this end he felt that it was essential that a chartered body, entitled to collect and hold funds and maintain missionaries in the colonies should be founded. On 16 June 1701 the Society for the Propagation of the Gospel began its long record of service, duly incorporated with a Royal Charter.

We have noticed earlier how King Charles II was happy to offer a bounty of £20 to any priest who was prepared to go to the Colonies. In Maryland and in Pennsylvania a tax of one penny on each pound of tobacco paid the stipends of the Anglican Clergy. And the royal charter of the SPG was itself a significant token of the relation between the State and the Established Church. As in the possessions of Spain and Portugal, of Holland and France, so it was assumed as but natural, in the overseas possessions of Britain, that the Church of the Metropolitan Country must have the privileges of an Establishment in the Colonies. The SPG with its royal charter is a link with the world of Pope Alexander VI. He had reconciled the rival ambitions of the Spanish and Portuguese conquistadors by dividing the newly discovered lands between them. But in doing so he 'had emphasized the Christian element in these discoveries and conquests, and had laid upon the Christian powers the responsibility to find and support missionaries, and at a later date to found and endow bishoprics'.[4] Thomas Bray and the SPG were in a great and venerable tradition. But it was the end of an age.

The great achievements of the SPG were to be made in an age when it was finally determined that Establishment of religion could not be exported to Asia and Africa and the Islands of the Pacific. Yet the idea of Establishment died hard. Royal letters, which were to be read in churches, continued from time to time to be issued by Royal Warrant well into the nineteenth century, exhorting congregations to subscribe to the SPG. And something like a quasi-Establishment maintained itself in the minds of many churchmen, even though it possessed no legal authority. Something of this curious story I have related in the first chapter of my book *Social History and Christian Mission.*[5]

We shall come across the influence of Thomas Bray again at a later stage. But now we must turn to the tumultuous events of the eighteenth century which were to exercise so profound an influence on the missionary movement of all the Churches, and not least of Ecclesia Anglicana.

It is difficult to exaggerate the difference in the climate of men's minds between those who founded the SPCK and SPG, the two first Anglican Missionary Societies, and those who, a hundred years later, in 1799 founded the Church Missionary Society. For an understanding of the differences I refer to what, in my judgement, is far and away the most percipient study of John Wesley and the eighteenth-century Evangelical Revival, a study written by Fr Maximin Piette of Louvain, with the title *John Wesley in the Evolution of Protestantism.* Here are two quotations. After listing the names of some of the distinguished scientists of the end of the seventeenth and the early part of the eighteenth century he writes

> Illumined by the torch of their inspiration and experiments, it [the eighteenth century] was destined to discover and to tame the hidden powers of nature. Untold conquests in the material world: a whole universe waiting to be explored: the universal interdependence of all created things: the minute scrutiny of starry spheres and heavenly firmaments; the foundation and basic laws of the whole of modern chemistry! Eighteenth century: Century of Reason: a victorious and triumphant century indeed![6]

Savour that quotation! The great geographical explorations of the age of Pope Alexander VI had ushered in a revolution in human thought, and precipitated a social and religious ferment. This later age of exploration into the world of nature was to have a comparable revolutionary effect.

That is the context in which Fr Piette sets the significance of John Wesley and the tidal wave of new spiritual life of which he was pre-eminently the expression.

His missionary effort [says Fr Piette] was to be a crusade in favour of a Christian life. He did not bring forward learned theories, but he presented experiences as lived in every-day life. Since experiment was shown to be so extraordinarily fertile in the field of natural sciences, might he not expect as wonderful results in the spiritual life? Such was his thought. Spiritual experiences rely for their full effect on a two-fold state of mind: the consciousness of sin on the one hand and the assurance of salvation *hic et nunc* on the other. The transition from one state of mind to the other was accomplished in a flash, by the crisis of conversion known as the New Birth. To justify his experimental method, Wesley appealed to the practical results of his preaching; the moral betterment of his hearers. The justification by faith which he preached was nearer the doctrine of the Council of Trent than what he contemptuously called Luther's crazy solifidianism.[7]

That is a very important assessment of John Wesley, though I think the full argument of Fr Piette's book points even more emphatically to the truth that the deepest elements in Luther's own experience had been obscured in controversy and quite lost to sight in the Lutheran scholasticism of the seventeenth century. What Wesley really did was to recover the depths of the Pauline experience in Rom. 7 and 8 which St Augustine of Hippo had so forcefully emphasized, and which was Luther's own personal experience. Wesley brought them down to the level of the personal experience of the miners of Bristol and the prisoners in the slums of the cities in what was the beginning of the Industrial Revolution. The explosive force of this experimental religion profoundly influenced the future of English religion and proved to be the single most dynamic inspiration of the modern missionary movement within Anglicanism and in Protestantism generally.

We have seen how Thomas Bray envisaged the missionary

work of the Church as an activity to be strongly supported by
the State, Church and State being still conceived in terms of the
medieval synthesis. By the end of the eighteenth century the
whole shape of society was being changed. Experiment in
the world of science was being paralleled by experiment in
the forms of government. The American Revolution and the
French Revolution brought finally to an end the age of
the Christian prince. All institutions were under attack, as was the
moral fabric of society. Here is the significance of the Evangelical revival in the English-speaking world. In an age of experiment men responded eagerly to an experimental religion whose
cardinal beliefs were extremely simple. And from this follows
the fact that the corporate expression of this religious movement
took the form of small voluntary associations for mutual study
and mutual encouragement in the Faith. The forerunners of
these, as far as England was concerned, were the religious
societies at the end of the seventeenth century, with some of
which Thomas Bray had been himself involved, and which
played a part in the founding of the SPCK and SPG. John
Wesley's 'Holy Club' at Oxford was another such. And the
Class Meetings which he established were a further expression.
This was a form of association that was wholly congenial to the
religious spirit of the eighteenth century and proved to be the
cement which saved Evangelical religion from disintegrating
into individualism. These religious societies had their own
strict discipline. And one issue from that discipline was a
highly organized philanthropy.[8]

Now, this whole movement of thought and experience, and
of a latent capacity for organization and corporate responsibility, penetrated the Anglican Church, not surprisingly,
inasmuch as John Wesley was himself an Anglican. Already,
however, independently of John Wesley's influence a number
of Anglican clergy had arrived at his spiritual experience and
were preaching this recovered gospel. I use the word 'recovered' deliberately because, at least in the Church of England,
a period of spiritual aridity marked much of the Church's life.
But these Anglican clergy, like the followers of John Wesley,
were viewed askance by the authorities in both Church and
State. Their 'enthusiasm' appeared to be altogether too closely
akin to the mood of revolution which was fermenting through-

out the national life. So, when a number of clergy and laity, all deeply moved by the Evangelical revival, met together to form a Missionary Society which would seek to take the gospel to the heathen world, they were viewed with deep suspicion, not least by the leaders of their own Church.

This same group was, on Christian grounds, deeply committed to seeking the abolition of the Slave Trade and of slavery. This campaign in turn came in for fierce resistance by vested interests. It looked as if this Evangelical religion was not only an embarrassment to the Church but a potential threat to the Constitution, and certainly a serious challenge to some commercial interests.

The Evangelicals who founded the Church Missionary Society were, for all these reasons, extremely unpopular. They had, themselves, to proceed with their undertaking as a voluntary society, without benefit of ecclesiastical support. In the sequel this suspicion of enthusiasm together with the general episcopal apathy with regard to evangelism secured the firm establishment, at the heart of the Anglican Missionary expansion, of the voluntary principle. The essence of this principle is that persons sharing a similar spiritual experience, a similar concern for proclaiming the gospel, and a general agreement as to the best means of doing so, should form Societies for this purpose.

One providential result of this development at the end of the eighteenth century was that there was no risk of these voluntary societies receiving any form of state support. The earlier missionary movement of modern times had been vitiated by its too close association with the empires under whose patronage it had developed. At the end of the eighteenth century there were still powerful influences which would have found their natural expression in state-sponsored missions. The story behind the passing of the East India Act in 1813 and the resultant Church Establishment in India shows that this was a danger barely averted. There was, at least, in the first quarter of the nineteenth century, a by no means negligible danger that the Church of England might attempt to conduct its expansion abroad as a department of State.

One small but interesting illustration of this is to be found in the record of how the Anglican episcopate was established in the United States of America. Thomas Bray had argued urgently, but unsuccessfully, for the consecration of bishops for the American colonies. So, when the episcopal clergy in Connecticut in 1783 chose Seabury as a man suitable for consecration and sent him to England, it proved impossible for the Archbishop of Canterbury to proceed with his consecration for a number of reasons which included the fact that the United States was a nation outside the Empire, and that a bishop would be unable to take the oath of allegiance to the British Crown. In the sequel it was three Scottish bishops who consecrated Seabury on 14 November 1784 as the first Anglican bishop in the United States.

In 1786 an Act of Parliament was at last passed which empowered the Primate to consecrate persons who were subjects or citizens of countries outside the King's dominions. But an ominous clause in the Act showed the continuing threat to missionary expansion. It read:

> Provided also, and be it hereby declared, that no Person or Persons consecrated to the Office of Bishop in the Manner aforesaid, nor any Person or Persons deriving their Consecration from or under any Bishops so consecrated, nor any Person or Persons admitted to the Order of Deacon or Priest by any Bishop or Bishops so consecrated, or by the successor of any Bishop or Bishops so consecrated, shall be thereby enabled to exercise his or their respective Office or Offices within His Majesty's Dominions.[9]

American bishops and clergy visiting England were treated as laymen and were not permitted to officiate or preach!

It was the voluntary principle, as represented by the Church Missionary Society, which set the pattern which in due course rescued the Church of England from this dilemma and made its expansion into the Anglican Communion possible.

God does sometimes use revolutionary impatience to serve his purposes!

Having established the important significance of the voluntary principle and its application in the creation of voluntary societies committed to missionary work overseas, certain supplementary points may help to explain the expansion of the Ecclesia Anglicana.

Sea-power, together with the initiative in commerce provided by the Industrial Revolution, combined to create an extraordinary urge to explore the world and with it to create areas of British political influence which gradually took the form of an Empire. Further to this a genuine moral earnestness throughout Society, itself in large measure the fruit of the Evangelical Revival, combined with more commercial motives to establish in the popular mind the obligation on Britain to promote 'Christianity and Civilization' wherever, in the nineteenth-century understanding of both terms, neither as yet existed. This in itself was an encouragement to the missionary enterprise. The attack on slavery was the philanthropic parallel to missionary endeavour.

We turn now to an important point about the relationship of the Evangelical Missionary Societies, which were Anglican in doctrine and practice, with the Established Church in England, and more particularly with the Episcopate. Charles Simeon, Vicar of Holy Trinity, Cambridge from 1782 to 1836, the outstanding Evangelical leader of that period, was a deeply committed churchman. And it was his influence, more than that of any other man, which kept the Evangelicals within the Church of England, when episcopal antipathy might well have led them into schism.[10]

It was his influence which sent out able and devoted men to act as chaplains in the territories of the East India Company at a time when no missionaries were permitted in India. He was a devoted supporter of the Church Missionary Society. Indeed it was his own prophetic enthusiasm, which terminated a period of anxious discussion about the possibility of founding such a society and which pressed for immediate action.

The earliest document of the Society is entitled an *Account of a Society for Missions to Africa and the East instituted by Members of the Established Church, 1799*. Its opening sentence reads: 'Of all the blessings which God has bestowed upon mankind, the Gospel of our Lord and Saviour Jesus Christ is the greatest. It is the sovereign remedy for all the evils of life, and the source of the most substantial and durable benefits.'[11] Appreciative recognition is given in that document to the work of the SPCK and SPG, it being noted that they are primarily engaged in the British Plantations in North America. It further observes with regard to the SPG that 'the primary and direct object of this society has been rather the religious benefit of the British Colonists, and those Heathens immediately dependent upon them, than the conversion of the Heathen in general'.[12] It goes on: 'Room, therefore, is still left for the institution of a society which shall consider the Heathen as its principal care. The whole Continent of Africa, and that of Asia also (with the exception of a few places) are still open to the missionary labours of the Church of England. To these quarters of the globe, therefore, the promoters of the present design turn their chief attention.'[13] The founders, having already decided that the new society was to be founded on 'the Church principle' here affirm 'that as members of the Church of England they consider its doctrinal articles as exhibiting the standard of that faith which it should be their endeavour to propagate'.[14] One whole page of the *Account* (p. 8) deals with the Society's loyalty to the episcopal principle, a loyalty which has characterized the Society ever since.

What is to be noticed, however, is that nowhere in Africa or Asia were there any bishops of the Church of England. The absence of bishops in North America had not deterred Thomas Bray from sending missionaries. A similar lack did not deter the CMS from doing so. For both, the setting forth of the gospel was the priority. It was indeed only after the rise of the Oxford Movement in the middle of the nineteenth century that the idea was advanced that a mission could only properly be undertaken under the leadership of a bishop. Of the importance of a bishop, and an episcopally ordered ministry, for the due upbuilding of the Church, there has never been any doubt in the missionary expansion of the Ecclesia Anglicana. What has never been considered by Evangelicals within our Church is that missionary work, in the way of primary evangelism, cannot be undertaken without episcopal supervision. And events seem to have justified this Evangelical conviction. Some of the largest Anglican Churches today, if numbers are relevant, whether in Asia or Africa, have in fact been pioneered by missionaries, often laymen, before it was possible to achieve the appointment of a bishop. Nevertheless, the Evangelical Societies in the Church of England have been as assiduous as any in seeking the formation of an Episcopate, at first missionary, and, as soon as possible, indigenous, once a Christian community had come into existence.

At an early point in this essay, note was made of the importance of the Book of Common Prayer in the history of Anglicanism. We have seen Thomas Bray deeply concerned to ensure the availability of prayer books in the American Colonies. We have seen the foundation of the SPCK with the meeting of this need as one of its objectives, ever since maintained. The Church Missionary Society has been no less assiduous. There is a letter written by Henry Venn, the Chief Secretary of the CMS from 1841–72, under the date 28 September 1849, in which in reply to some objection he writes

> The Church Missionary Society uniformly sends out the prayer book with the Bible, wherever a Christian Church exists, and has done more to extend the use of the prayer book in different languages than has been done by any other society or agency since the prayer book existed.
>
> The Society has translated and used it in Tamil, Telegu, Malayalam, Singhalese, New Zealand, Hindi, Mahratta, Maltese, one of the dialects of Abyssinia, and of several of the American Indians.[15]

There is another sequel to the voluntary principle, represented by the CMS and by many other societies. This has proved to be of incalculable importance in the development of the Ecumenical Movement. Because today the Ecumenical Movement has received the blessing of ecclesiastical authority in all the Churches it is sometimes forgotten that it was pioneered by the missionary societies, long before any Church was prepared to commit itself to thinking out the principles of ecumenism. One of the earliest experiments in closer fellowship between Christians took place in Bombay in 1825 when CMS missionaries joined with Congregational, Presbyterian, and Brethren missionaries to form what they called the 'Bombay Union' to promote the discussion of common problems, to discover areas of agreement and the means of avoiding friction, and to agree on the requirements for baptism of native converts.

It would be disingenuous to pretend that within the missionary movement there has not been tension between the very different philosophies of mission represented by the SPG and

CMS, and the other societies associated with one or other of these traditions. The SPG (now the USPG since its union with the Universities Mission to Central Africa) has faithfully followed the Ignatian rule of 'doing nothing without the bishop'. And their work has been very greatly blessed to the building up of the Church all over the world. The CMS, and kindred Evangelical Societies, while faithful to the principle of episcopacy for the general ordering of the Church's life, have set their priorities elsewhere. When a bishop has been available they have readily acknowledged his leadership. But if he was not available, and often he was not, they have gone on with their evangelism undeterred. As a result they have found themselves pioneering co-operation with the societies of other churches, and promoting schemes for church union, well ahead of the official endorsement by the Church.

Tension there has been, but it has been more creative than destructive, and its less happy effects have been greatly reduced by the fact that the two traditions have been worked out for the most part in different geographical areas.

However, there is one consequence of the history which is here traced out and that is the absence of any generally received methodology of mission in the Anglican Communion. What can be claimed is that there has been something like a common development due to the liturgical unity provided by the Book of Common Prayer, and by the acceptance of an episcopal ordering of the Church as the norm for practice.

Further to this there has been a common structural progress which can be described in terms of three stages—first, has come the period of exploration—a probing to see whether the gospel was to win a response; second, once a response had come, there was the setting up of a scaffolding consisting of foreign missionaries, the bishop normally being one of them, who created the 'form' of the local church, providing for its ministry and for its consultative procedure; third, came the period in which under its own indigenous leadership the local church has taken responsibility for its own affairs.

That is to describe a process by analysing it. The development has taken place at a varied pace, and not without many periods of friction and regress. Meanwhile there must be few who know the actual situation in the Church overseas who are altogether convinced that a heavily westernized pattern of church organization is sure of survival in its traditional form. This is not to hold any doubts about the reality of the Church itself, but only about its present structure.

Partly in order to strengthen the local churches of the Anglican Communion in Asia and Africa, there has been in this century, and more particularly since the end of the Second World War, what is known as Provincial development. Provinces consist of a number of dioceses under an archbishop which together form an autonomous unit within the Anglican Communion. While all are self-governing, few in Asia and Africa are anywhere near self-supporting. And in a grimly adverse economic, and sometimes political, climate they have to face problems which do not make it easy for them to be self-propagating as they would wish to be. Yet this Provincial development is important. Among other things it achieves two objectives. It does in some measure rescue the local church from being victimized as a surviving embodiment of colonialism, while, with the links that all the Provinces have with each other in the Anglican Communion, there is some safeguard against the local church surrendering to a narrow nationalism. In the second place it provides a sufficiently large unit to be able to negotiate responsibility with other churches towards the goal of church union.

Within very strict limitations of space this general outline, grossly oversimplified as of necessity it is, is offered as one interpretation of the missionary expansion of an island Church into a world-wide Communion.

NOTES

1   K. S. Latourette, *A History of the Expansion of Christianity*, vol. III, p. 277.

2   Ibid., p. 277.

3   H. P. Thompson, *Thomas Bray* (London 1954), p. 10.

4   Stephen Neill, *A History of Christian Missions* (1964), p. 142.

5   Max Warren, op. cit. (London 1967), pp. 15–35.

6   Maximin Piette, op. cit. (London 1937), p. 98.

7   Ibid., p. 475.

8   See Max Warren, *The Missionary Movement from Britain in Modern History* (London 1965), pp. 31–4.

9 H. G. G. Herklots, *The Church of England and the American Episcopal Church* (London 1966), pp. 100–1.

10 For chapter and verse to support these generalizations see Max Warren, *The Missionary Movement from Britain in Modern History* and *Social History and Christian Mission*.

11 *Account*, op. cit., p. 2.

12 Ibid., p. 7.

13 Ibid., p. 7.

14 Ibid., pp. 10–11.

15 CMS Archives, G/AC1/7, pp. 188–90, 28 September 1849, Letter to Miss Primrose.

Missionary Vocation and the Ministry
The First Generation

———————•◄••►———————

A. F. WALLS

The modern missionary movement was a child of the Evangelical Revival, but it was a late child. In Britain half a century separated the period when John Wesley's heart was strangely warmed and the Countess of Huntingdon began to let Whitefield loose in fashionable drawing rooms, from the period when men met in conclave to consider, as a practical proposition, the evangelization of the world. They then estimated the world's population at 731 millions; and Protestant Christians were, for practical purposes, confined to western Europe and the North American eastern seaboard. They had no assembled missionary tradition, no gathered experience, little knowledge of the practical problems to be faced. The only reason they had to expect success was in the biblical prophecies: their conviction that in due time the earth would be full of the knowledge of God as the waters cover the sea.[1] It is hardly surprising that there was no rush to be in the first generation of missionaries, and a matter of interest to see where the founders of societies expected, and where they found, the personnel for the task which possessed them.[2]

In his *Enquiry*, an extraordinarily influential work for one published in the provinces by a man of only parochial reputation, William Carey assumes that the man who has accepted the call to the Christian ministry must be ready to receive it to the mission field also:

> ... And this would only be passing through what we have virtually engaged in by entering the ministerial office. A Christian minister is a person who in a peculiar sense is *not his own*; he is the *servant* of God. . . . He engages to go where God

pleases, and to do, or endure what he sees fit to command, or call him to in the exercise of his function. He virtually bids farewell to friends, pleasures, and comforts. . . . . It is inconsistent for ministers to please themselves with thoughts of a numerous auditory, cordial friends, a civilized country, level protection, affluence, splendour, or even a competency. . . . . I question whether all are justified in staying here, while so many are perishing without means of grace in other lands.[3]

And he is ready to prove his point: for when, as a result of his influence, a missionary society is founded, he is ready to go as one of its first agents.

Carey was, of course, by any reckoning a remarkable man; yet he represents a type bred among the English Dissenters and the Scots seceders: independent, hard-working, developing their own tradition of learning. Many such ministers had practised trades or crafts before their call, and some might, as Carey had for some time done with his cobbling,[4] continue with them thereafter. There was certainly nothing incongruous in itself in a shoemaker becoming a missionary: this was the way men came into the home ministry.

People with this tradition did not have such a complicated view of missionary service as those ministers of the English and Scottish establishments who wanted to encourage missions. These took for granted, as Carey had done, that a missionary was essentially a preacher, and that a preacher should normally be a minister. But for them the minister was the representative of the established Church in society, and as such entitled to a measure of respect. This is turn implied a degree of education and social accomplishment which would not disgrace it.

Among early writers on missions with this background, it is remarkable to find that few seem to *expect* much response from ordained and beneficed clergymen as missionary recruits. Melvill Horne says in so many words that he does not expect it—though he immediately apologizes lest he has been too harsh on his own Church.[5] No, it is clearly too much to expect that a man who has a benefice, and the security which it provides— and which may have taken quite a bit of getting—will give it up for the hardships of Sierra Leone or Tahiti. Horne does not say so, but perhaps it was also expecting much of hopeful unbeneficed clergy that they should give up their place in the queue, and lose, probably for ever, that benefice which to the forty pounds a year curate must have seemed the best blessing of earthly existence. Jane Austen, always a most accurate observer of these things, puts the point well in the dénouement of *Mansfield Park*. Mary Crawford, surprised and abashed at Edmund Bertram's profound seriousness, says to him: 'A pretty good lecture upon my word. Was it part of your last sermon? At this rate you will soon reform everybody at Mansfield and Thornton Lacey; and when I hear of you next, it may be as a celebrated preacher in some great society of Methodists, or as a missionary into foreign parts.'[6] Edmund was a beneficed clergyman; and at the time (1811–13) that *Mansfield Park* was written, no former holder of an English benefice was, in the proper sense of the term, 'a missionary into foreign parts'.

A similar conviction is implied in a sermon by Thomas Haweis, one of the few prominent Anglicans to support the London Missionary Society, preached at the Society's inauguration in 1795.

Whom shall we send, and who will go for us? I answer, such as the Lord hath prepared and qualified for the arduous task. Men, whose lives are not dear unto themselves, but ready to spend and be spent in the honourable service. Men, really moved by the Holy Ghost to devote themselves to the work... Men, who have an internal evidence of the Spirit, *witnessing, with their spirits, that they are the children of God;*—a divine ardour, prompting them to prefer the salvation of men's souls to every earthly consideration. ... Such are the men the great Shepherd and Bishop of Souls sends, such are the instruments we must seek.[7]

But where are such people to be found? Haweis has a quite explicit answer:

Nor need we despair of finding them, if not in the schools of learning, or the seminaries of theology, yet among the faithful, in our several congregations.[8]

Haweis, that is, not only expects no recruits for the mission field from the home ministry: he does not expect that the ordinary sources of supply of the home ministry will produce recruits either.

> Not that the knowledge of the dead languages, however desirable, is essential to the communication of Gospel truth in the living ones. A plain man—with a good natural understanding—well read in the Bible,—full of faith, and of the Holy Ghost,—though he comes from the forge or the shop, would, I own, in my view, as a missionary to the heathen, be infinitely preferable to all the learning of the schools; and would possess, in the skill and labour of his hands, advantages which barren science would never compensate.[9]

The missionary needs spiritual qualifications, a knowledge of the Bible, and common sense. Competence with a mallet or a saw is all to the good, but formal education is not necessary— which is as well, for educated people are most unlikely to offer.

For many people who heard that sermon, this presented no difficulty: some outstanding Dissenting ministers did come from the forge or the shop, and had acquired much skill in dead languages as well. But Haweis was an Anglican, and knew quite well that no bishop was likely to ordain a man from the shop or the forge just because he knew his Bible. Haweis can answer this argument only with the big stick; unless the bishop (or presbytery) is born again, he cannot tell who is and who is not fit to be a missionary:

> I am, my brethren, an Episcopalian, and by choice, as by education, attached to the Established Church, and wish to see her a glory in the earth. . . . Yet I am no bigot. I neither suppose salvation restricted to her pale, nor the approbation of her rulers, however desirable, essential to an evangelical mission. Indeed it is an axiom, to which every real Christian will accede, that no dignity of office, whether Bishop or Archbishop, nor a whole Presbytery, however wise or learned, if they have not themselves experienced the divine call, and been inwardly moved by the Holy Ghost, to take the sacred ministry upon them. . . . such men, I say, can be no more capable of judging the qualifications of a missionary, than the stupid Omiah to solve the most difficult proposition in

Euclid, or a deaf man to decide on the beauty of harmonical composition.[10]

This being so, missionaries will be chosen by

> such as have themselves been taught of God; and whose age and experience, in the good ways of our Saviour, enable them to discern between the ebullitions of mistaken zeal and the deliberate devotedness of one truly sent and moved by the Holy Ghost.[11]

—in other words, by such people as shall form the London Missionary Society's committee.

Haweis was a survivor of an older type of Anglican Evangelical who cared little for ecclesiastical regularity, and had many brushes with authority. For him, therefore, if the bishops were so obtuse as not to see where the interests of the gospel lay this was a pity, but neither the missionary society nor its missionaries were any the worse for lacking episcopal countenance.[12] But the newer generation of Evangelicals, that typified by Simeon, could not so readily divorce the interests of the gospel from the discipline of the Church.

It was such men who formed the society which became known as the Church Missionary Society. For their purpose the pre-existing Society for the Propagation of the Gospel, the quasi-official organ of the Church of England overseas, even if it were to undertake more obviously missionary work (as indeed it had done at various times in its history) was inappropriate, for it was not committed to the gospel as the Evangelicals understood it; and the ostensibly non-denominational London Missionary Society was inappropriate since it was not committed to the Church as Anglicans understood it.[13]

But the Church as Anglicans understood it had an episcopally ordained ministry: it follows that an Anglican missionary society might be expected to have episcopally ordained missionaries. If, however, such are not forthcoming—and, as we have seen, there seems to have been little expectation that they would be—and if those who do offer for service are not of the social class and type of education normally expected of the clergy, would it be right, even if it were possible, to seek regular ordination for them? To those who argued that social refinements were unnecessary on the mission field, others were quick to reply that once a man was ordained he was an English clergyman for life; and if a vulgar man were ordained for missionary service, what would prevent his coming back and taking a benefice for which he might be socially unfitted? Might not adventurers and social climbers offer for missionary service simply as a short cut to higher status?

These questions are solemnly discussed in a memorandum drafted by John Venn shortly before the foundation of the CMS:

> It is obvious that the Church of England can allow no persons to officiate in any respect as Ministers who have not been *episcopally ordained*. Episcopal ordination, bearing respect to the present improved state of society in this island, is justly conferred upon those only, whose education and learning qualify them for the rank the English clergy hold in society. It is evident, however, that a missionary, dwelling among savages rude and illiterate, does not require the same kind of talents, manners or learning as are necessary in an officiating minister in England. But ordination admits not of distinctions correspondent to the degree of refinement in society. He who is once episcopally ordained, though with the sole view of acting as a missionary to the heathen, would possess the power of officiating, and holding any benefice to which he might be presented, in the English Church. This circumstance necessarily requires extreme caution in ordaining persons for the purposes of missions only. For what security can be afforded, that a person of inferior station, offering himself upon this ground for orders, is not influenced by the desire of a more elevated rank in society or of a life of greater ease, rather than by a pure zeal for the salvation of the heathen?[14]

Venn's answer is to suggest that a lower order of unordained missionary be created, with the title of catechist. Conscious of the breach with normal Anglican order, he enters on an excursus on early church history to prove that there were catechists in the primitive Church who acted as evangelists, apologists, and instructors of converts—the very duties expected of missionaries. In the early Church too, the office of catechist was regarded as probationary for higher orders. Therefore, if a catechist should serve worthily on the mission field, there was excellent precedent for his eventual ordination.

The office of catechist was patently designed to permit the employment of unordained men in a missionary capacity by an Anglican society; and it was deemed necessary because at its commencement there was no real expectation of ordained or ordainable men coming forward in sufficient numbers. Even so, there was such strenuous opposition among the firmest supporters of the Society to so irregular an expedient that it was quietly abandoned.[15]

In the discussions which led to the formation of the Society it had been Simeon himself, that pillar of church order, who had said, apropos of missionary enterprise, '*When shall we do it?* Directly, not a moment to be lost. . . . *How shall we do it?* It is hopeless to wait for Missionaries. Send out catechists.'[16] The abandonment of the catechist scheme seemed to bear out the truth of his words. It did appear hopeless to wait for missionaries. The Committee wrote to Evangelical incumbents all round the country, but none could produce any candidates. In Cambridge Simeon put the question before his pious undergraduates, and was saddened to find not one responded.[17]

The CMS was thus reduced for several years to the invidious position of issuing reports with nothing to report, and holding meetings about what they hoped to do in future. No doubt, they could have made a start had they been able to send out men of the same sort of background as most of the early missionaries of the Baptist, London, and Scottish societies; but the insistence that none such should be sent except as, or at least in the company of, ordained men, effectively foreclosed any such possibility.

Meanwhile, the London Missionary Society had made its start with candidates recruited on the principles laid down by Haweis. A small operation was mounted in Sierra Leone, but the main thrust was to the Pacific islands and in 1796 a party of thirty missionaries, plus wives and children, set out.[18] Four of them were Dissenting ministers. The others included six carpenters, two weavers, two tailors, two bricklayers, two shoemakers, a harness-maker, a gardener, a cooper, a hatter, a shopkeeper, a linen draper, a gentleman's servant, a blacksmith, a surgeon (at that time, of course, an occupation mainly concerned with sawing off damaged limbs, and still associated with the barbers), a cotton worker, a linen draper, and a cabinet maker.[19] There were also six wives and three children. All had been examined by the LMS Committee. They were to live as a church and family, preach, maintain the mission, and teach European trades (which it was assumed the islanders were anxious to learn).

The first casualty was at Portsmouth; one of the wives was so seasick as to be unable to face another 27,000 miles of it, and her husband left too. The rest of the party made a quick passage, and distributed themselves between Tahiti, Tonga, and the Marquesas Islands. One refused to go ashore; two others left next time the boat came. At the first sign of violence erupting, eleven others left, and the thirty were reduced to fifteen, the wives to one. Three of the men were murdered in eruptions of violence, and four went back after a few years of service. Three married pagans and settled down, two of them giving up all profession of Christianity.

Here were thirty people who apparently met the qualifications laid down by Haweis, yet only a handful were left after five years. The rest had collapsed under the strains, physical, mental, moral, spiritual, which a mission imposed. One of the many questions which this created for the promoters of missions must have been whether Haweis was right to say that education was irrelevant to missionary service. In the first place, there was a language to be learned, and only two of the Tahiti party ever mastered the island tongue as missionaries. Again, less obviously, there was what today we call culture shock; the experience of living in a society whose manners, customs, and values are quite different from one's own. Some of the missionaries seem to have been incapable of the major intellectual effort required to grapple with this and work out its implications for their own life in that society, and conceivably their defective education and narrow experience—for some were very young—may have been partly to blame.

But having said all this, when one looks at the core of the party who remained, the generalizations collapse. The outstanding figure among them is Henry Nott. He became leader among them by sheer decision of character; he acquired the greatest mastery of the language; was the first to preach in the vernacular; and worked solidly for twenty-seven years at the translation of the Bible without leaving the island (save for a few months in Australia to get married), learning Hebrew and Greek to make himself a better translator. After twenty-seven years, and not before, he returned to Britain to see the Bible through the press; having done this, he returned to Tahiti, and worked there, with one sole break, till his death in 1844, a period of nearly fifty years in all. Yet Nott was a bricklayer by trade, had little formal education, and when the party sailed he was only twenty-two years of age.[20]

This is important because it shows that in a sense Haweis was right: some plain men with no obvious acquisitions but the Bible and common sense, were among the best missionaries. Apart from their personal qualities, their other skills were valuable: they were much more use at building churches and houses and schools than many a vicar from Eton and Cambridge would have been. And their background was an advantage in other ways. People like Nott, who were labourers or craftsmen, were not used to comfort at home; they never missed things which it might have been a privation to the beneficed clergymen to surrender.

Men of this type provided the staple missionary product in both England and Scotland for more than half a century. The Scottish establishment was not more accommodating than the English. From the famous 1796 Assembly debate, which by a masterpiece of minuting managed both to approve missions in principle and to prevent anything being done about them in practice,[21] until 1824, when the Assembly instituted its own mission, Scottish candidates could reach the field only through the Scottish Missionary Society,[22] or through English-based agencies such as the LMS. A goodly number did so; but a wholly disproportionate number of these came from the Secession churches, especially that of the Burgher Synod, and from the Scottish Congregational churches. Rather typical (in their background, not their careers) were the first four candidates of the Edinburgh and Glasgow societies, who all went to Sierra Leone:[23] a student from the Burgher Divinity Hall, Henry Brinton of Selkirk; a Glasgow tailor, Robert Henderson, who gave up being a missionary to become an atheist lecturer;[24] a

Clydesdale weaver, Duncan Campbell, who found a berth in the Slave Trade in the Sierra Leone hinterland; and a gardener from Inverkeithing, Peter Greig, who was murdered for his possessions.[25] In the course of 1802, the CMS did receive an application which could have transformed the conception of the missionary: Henry Martyn, Fellow of St John's College, Cambridge, and Senior Wrangler the previous year, had become convinced of his vocation, and the Committee rejoiced. But it was not to be. The family fortunes collapsed and Martyn was left as the only support of his family. He could no longer go as a missionary: he could not afford it. Some years later, indeed, he was to reach India, and his brief life has become one of the best known and most moving stories in modern missionary hagiography. Yet technically he was never a missionary; he was a chaplain of the Honourable East India Company, receiving a substantial official stipend.[26] Some remarkable men, both before and after Martyn, with the same missionary heart and outlook, served as chaplains to the British monopoly company, and one of them, Claudius Buchanan, probably did more than anyone else to arouse active and widespread public interest in missions in India;[27] but they were not regarded as missionaries by their employers, and they did not come through the missionary societies.

While Martyn was making his first application to CMS, the Society was gaining its first regular recruits. Help had come from an unexpected source.[28]

Through the German church in London, the Society made contact with the Missionary Seminary in Berlin. The forces which had produced the missionary societies in the English-speaking world were at work on the Continent also, where seminaries and systems of training for missionaries developed. What the Continental promoters of missions lacked was any means of stationing missionaries when trained. So an arrangement was concluded between the institution with the men but no means and the society with the means but no men, and the long period of co-operation between the Society and European agencies began. Should anyone cavil, the CMS could point to a long history of mutual recognition of the Church of England and Continental Protestant churches, especially Lutheran churches, and to the long-standing use by the impeccably

Anglican Society for Promoting Christian Knowledge of Lutheran ministers, Danish and German, as its agents in India. There was even the understanding that (since there was no bishop nearer than London) the ordination of native ministers might be performed by Lutheran missionaries according to the Lutheran rite. And the practical problems which had bedevilled CMS recruitment from the beginning were settled at a stroke. There was no need now to labour along a tortuous and uncertain path to seek ordination for 'plain men' with Evangelical principles unacceptable to most bishops; the missionaries could receive Lutheran ordination in Germany. There was no longer a need to rack the consciences of the sticklers for church discipline on the Committee by expedients about catechists. And there was no longer a fear of an unsuitable person coming back from the mission field and aspiring to an English benefice. The advantages of accepting ordained Lutheran missionaries as though they were Anglicans were manifold.

The first two students from Berlin were accepted in 1802. They stayed in England for further study of theology, English (the first meeting with the Committee had been hampered by the fact that the candidates knew no English and the Committee no German), and Susu. They went back to Germany for Lutheran ordination and arrived in Sierra Leone in 1804, thus enabling the Society to get its first missionaries on to the field some five years after its institution.

The relationship—first with Berlin, then with Basel and St Christhona and to a lesser extent with other continental bodies—was not always easy, and there were many abrasions.[29] But the German contribution to missionary operations was crucial. Of the twenty-four missionaries sent out by CMS in the period up to the end of 1815, no less than seventeen were Germans, and only three were ordained Englishmen.[30] If we take the earliest and most dangerous field, West Africa, in the same period, the total is even more striking: all appointments except for one schoolmaster were Germans.[31] After 1815 the balance changes. That year saw the departure of the first two CMS missionaries to receive Anglican orders, both having been ordained on the title of English curacies,[32] and also of the first English university graduate, like Martyn an ordained Fellow of St John's College, Cambridge.[33] The following year saw two more English clergymen setting out for India via English curacies;[34] and the only Germans who went out that year were recruited in London and not through the seminaries.[35] Next year, 1817, saw fourteen recruits getting out, much the largest number in any year so far; and seven were English clergymen and only four Germans.[36] From this point onwards the Germans, though they provide some of the most illustrious names, are only a supplementary source of recruitment, and it gradually became normal for missionaries from the Continental seminaries to receive Anglican ordination. But Lutheran ordination, which came to be a stumbling-block on the path of good relations between CMS and its Continental associates,[37] was in the early years a mighty convenience. As had been foreseen, it enabled the ordination of suitable local candidates as early as 1820.[38] It was also possible for lay missionaries, such as W. A. B. Johnson and Henry Düring, who had been discharging the pastoral office with great effectiveness, to be ordained on the field without the long journey to Britain and the uncertainties of appeal to bishops.[39]

We have already noticed a change in the CMS recruitment pattern after 1815. This is not the place to consider the reasons, save to say that these have nothing to do with any sudden attractiveness of the mission field to the younger sons of country gentlemen, but may have something to do with the Society's new method of organization which must have made many people in the parishes feel for the first time that the missionary cause was something to do with them,[40] and certainly something to do with a newly acquired accessibility to the episcopate.[41] But it is worth noticing that the period of improved recruitment from Britain takes place just at the point when missionary service is becoming notably dangerous: at the point when CMS has concentrated its African operations in the Sierra Leone Colony, and there is a fair presumption that any-one who goes to Sierra Leone will die there or be broken for life.[42] As at later times in the history of the missionary move-ment, it appears that, whatever factors adversely affect recruit-ment, the presence of physical danger does not necessarily do so.

But the typical missionary long remained, as he had been in

the first generation, a man of humble background and modest attainments. Besides a sprinkling of men who might have, and in some cases actually did, minister in their own countries, it was the journeymen, artisans, and clerks who came to the mission field from England. From Scotland the missionaries came (much more frequently than in England) from the farm or the croft, like James Henderson, or from the factory, like Livingstone, or from the south-bound work-hunting emigrants, like Moffat, who was a gardener on an English estate. The mention of these names is itself a reminder, however, that many men who would not have been considered for ordination at home, in order to reach the mission field, or in order to be more effective there, set themselves to intellectual effort and acquired learning and skills far beyond anything which would have been required of them in their ordinary run of life. The fact that some of them became legends, and the not less important fact that many displayed the ministerial charismata in a high degree, were to have their own effect in the transformation of the ministry.

NOTES

1 For the importance of the prophecies, cf. J. A. de Jong, *As the Waters cover the Sea. Millennial expectations in the Rise of Anglo-American missions 1640–1810* (Kampen 1970).

2 On the background of nineteenth-century missionaries, and helpful reflection thereon, see M. A. C. Warren, *Social History and Christian Mission* (London 1967), esp. ch. 2.

3 William Carey, *Enquiry into the Obligations of Christians to use Means for the Conversion of the Heathens* . . . (Leicester 1792), 71ff.

4 'Not even shoemaker, sir: just a cobbler', said Carey to a sneering army officer. S. Pearce Carey, *William Carey D.D.* (London 1923), pp. 34f.

5 Melvill Horne, *Letters on Missions addressed to the Protestant Ministers of the British Churches* (Bristol 1794), cap. 1.

6 Jane Austen, *Mansfield Park*, vol. 3, ch. 16 of the original edition; Oxford Illustrated Jane Austen, p. 458.

7 A large section of the sermon, with many other addresses and documents associated with the birth of the LMS is printed in R. Lovett, *The History of the London Missionary Society 1795–1895* (London 1899), I, pp. 26ff.

8 Ibid., p. 27.

9 Ibid., p. 28.

10 Ibid., pp. 28f.

11 Ibid., p. 28.

12 Haweis had planned a Tahiti mission as early as 1789, employing two students from the Countess of Huntingdon's Connexion; and he tried (at their insistence) but in vain to secure for them episcopal ordination. See A. Skevington Wood, *Thomas Haweis 1734–1820* (London 1957), pp. 170ff, 177ff.

13 On the origins of the CMS see Charles Hole, *The Early History of the Church Missionary Society for Africa and the East to the end of A.D. 1814* (London 1896) and Eugene Stock, *History of the Church Missionary Society* i (London 1899), pp. 58ff. Hole's book is often virtually a calendar of the documentary sources.

14 Venn's memorandum is printed as an appendix to M. Hennell, *John Venn and the Clapham Sect* (London 1958), pp. 280–4.

15 Hennell, op. cit., pp. 243f.

16 W. Carus, *Memoirs of the Life of the Rev. Charles Simeon M.A.* (London and Cambridge 1847), p. 169.

17 Hole, op. cit., pp. 56ff, 61f.

18 The story is told with frankness by Lovett, op. cit., ch. 3.

19 The party are listed in J. Sibree, *London Missionary Society: A register of Missionaries, Deputations etc. from 1796 to 1923*, nos. 1–30; cf. Lovett, op. cit., p. 127 for their trades.

20 See Sibree, no. 23; Lovett, op. cit., pp. 117–305.

21 *The Principal Acts of the General Assembly of the Church of Scotland* convened at Edinburgh, the 19th day of May 1796, Edinburgh 1796, sub 27 May.

22 Originally separate societies were set up in various parts of Scotland; the Edinburgh and Glasgow societies both contributed men with the LMS to a Sierra Leone party in 1797. Later the Edinburgh society took the name of Scottish Missionary Society.

23 Cf. William Brown, *History of the Propagation of Christianity among the Heathen* (Edinburgh and London 1854), ii, pp. 415–56. Brown (a minister of the Burgher Synod who was unable on health grounds to go to the mission field) was Secretary of the Scottish Missionary Society.

24 But he considerately repaid to the Society the money spent on his training—W. L. Mathieson, *Church and Reform in Scotland* (Glasgow 1916), p. 81.

25 Greig's brief service has produced a brief biography: see George Smith, *Twelve Pioneer Missionaries* (London 1900), pp. 122–36.

26 On Martyn's application see Hole, pp. 86f, 91, 93, who points out that a formal candidature, as distinct from notice given, was hardly in question in 1802; Martyn was still under age for priest's orders, and was not ordained deacon until October 1803. Before this date the Committee had already decided he would be wasted in West Africa.

27 Especially with his *Memoir of the Expediency of an Ecclesiastical Establishment for British India* ... (London 1805). (See the forthcoming new edition with introduction by A. K. Davidson, which indicates the effect of the *Memoir* and *Christian Researches in Asia with notices of the translation of the Scriptures into the oriental languages* (Cambridge and London 1811).

28 On what follows see Hole, pp. 84f, 114f; Stock 1, pp. 82ff.

29 Cf. J. Pinnington, 'Church Principles in the early years of the Church Missionary Society: the problem of the "German" missionaries', *Journal of Theological Studies* NS 20 (2) (1969), pp. 523–32. Not all the students were Lutherans: some were Reformed; the Basel seminary was non-denominational.

30 *Register of Missionaries (Clerical, lay, and female) and Native Clergy* (CMS. 1896 and 1905), nos. 1–24.

31 *Register*, loc. cit. The first CMS missionaries, Renner and Hartwig, went first to Sierra Leone (the name then strictly applied only to Freetown and its immediate environs), but with explicit instructions to work in the hinterland. Until 1816 the centre of operations was in the Rio Pongas area, addressed to Susu-speaking peoples, with an entirely German staff, but there were occasional appointments to other places, such as the Isles de Los and even, during its British occupation, Goree. Later attention was diverted to the new recaptive population in Freetown and the villages of the peninsula, and the Rio Pongas mission was gradually wound down, its staff transferred to Sierra Leone. Several English schoolmasters went to Sierra Leone, but no ordained English missionary before 1824.

32 William Greenwood had been ordained deacon in 1813, and served eighteen months as curate at Knutsford; Thomas Norton was ordained deacon in 1813 and priest in 1814, and served a curacy in York. Both had previously offered for missionary service, and studied for some years under Thomas Scott, the commentator, who was in charge of CMS training. Both went to India. *Register*, nos. 21 and 22.

33 William Jowett (*Register*, no. 24) was Twelfth Wrangler in 1810. He was a missionary of the Society in Malta and later became Clerical Secretary of CMS.

34 Benjamin Bailey and Thomas Dawson had served Yorkshire curacies, but for much shorter periods than their predecessors. *Register*, nos. 29 and 30.

35 Henry Düring and the celebrated W. A. B. Johnson were both Hanoverians who, like many of their compatriots, had sought work in the other dominions of the Hanoverian crown. Johnson underwent an evangelical conversion in London and was in attendance at Surrey Chapel when he offered as a schoolmaster (W. Jowett, *Memoir of the Rev. W. A. B. Johnson* (London 1862)). Christopher Jost, who went out

at the same time as Johnson and Düring, and like them as a school-master, was a member of the Savoy church in London, whose minister, Dr Steinkopf, had been the original link between the CMS and the Berlin Seminary.

36 *Register*, nos. 31–44. One of the English clergymen was sent to Malta, the rest to Ceylon or India. One German in Lutheran orders and two English lay schoolmasters went to Sierra Leone, the other Germans and one schoolmaster to India.

37 Cf. Pinnington, art. cit. Many of the Lutherans, not unnaturally, objected to a second ordination.

38 The celebrated Muslim convert Abdul Massih had worked as a CMS catechist, and William Bowley (see *Register*, no. 68), a Eurasian, had done excellent work in Indian congregations. Bishop Middleton declined to ordain them on the ground that he had no authority to ordain natives of India. After receiving Lutheran ordination in 1820 they were given Anglican deacons' ordination in 1825.

39 Johnson and Düring, who had not had seminary training, were given Lutheran orders by their Sierra Leone colleagues in 1817.

40 Cf. Stock, op. cit. i, pp. 129–43.

41 The first Evangelical to be consecrated, Henry Ryder, became Bishop of Gloucester in 1815 (translated to Lichfield 1824). He was concerned in the ordination of six out of the seven English clergy who sailed in 1817, and for the first time English curacies were not required as a title to ordination. See G. C. B. Davies, *Henry Ryder, the first Evangelical Bishop* (London 1958). Apart from Ryder, who was on the CMS Committee, several other bishops were by this time willing to lend the CMS more countenance.

42 Of twenty-seven missionaries sent to Sierra Leone before 1820, fifteen had died before the end of that year. In 1822 a total of twelve CMS missionaries (including wives) died in Sierra Leone. P. D. Curtin, 'The White Man's Grave: image and reality 1780–1850', *Journal of British Studies* i (i) (1959), pp. 94ff, and *The Image of Africa* (Madison, Wisconsin 1964), ch. 3 and 5 offers evidence to suggest that many must have been the victims of treatment as much as disease.

In defence of
Early North African Christianity

IEUAN P. ELLIS

An important theme in the first volume of Professor C. P. Groves's history of missions in Africa is that the North African Church of A.D. 200 to 700 failed to evangelize the surrounding peoples and so was swept away in the advance of Islam.[1] A more recent writer, Dr Cecil Northcott, has expressed it bluntly: 'In the centuries from A.D. 200 to A.D. 700 Christianity missed its supreme chance of expansion in the immense land empire, from the North African coast to the tenth parallel of Latitude north, where today Islam is dominant through its own missionary zeal.'[2]

On this view effective early Christianity in Africa was limited to the Latin-speaking Church in the north-eastern area of what is now known as Tunisia (with some extension into Algeria), but this Church never reached great depth in its own area and even less in neighbouring territory. On this depended great things, no less than the first opportunity to evangelize Africa, and this was lost. The underlying argument is that the Christian Church bungled its first two chances in regard to Africa and only succeeded with the third, in the European and American missionary movements arising out of the Protestant Evangelical revival of the eighteenth century. This leads Professor Groves to give scant justice to the achievements of early Christianity in Africa and to the Portuguese missions. In particular, his account of the North African Church and of its relation to Christian expansion in Africa needs some re-interpretation.

In the first place, the make-up and extent of the Church in North Africa need to be clarified. Fuller research, aided by archaeological work carried on since before the 1939–45 war, suggests that it was more than a narrowly-based, urbanized structure. More penetration took place among the native population than was allowed by, for example, Westermarck.[3] Older scholars have been bedazzled by the personality of Augustine and have failed to take due account of the vigorous Christian witness in areas away from Carthage and other large towns. While it may be extreme to talk of two Churches in Africa, the Donatist evolution suggests that a distinct group existed in some ways independently of the Latin Catholic Church. One factor in this evolution was the conversion (possibly in so short a period as between A.D. 240 and 275) of the population in Numidia and Mauretania Sitifensis. The links in thought between Catholics and Donatists were certainly close: their leaders alike spoke in the superb 'professional Latin' of the African Church; spokesmen for both agreed that they were united in doctrine; and the Latins, despite their Romanization, were recognizably 'African' in outlook. Augustine is in direct succession to Tertullian and Cyprian, both of whom Catholics and Donatists held to be their common fathers. But there were differences in ecclesiology, and 'non-theological factors' affected the cleavage.

The Donatist controversy should not, therefore, be dismissed as a split within one camp or as a theological squabble which diverted energies from evangelism. Professor Groves shows a similar misunderstanding of the position in Egypt when he speaks of 'Coptic-Melkite squabbles'. But, if anything, the Coptic and Donatist movements may be evidence of the strength of the 'native' Christians. Indeed, the Donatists claimed that they possessed the true faith in Africa and were the Catholic Church of their land, and they established a bishopric in Rome to validate their position in the eyes of the Christian world.[4]

Professor Groves holds that 'the churches clustered most thickly round Carthage', but the excavations of various teams show the extent of Christianity in other areas, still predominantly urbanized but also partly 'rural'. Berthier and Martin investigated seventy-two sites which produced 200 churches and chapels in small towns and villages in Numidia. The Donatists drew a good deal of their strength from these small sees.[5] Other excavations have revealed churches in Mauretania Sitifensis (part of the modern Algeria) and in the southern part of Tunisia; and there are churches in the Nemenscha country extending south from Tebessa towards the Sahara. Most of these churches appear to have been Donatist, but some were Catholic. Numbers were about equal in the province of Tripolitania and Mauretania Caesariensis. A considerable area of country in this part of Africa seems, therefore, to have been evangelized, without denying the existence of what Courtois called *l' Afrique oubliée*, the forgotten Africa of the great mountains and deserts which neither Donatists nor Catholics were able to reach.

In this light, the absence of Berber scriptures may appear less significant. The question of the languages of the region is a difficult one. An agricultural population of probably mixed Libyan (Berber) and Punic origin was firmly established in the hinterland from the first century A.D., but while Berber was known as a living language in some sense over the whole length of Latin North Africa, it was less literary than Punic and did not figure in the competition of the various languages (Latin, Punic, and Greek) for universal written purposes. Bi-lingualism (Libyan and Punic) would be found even among the poor. Certainly, parts of the Bible were translated into Punic, and Augustine speaks of Punic speakers even in his congregation at Hippo (the contention that he meant Berber speakers is disputed), while he himself composed Punic hymns against the Donatists. It is possible that Augustine's reference may suggest a resurgence of Punic culture following on Donatism as a nationalistic movement.[6] W. H. C. Frend suggests that the Donatists' intense veneration for the scriptures may have militated against translation into the vernacular, since it was the 'primitive', Old Latin version which they viewed in this way. This, the Bible of Tertullian and Cyprian, became peculiarly their own scripture, for the Catholics used a newer version. The existence of Punic translations may suggest that, had time been with them, the Donatists would have produced a vernacular scripture like the Copts.[7]

In seeking to explain the collapse of the North African Church, three factors should be taken into account. First, the Church was in a weak condition as a result of the Vandal persecutions. Catholic and Donatist alike suffered, and the century of Byzantine influence saw no great recovery.[8]

Secondly, there had been no satisfactory resolution of the
Donatist problem. The native Christians—unlike the Copts
in their struggle with the Melkite Church—never achieved a
lasting measure of independence or became a fully-organized
national Church. Their association with the rebellious Gildo
was fatal for their cause, and after their defeat at Augustine's
hands at the Council of 411 they were virtually proscribed.
Thirdly, there is the question of whether it is possible to speak
of a 'Berber religious continuum', i.e., that the Berber retained
his fundamental religious convictions in the transfer from one
monotheistic religion to another. Thus the apparent mass
apostasy of former Donatists, as well as the recently converted
native kingdoms who threw off their Christian allegiance
without any great compulsion from Islam, could be compared
with the mass conversion to Christianity of the second half of
the third century in the same region. A more certain factor
would have been the hatred of Rome which had dominated
their Donatism. A non-classical religion such as Islam would
not be unwelcome, since 'official Christianity' was represented
by a Romanized form. 'Dissent may have prepared the way for
Islam.'[9]

Professor Groves's argument, which he derives from this
reading of the facts, should also be examined. In effect, the
North African Church lost Africa to Christianity: '. . . the first
opportunity came and went. And it was not repeated. The
chance to enter Africa from the north was not given again.'[10]

Three objections spring to mind here:

1. *Can* the North African Church properly be singled out in
this way? Islam stretched from Egypt to Spain by the eighth
century, and its superior 'missionary zeal' turned south from
many spots. The Christians of North Africa had occupied a
smaller area. In any case the Coptic Churches, which had a
history as long as the North African, were as favourably placed
for the evangelization of the continent. The Nile presented an
artery which stretched into the heart of Africa. Professor
Groves admits that some success was achieved by the missions
from Egypt.

2. How much time was there for the task of evangelism? It is

unrealistic to speak of an unbroken period of 500 years from A.D. 200 to 700. Persecution did not cease until 313, the worst and most severe having caused havoc in the Church only a few years before this, and by 429 the Vandals had arrived and with them the century of the 'Babylonian Captivity' and widespread persecution. The period of Byzantine influence which followed this was not much more than a century in length (expulsion of the Vandals 533, first arrival of the Arabs 647, capture of Carthage 697), and it was during this century that, as Professor Groves shows, some evangelistic work was attempted.

3. How useful is it to talk in terms of 'evangelism beyond the borders'? In the case of Proconsular Africa there were grave physical barriers, the steeply forested areas in the north-west and the deserts to the south, which made any large-scale penetration of the interior—as the Roman legionaries found— impossible. If in the two centuries of its evangelistic opportunity the North African Church, from its particular corner of Africa, had missionized to 'the tenth parallel of Latitude north', it would have been a phenomenon without equal. The Islamic mission in the same area took far longer than two or three centuries. In any case Islam had what Christianity never had: the energy of the Roman empire had been largely spent by the time that Christianity triumphed; there was no new vital force to overrun half the world such as that Arab advance which gave the new faith its astonishing success in the eighth and ninth centuries.

A good deal more may be said in defence of early African Christianity. E. W. Blyden saw the North African Church as one of the great gifts of his race to Christianity: it demonstrated that Africans were in the Church from the outset and confounded Anglo-Saxon apologists who held that men from the dark continent were latecomers to Christianity.[11] Acts 13.1 was highly significant for Blyden: among the five leaders at Antioch were 'Symeon called Niger and Lucius of Cyrene', so men with African associations stood alongside Paul and Barnabas.

Blyden's perspective is important. The total collapse of the great North African Church must remain a puzzle and a challenge, though the many factors in it may not be reduced to a simple theological formula on the lines that 'to fail to share the faith with all around is to let it die'.[12] The theological achievement of the Church as teacher of the West has always been recognized. Blyden quoted Dean Milman: 'Africa, not Rome, gave birth to Latin Christianity.' But the North African Church may also have a meaning specifically for the African churches of today and for their contribution to the evolution of world Christianity. The question being asked here is about the nature of the thought which the North Africans expressed more distinctly than other Western churches, and whether this may be termed indigenous. There is an obvious need for caution. Blyden himself thought that the North African Church had not become indigenous, but he was repeating a fashionable point of view and wanted to emphasize the Ethiopian Church, against Western denigrators, as the first which had taken note of the needs and thoughts of the African. Attempts to derive distinctive North African thought precisely from the Phoenician and Jewish (in contrast to Greek) elements in pre-Christian North Africa have gone beyond the evidence available and met with much criticism, as also the claim that the Donatists in their art and liturgy became a native Church.

However, there is at least one distinctive element in North African thought, particularly in Tertullian and Cyprian, which cannot fail to be noticed, and this is the emphasis on the Spirit. It determines the ecclesiology of both teachers. For Tertullian, in a real sense, the Church is the Spirit; radical obedience to the Spirit is the mark of the Church. A congregation insensitive to this and not manifesting the charismatic gifts cannot have the Spirit. The thought appears to harden in Cyprian to become an emphasis on the possession of the Spirit in the Christian ministry, but Cyprian is as sure as Tertullian that there can be no Church without the Spirit and that the Spirit will manifest his presence plainly. This approach explains the distinctive physical appearance of the African churches for, frequently, the baptistery was the largest room in the ecclesial building. For the African Christian baptism could never be a formality.

Tertullian vividly described the experience of new life and rebirth undergone by the neophyte, and as vigorously insisted on rebaptism for any who had received the sacraments of unspiritual ministers, for the sense of rebirth could never have been present in those other services.

Such a charismatic preoccupation cannot be Tertullian's own, however forcefully his particular language expresses it. This is important in relation to the question of Montanism in North Africa. Tertullian, as everyone knows, became a Montanist. Did Montanism receive a more ready welcome in North Africa than in other churches in the West, and, indeed, was it in a sense a revival movement in the North African Church? Montanism was certainly found in Gaul (Alexander the Phrygian, who 'was not destitute of the Apostolic gift'[13]) and in Rome itself, before falling under the ban. However, its distinctive literary expression in the West came from the Church of North Africa. The great Latin martyrology, the passion of St Perpetua and her companions (A.D. 203–4), seems to be a Montanist utterance.[14] Augustine could still quote it 200 years later and in some churches in Africa it had the status of canonical scripture. Belief in a movement of new prophecy would seem to be essential in a congregation which believed in the direction of the Spirit who could still make revelations to men, in the name of Jesus.

But it is important to see Montanism as a complement to already existing African thought; and that both modifies Montanism itself and puts its alleged challenge to authority in a different light. It was as an African Montanist that Tertullian separated from the Church. Schism is the major sin, the breaking of unity and separation from the Spirit; but the separation from the Spirit may already have happened if the congregation does not heed his voice; both standpoints were possible on the North African argument. Hence in some circumstances the categorical necessity of schism. The question then is: Is Tertullian properly to be regarded as a 'schismatic'?

It is obviously impossible to speak of a continuity of African thought from Tertullian's day to our own. The distinctive theology, if it was such, of North Africa died with the Muslim onslaught and was, perhaps, already dying as the remaining

Donatist congregations declined in the sixth century. But there is some point in bearing the North African Church in mind. It has been claimed that the modern Church in Africa may go the way of the North African Church because of the many native churches that have sprung up in the continent manifesting schismatic tendencies. But this argument is as superficial as the other which makes the North African Church the subject of a cautionary missionary tale with a tragic ending. The North African belief in the Spirit was never a charter for independent congregations breaking out one after the other; witness Cyprian's concern in *De Unitate*, the first Latin treatise on unity, and the way that this concern was demonstrated to the West by the seven councils of the African churches between A.D. 251 and 256. Then, more than eighty bishops, on one occasion, could be seen together manifesting the Spirit-given harmony.

What the North African Church stands for is the principle of responsible autonomy and continued deference to the Spirit in case mere expediency or a quite mechanical notion of unity should become dominant. In any case, it is wrong to speak of 'schisms' or schismatical tendencies in North Africa; there was only one schism, strictly speaking, and it had existed in principle ever since Tertullian made his stand. And in the Christian Church after 313, North Africa was not the only area where incipient nationalisms took a religious expression in separatist movements.

Tertullian and Cyprian stand as a corrective against any mechanical understanding of unity, but they believe in unity because of the Spirit. The modern Pentecostal movement among the churches in Europe, America, and Africa demands urgent theological exploration, but it defies easy analysis because its elements are so diverse, and we may have to reckon with a 'spirit' phenomenon that is older than Christianity itself and is, perhaps, alien to it. That was also true of Montanism, particularly in its Phrygian element. One lesson of the North African Church is that its awareness of the Spirit enabled it to contain such a movement, and it was the alleged schismatic Tertullian who helped to rescue the Western Church from the modalist heresy precisely because of his insistence on the essential personality of the Spirit.

NOTES

1 Cf. C. P. Groves, *The Planting of Christianity in Africa* (London 1948) 1, pp. viii, 59, 83, 89, etc.

2 Cecil Northcott, *Christianity in Africa* (London 1963), pp. 57–8.

3 E. A. Westermarck, *Ritual and Belief in Morocco* (London 1926) 1, pp. 13, 133.

4 W. H. C. Frend, *The Donatist Church* (e.1, Oxford 1971), pp. 164, 195.

5 Ibid., p. 53.

6 But see Peter Brown, 'Christianity and Local Culture in Late Roman Africa', *Journal of Roman Studies* 58 (1968), pp. 85–95, who challenges any easy identification of 'nationalism' with opposition to Latin culture. Cf. also, in the same issue of *JRS*, Fergus Millar, 'Local Cultures in the Roman Empire: Libyan, Punic and Latin in Roman Africa', pp. 126–34, and Ramsay MacMullen, 'Provincial Languages in the Roman Empire', *American Journal of Philology* 87 (1966), pp. 1–14.

7 The comparison with the Copts may also suggest another reason why Berber scriptures were not produced. 'North Africa', in the sense in which the term is used here, may be compared with the region of the lower Nile, which was later in producing its own Coptic scriptures because of the fact that the Bohairic-speaking group were more literate in Greek. The Donatists were hardly non-literate in regard to Latin, and by the time of the fifth century (if this is the date to be assigned to the Bohairic text) they were already in decline.

8 Cf. lists of bishops in Groves, op. cit., vol. 1, p. 67.

9 Frend, op. cit., p. 335. I am aware that Frend's views, and those of other writers, on the continuing element in Berber religion have been disputed.

10 Groves, op. cit., 1, p. viii.

11 E. W. Blyden, *Christianity, Islam and the Negro Race* (Edinburgh U.P. 1959), p. 165.

12 Groves, op. cit., 1, p. 89.

13 See letter of the Church of Lyons and Vienne, in J. Stevenson, *A New Eusebius* (London 1957), p. 38.

14 Timothy Barnes, *Tertullian, A Historical and Literary Study* (Oxford 1971), p. 77.

An East African Ismaili Ginan

NOEL Q. KING

In long, patient conversation on the ship coming out and in the enchanted gardens of Legon Hill, Canon Sawyerr taught me to pay heed to 'the ordinary devotions of ordinary people' as a source of religious study, and spoke of the welcome Africa had for 'people from outside who genuinely become indigenous and claim no privileges'. In paying the respect of *pietas* to my academic godfather (sponsor) into Religions African, I seek accordingly to draw attention to the study of one of the groups of Asian origin who long ago made Africa their home. The Ismailis may well have been on the East African coast before the Portuguese, using the monsoon to bring them from Cutch, Kathiawar, and Gujerat in western India.[1] When the Sultan of Muscat and Oman made Zanzibar his headquarters in 1840, Ismailis joined with Arabs and Swahili in the movement to penetrate the hinterland. By the start of the colonial period they were well known as economic pioneers and small business-men; with the opening up of communications and under the leadership of His Highness Aga Khan III, Sultan Muhammad Shah, who was Imam from 1885 till 1957, they were to be found in residence from Somalia to South Africa, from Kenya, Tanzania, and Mozambique as far inland as Zaïre and Zambia. On the coming of independence, their community was known for its support of rising African politicians and for seeking the rights and duties of citizenship.

Their religion was the constant factor which held the Ismailis together. When all around was changing, though they adapted their way of life almost completely, they kept the central point of their religion—devotion to the Imam—inviolate. During the century with which we are dealing, the *ginans*, religious 'gnostic' lyrics sung by groups of believers, were a form of devotion which contributed to this love of the Imam and to holding the community together. We can take as an example the *ginan, Eji unchare kot bahu vechna.* Since the sound of the words is so important it is necessary to give a transliteration as well as a rough paraphrase (for indeed translation is impossible).[2]

Eji unchare kot bahu vechna,	The castle is high and impregnable,
Niche vahe dariya;	the sea is down below, I am a fish in
Hun re dariyavanti machli,	that sea. O Master, come to my
Sahinya taran av	rescue

Chorus	*Chorus*
Hun re didār vina bavari,	I am beside myself without the
Sajan ghre av, valam ghre av;	vision of you, O my beloved, my
Bando bhulyo tāri bandagi,	dear one, come home.
Sahinya surat batāv,	Though thy slave was forgetful of
Hun re didār vina bāvri	thy service, O Lord, show thy face:
	I am beside myself without the
	vision of you.

Eji agar chandan ni kotdi,	Thy dwelling is of incense and
Sufal rachiya kamad;	sandal, and the door is created out
Tala didha che premna,	of good deeds. It has a lock of love,
Sahinya kholan av	beloved, come to open.

Eji pinjar padyo parivārno,	I have become a prisoner of things
Koik bujat jan;	temporal which can be understood
Mere tan ki vedna,	by those who know. Beloved, slake
Sahinya tapat bujāy	the heat and agony in my self.

Eji itna kop na kijiye,	Do not be so wrathful, my beloved,
Sahinya deeje didār;	vouchsafe me thy vision. By Pir
Pir Hassan Shahji venti,	Hasanshah I beseech thee to come
Sahinya taran av.	to my rescue.

The family likeness between this *ginan* and the stuff of mystical lyrics in Judaism, Christianity, and *sufi* Islam is immediately apparent. Equally its kinship to the Indian medieval mystical movement is unmistakable, a great number of analogies from the anthology which is the *Shri Guru Granth Sahib* of the Sikhs, the 'psalms' of the Maharatha Saints, and the poems of Kabir, spring to mind. A scholar qualified to speak of the music which is laid down as accompaniment for these lyrics would be able to press the analogies still further.

There is no one 'official' exegesis of a *ginan*, but each individual and group is encouraged to make it their own by relating it to themselves. Obviously, 'the beloved' is the Imam, and an Ismaili rejoices in the Imamate much as certain Anglicans rejoice in Mother Church as a continuation of the incarnation. The intensity of emotion and devotion generated by a *ginan*, either in group singing or in recollecting it in tranquillity, is immense. Sometimes a *ginan* is chosen by a preacher (*wa'ez*) as his theme: and his sermon, especially if he sings snatches from the lyric, becomes a deep and vivid experience. He will bring the *ginan* right home—to a Mombasa community 'the high, high fort' becomes Fort Jesus; and again, they are awaiting their own Imam as his jet circles the airport, lands, and he, 'the one of ones', steps out.

The *ginan* has served the East African Ismailis well, but the young people use English and Swahili more than Gujerati. The language used in the *ginans* is archaic in any case. The community is outstanding in the efforts it makes to keep up its religious education, but insists that its teaching must never become merely antiquarian. The way ahead is for the *ginans* to be put into English, Swahili, Luganda, and so on, if a poet of genius can be found. Such ability is not absent among the Ismailis of East Africa. The music will haunt and enrapture, no matter what the language of the words may be.

NOTES

1   The normal transliteration in use in East Africa has been used throughout. The writer is indebted to Abdul Adatia, Rohit Barot, Aziz Esmael, Yasmin Kanji, Azim Nanji, and others for assistance in his Ismaili studies. They should not be held responsible for the views expressed or the errors committed. I regret I am not able to give full notes and references, being marooned by the banks of the Isis.

2   This *ginan* is number seven of *A Selection of Ten Holy Ginans*, prepared and published by the Shia Imami Ismailia Association for Kenya (Mombasa 1964). It also appears in the original Gujerati of various lithographed collections collated by me in Bombay. The text used is eclectically chosen from these and the translation is not based on any one hitherto published. By comparing editions in many *ginans* it is possible to trace over the years a changing of words to eliminate possible Hindu connotations. The *Pirs* met their Khoja converts where they were and led them forward by 'accommodation' over a period of centuries.

The Contribution of
Studies on Religion in Africa
to Western Religious Studies

H. W. TURNER

All study of African Christianity is potentially fruitful for
Western scholars, but it is in the area of the independent
churches and new movements that certain issues appear more
sharply defined and Western methods falter more visibly when
faced with such unfamiliar phenomena.

After some general considerations, partly methodological, I
shall survey some of the benefits from these African studies for
the familiar Western fields of biblical studies, church history,
missiology and ecumenics, systematic theology and Christian
ethics, and the history and phenomenology of religion.

The scholar used to Western facilities and the procedures that
derive from these soon finds himself under various limitations in
Africa. There are, firstly, limited library resources; indeed many
of the familiar tools, especially in the historical field, are
entirely absent. This means that one has to search out the
primary source materials, to locate, collect, classify, bind, and
deposit in archives the kind of documentary materials that are
taken for granted in Western countries, and also to collect the
oral tradition that new recording and storing devices make so
much easier. This exercise provides a new feeling for the
importance of such primary sources and a new eye for what
can be turned to account as a source of information and understanding—indeed for the very idea of what constitutes data in
any field.

This same limitation of resources coupled with the difficulty
of communications within the African continent encourages
concentration on study of what is at hand in living concrete
form, the local religious forms. The abundance and variety of

these provide a rich and fascinating field of study for a wide range of religious disciplines.

Upon return to a Western milieu one immediately notices the almost entire absence of equivalent serious local and contemporary studies, and the failure to collect the documentary and oral data for these. Where would one find a collection of the invaluable if voluminous weekly literary productions of the Christian religion in a Western country at the parish or congregational level, or even of the domestic periodicals of the various denominations? Yet this is a grass-roots index of what is going on, and ought to be a major resource for the academic articles in the learned journals. The main exceptions seem to be studies of the more exotic or minority groups, and usually by the sociologists of religion, to whom we appear to have consigned what is local and contemporary. A more comprehensive view of the full range of relevant data can have a profound effect on the whole nature of a subject-discipline. In this sense our Western studies of Christianity remain distorted in so far as they take little account of Christian forms in non-Western cultures and of local and contemporary forms in all cultures.

BIBLICAL STUDIES

When we turn to the biblical field we discover that many portions of the Scriptures that we tend to pass over or ignore are taken seriously by African Christians. For example, there is the attention given to dreams, both in the Bible and in traditional and in Christian Africa. In the Bible dreams are recorded as a means of revelation at many critical junctures and for many prominent figures. There is, however, exceedingly little theological discussion of dreams in Western studies, for we tend to relegate them to the realm of the pathological, or to gloss over them in Scripture exegesis as merely a cultural or literary form, or as belonging to a primitive stage of religious experience.

Are the biblical and the African worlds merely primitive, as compared with ourselves? Or is it rather that the Bible is indeed a 'book for all cultures', and that in its ceasing to speak to our culture at this point we learn more about ourselves than we do about our Scriptures? Perhaps what we lack at this point is suggested by the intriguing advice of a leader in an independent

African church to his members when he exhorted them 'to learn to dream like a Christian'.

However this may be these churches certainly reveal some of the ways in which our own scriptural study is culture-bound. They also contribute to discussions of the canon of Scripture itself, and in at least two ways. Firstly, they may make a different evaluation and use of certain books as compared with Western evaluations. We recall Luther's judgement on James as an 'epistle of straw' and place that against the fact that both independent and older African churches which I have investigated on this point all make a greater use of James than of most other parts of the New Testament, and certainly greater use than we make of it. Further, the one independent church I have studied on this point made use of the whole Bible in its preaching; in comparison I think it would be easy to find many sections of Western Christianity where large areas of the Scriptures had never been used in preaching.

When it comes to the differential use of Scripture, which exists in all sections of the Christian Church, it is interesting to discover that something of a common pattern probably runs through both the West and Africa. My limited inquiries in both areas indicate, for instance, that Gen. 1—11 is used much more than Gen. 12—50, and more than most of the rest of the Old Testament; that John's Gospel rivals that of Matthew in usage, with Mark used least of the four; and that the Acts of the Apostles is used very little. If something of a common pattern in the differential use of Scripture extends even to such apparently 'way out' sections of the Church as the African independents (in spite of their own special quirks at some points) we have new evidence of the way the Bible actually functions across the Christian world, and the exciting possibility of being able to establish the broad lineaments of a world Christian norm for the differential use of Scripture.

CHRISTIAN HISTORY

How the historian of the Christian centuries must wish he could get behind the scanty or enigmatic documents and supply the missing evidence by stepping into a house-church in the second century, following an Irish missionary to Europe, talking to a medieval sectary, seeing for himself what the

Anabaptists were really like or what happened to vast crowds of simple folk when Wesley preached in the open fields.

In the non-Western areas of the Christian world, if he stops to look, he can often find living forms that come very close to a recapitulation of parts of the biblical and Christian centuries. Especially in the multitudinous African phenomena he will find many parallels to the earlier stages in the history of the people of God. Some movements have made a radical breakthrough from tribal religion and all magical practices in favour of faith in the one God they find in the Old Testament, but have not reached a Christian position. They may even specifically reject it, and actually call themselves by Old Testament names, as with Enoch Mgijima's Israelites in South Africa, and the Abayudaja or People of Judah in eastern Uganda today.

The Jerusalem community of the New Testament period is recreated before us in the first stages of other African movements, where we find pentecostal phenomena, communal living within the bond of a new faith, prayer and fasting, healings and miracles, the enduring of persecution, and missionary expansion with no resources other than the convictions of a new religious experience. And there are the African Galatians and Corinthians also, with their proneness to litigation and party divisions, their moral lapses, and their new legalisms.

At other times it is the second Christian century which we see before us in African form, with its loss of the full dimensions of the earlier Christology and soteriology, and its descent into legalism. We see too modern Montanisms, with their prophet founders and prophetesses, their New Jerusalem holy cities, their millennial hopes, and their replacement of the incarnation by the present revelations of the Holy Spirit.

When we observe the remarkable expansion of some of these African churches, across tribal and national boundaries and spanning great distances, and when we see some of the mass movements swinging whole sections of the population into the Christian orbit, as with Kimbanguism in the Congo, Harris in the Ivory Coast, or Joseph Babalola or Garrick Braide in Nigeria, we wonder if we are watching the way the Christian faith spread and took root in the tribes of Europe and the peoples of North Africa during the first great periods of Christian expansion.

Medieval popular movements and the non-establishment wing of the sixteenth-century Reformation both reveal many similarities with current African developments. Once again people leave the established older Churches with their higher prestige and better facilities and find their spiritual home in some despised, persecuted, poor, and ill-equipped African independent church because here they believe they find the really vital and powerful Christian religion, and the true original Church of God, uncorrupted by Western accretions and human distortions.

Many independent churches have regarded themselves as effecting a radical reformation in a Christianity that was corrupt and powerless because it had diverged from the biblical patterns. It is possible that the radical Reformers of the sixteenth century in Europe and of the twentieth in Africa have been equally misunderstood, and that the study of the latter could be most enlightening for our understanding of the former, as for many sections of Christian history.

MISSIOLOGY AND ECUMENICS

No mission society has ever said, We will teach this African member of our mission to read, train him a little in our ways, teach him some hymns, give him a Bible, and then turn him loose and have no further dealings with him, perhaps even put obstacles in his way or let him know that we think he is far from grasping the Christian faith. After thirty, fifty, seventy years, we will re-establish relationships and see what he has done with the little we gave him.

And yet the equivalent of this experiment has been performed time and again whenever an African with some mission or national church background has voluntarily separated himself or been forced on other grounds to do so, and has proceeded to establish a church of his own. When contact is re-established decades later we discover what has been happening when all mission or other controls and resources have been eliminated and unsophisticated Africans have been left to 'go it alone'.

Further, their idiosyncrasies, eccentricities (at least from Western viewpoints), emphases and insights, misunderstandings and heresies, strengths and weaknesses, may be taken as very similar to those within the older churches, but freed

from controls and inhibitions, allowed to develop in unsophisticated ways, and so writ large for all to see. The independents
therefore offer missiology a series of extensive, long-term,
unplanned, spontaneous, and fully authentic experiments from
which it may secure answers to some of its most difficult
questions. This is a unique contribution that we are only
beginning to appreciate and use.

For example, what is it that African Christians desire to
retain from Western Christian forms? It is not easy to answer
this question within churches established by and still connected with a particular Western tradition, but the independent
churches are better placed to answer for us, especially as their
members may be drawn from a variety of older denominations.
The answer seems complex, and here we can do no more than
note that the independents characteristically draw upon the
symbols, vestments, rituals, and hierarchies of some of our
traditions, but less upon the sacramental and sacrificial
emphasis that often accompanies these; at the same time with
their emphasis upon the Bible, preaching, and lay participation,
they exhibit more 'protestant' tendencies.

A similar question applies to the relationship with the forms
of African traditional religions and cultures. What are the
continuities and discontinuities in this connection, and are they
where mission policies have tended to place them? Here some
of the answers are both surprising and impressive. For example,
where missions have emphasized a break with African marriage
systems and required monogamy, the independents have commonly accepted continuity with the past here, and stressed the
break with the systems of magic as the vital point of discontinuity.

As a further question of missiological importance, we may ask
what are the most consciously felt needs, and what are the less
conscious but still urgent needs which a new religion must meet
if it is to be accepted? Again it is the independents who help
us to see the overriding African concern for spiritual power
from a mighty God to overcome all enemies and evils that
threaten human life and vitality, hence their extensive ministry
of mental and physical healing. This is rather different from
the Western preoccupation with atonement for sin and forgiveness of guilt.

As a less conscious but still vital need there is the demand for self-respect and for acceptance by the rest of the world. In the independents this is met by their conviction of their own independent standing in the sight of God, who has raised up African prophets as inspired leaders of African churches that will yet grow and speak new and precious things to the whole of mankind. The Western missiologist had probably not expected this sense of mission to him and to his world, and finds there was not much place for this factor in his missiological theory.

As a final question of the kind currently debated by the missiologists we may choose that of how churches grow. Some of the independents have achieved memberships to be measured in six figures, and some have spread over wide and diverse areas and even into the Western world itself. How have they done this without the usual resources of men and equipment organized by some sending body? The essence of the answer seems to be that they find a mandate in the revelation to their founder or prophet, and a gospel in their offer of spiritual power from the God who has given the revelation and who continues to manifest himself in healing or guidance or deliverance from the forces of evil. For their method they have preaching and testimony set in the context of joyous worship and for their chief instrument the Scriptures. This latter is noteworthy, for it stands in contrast to their relative neglect of the sacraments.

The related field of ecumenics must be dealt with more briefly. The practice of ecumenism has been extended in our time to include the Roman Catholic Church and the Pentecostal churches, and now in yet another direction towards the independent churches, especially those in Africa. In 1969–70 there was the epochal admission to the World Council of Churches of the Church of Jesus Christ through the Prophet Simon Kimbangu in Zaïre. Approval of the Kimbanguist Church seems to have depended less on doctrinal orthodoxy expressed in familiar ways than upon its dynamic Christian life. This is introducing a new dimension into ecumenism and into the basis upon which churches are prepared to recognize one another.

At the same time many African independent churches raise important theological questions and present old and possibly new heresies with which African theologians must deal. It has been suggested that we have here one of the stimuli towards the development of an African theology, which might well find some of its distinguishing characteristics reflected in the special features of these highly indigenous African churches. I am, however, not convinced that the limitations of a culture-bound white Western theology are best corrected by the development of other cultural theologies, black, brown, or yellow.

SYSTEMATIC THEOLOGY AND CHRISTIAN ETHICS

The independent churches of Africa present a number of questions in important areas of systematic theology, and above all in the doctrine of the Church, and in what is meant by the criteria of the Church. When an independent church applies for membership on a Christian Council it soon appears that the four classic notes of the Church as one, holy, catholic, and apostolic are very difficult of application, and that the different credal forms, or the Reformation marks of preaching, administration of the sacraments, and the exercise of godly discipline, help us little. The dissatisfaction already felt with all these criteria in Western quarters becomes explicit in the African context. Likewise the current Western search for more dynamic criteria, indicative of the inner life and vitality of a Church, is strongly encouraged when faced with an African independent church whose Christian existence and dynamic we can sense but never capture in our familiar categories.

It is the independent churches again that have exposed our Western tendency to informal or unconscious use as criteria of a Church, matters that have no business there. The main example is the common addition of the requirement of monogamy, with the implication that a body allowing polygamy, as many independents do, cannot belong to the people of God, the Church. This, as I have argued elsewhere, is an unbiblical and untheological procedure.

This same issue of monogamy versus polygamy also poses questions to our Western Christian ethics. Is polygamy marriage or adultery, within its own social system? Is there a new species called 'Christian marriage' which alone *is* marriage? Is there any difference in principle between marriage with its various systems, and the various systems of politics and economics, in the way they should be dealt with in Christian ethics? The concrete issue of polygamy in an ostensibly Christian Church context can stimulate the development of a more satisfactory theological ethic that does three things: separates this issue from the criteria of the Church, does justice to the polygamous system as a form of marriage, and yet establishes the Christian norm of monogamy.

Of other theological issues we must speak more briefly. In the realm of soteriology it is among the African independents especially that we see the 'Christus Victor' view of the work of Christ manifestly exhibited. To study the gospel of the independents expressed in terms of abundant life and divine power may open up neglected dimensions of the biblical sources of the Christian faith and of the gospel itself for our theologies.

It is a commonplace in the West to acknowledge that both the fact and the theology of the Holy Spirit have been neglected through many centuries. African independents have a pentecostal emphasis and indeed in Ghana like to be known as the 'spiritual churches', in this sense. Without condoning their commonly inadequate Christologies we can find in them another contributor to the ecumenical search for a Christian faith and practice less defective at this point.

There is one general point I would make about the importance of the study of this range of independent, popular, dynamic churches. Theology as a science depends upon access to its appropriate data in their most authentic and vital forms. If we regard the data of theology as being the revelations and acts of the Divine, the post-biblical and contemporary manifestations of these data will occur less vividly in a dispirited Western Church with declining numbers and morale. On the other hand, the data will be more evident and accessible in unsophisticated churches where the living God is taken seriously as present in the healing and conquering power of the Spirit, with a gospel-generated growth and a spiritual creativity and confidence. Here, at the growing edges of Christianity in its most dynamic forms, the theologian is encouraged to do scientific theology again, because he has a whole living range of contemporary data on which to work. It is not that these dynamic areas of the Christian world are free from imperfection;

but being full of old and new heresies they need theology and offer it an important task.

PHENOMENOLOGY AND HISTORY OF RELIGION

As a postscript to remarks that have concentrated on various sections of the Christian religious disciplines we must indicate some contributions that the study of Africa's independent churches is making to the general phenomenology and history of religion.

For example, it becomes apparent, especially in new movements that cannot be called independent churches, that the traditional tribal religions must also be investigated since these provide a major component of the new developments. Thus the history and phenomenology of religion are being led into an area that has largely been left to the anthropologists. For phenomenological study there is a rich reward, for these new churches and movements present an extensive contemporary and dynamic sampling from the characteristic forms of religion. There are new holy cities, sacred mountains, local sanctuaries, and tombs of the saints; new *langues des dieux*—holy words, revealed languages, and even revealed scripts; new festivals with rituals and symbols drawn from colours or from water or other elements. The historian of religion also has ample materials for studying the rise and development of new religious traditions in bodies that share in the 'rapid social changes' of our era, and can discover the emergence of myths and legends within a single generation. All this and more awaits the phenomenologist and historian of religion who can wean himself from preoccupation with the major so-called world religions and with the religions of antiquity.

In short, I commend the study of the independent churches and other movements of Africa, and of the rest of the world, to all the Western religious disciplines not merely as a highly specialized field of inquiry, but as a field pregnant with new ideas, new methods and procedures, new categories and points of view, for use throughout their work.

Harry Sawyerr's Patron
(Bishop T. S. Johnson)

MATEI MARKWEI

Although he was not the first Sierra Leonean to be a bishop, he was the first to be one in his own country. And herein lies his historical significance. He opened the way to that high ecclesiastical office in his own country for other Sierra Leoneans to aspire to it at home.

His position was not only unique but very challenging. Many eyes were on him. Unlike Bishops Crowther and James John-son, for instance, he had not been the builder of churches and the opener of new missionary stations. He was not the itinerant missionary who travelled many a hazardous path to preach the gospel and convert the heathen. He had been in the classroom for most of the time before his elevation. He was therefore prob-ably the first African to rise from the ranks of formal teachers to the position of a high pastor of the Church. The future of many other Sierra Leonean clergy in the Anglican Communion depended on his performance. That after him, two other Sierra Leoneans have been consecrated and one has attained to the position of Archbishop of West Africa[1] shows that when T. S. Johnson opened the door, he left it widely opened for all able Sierra Leonean clergymen of his persuasion 'to strive, to seek, to find, and not to yield'.

In his tribute to Senator George Norris, the late President F. D. Roosevelt gave four yardsticks to measure a person historically when he said: 'History asks: Did the man have integrity? Did the man have unselfishness? Did the man have courage? Did the man have consistency?'[2] If we measure the life of T. S. Johnson with these, there is no doubt that he comes out answering all the questions in the affirmative. Because of this, the Church that he faithfully served and many that knew him have etched his name in gold.

In 1962 the Sierra Leone Church (the full-grown daughter of the Church Missionary Society) founded a school in his memory. The Reverend Canon Harry Sawyerr refers to him as 'Scholar, Teacher, Theologian, Evangelist: A Father in God and my Patron'.[3]

T. S. Johnson was born on 23 September 1873 and named Edowu because he came after twins. His father, James Johnson, was of the liberated African stock. The story still goes on in the family that T. S. Johnson's grandfather, Agbogay, was a young man when he was sold into slavery. He was liberated on high seas and sent to Freetown. After serving the customary months in the King's Yard,[4] he was sent to Regent village which was then under the able leadership of a dynamic German missionary—the Reverend W. A. B. Johnson.

The Reverend Johnson's arrival in Sierra Leone had coincided with the closing of the Rio Pongas and Susu Missions (which the CMS had engaged in without much success) and the opening of the CMS work among the liberated Africans. Bishop Johnson later wrote that while the Nova Scotians brought their Christianity with them when they came to Sierra Leone, the liberated Africans, captured on the high seas, who had never landed in America, continued to worship their false gods and idols to which they had been accustomed. Because of this, missionary work among them became very necessary.[5] Governor MacCarthy who had strongly felt this necessity, heartily welcomed the move to close the Susu Mission and was glad to use the CMS missionaries for the work among the liberated Africans. He appointed these missionaries as superintendents of the villages and their duties included teaching, preaching, converting, and reforming the villagers.

With the appointment of superintendents also came a new Government policy—to mix the tribes in the villages so that each village could become a heterogeneous group. In 1816 therefore, when the Reverend W. A. B. Johnson was appointed to Regent, the first group of Ibos was also sent there to mix with the former Vai. Among the later groups of Ibos added to the village community was Agbogay who at baptism took the name Johnson after that famous missionary.

T. S. Johnson's paternal grandmother was also a liberated African from Ilesha, Nigeria. According to the family legend, she was a very young girl who was put in the charge of a nurse. This nurse arranged with slavers to sell her. After arrangements had been completed, she was sent to the place to fetch some beans from a friend. Because she loved beans, she ran on the errand only to be taken into slavery.[6] Luckily for her, the ship carrying her to America was intercepted and she was liberated and sent to Freetown. Being a young girl, she was sent at once to Charlotte village where a school had been founded for the training of liberated African girls. She was at Charlotte for five years before she was thought of age and was married to Agbogay Johnson of Regent village. Out of this union came James Johnson, the father of T. S. Johnson.

Agbogay Johnson died a few years after the birth of his son and left his wife to eke out a living for herself. After some time at Regent, she migrated to Hastings taking her son with her. At Hastings she remarried and so James Johnson came under a stepfather who did not believe in schooling. His opinion was that nobody fed on book learning but on the products of the field. But when later the family moved to Waterloo, James determined to learn how to read and write and so started to tutor himself while working with his stepfather on the farm.

When he came of age, James Johnson got married to one Nancy Nicol, the daughter of a prosperous farmer at Benguema. After his marriage, he determined to follow the steps of his father-in-law. He had barely started his farming when an opportunity offered itself. The Government boats often brought provisions from Freetown to Waterloo; besides these, there were a lot of people who traded between Waterloo and Freetown and needed transport, which in those days, was mainly by boats. James not only became supervisor of Government cargo but also built boats that plied between Freetown and Aepayachain—a convenient port between Waterloo and Cole Town. He stopped his work as a 'super-cargo' when he lost a bag of money when one of his boats overturned in midstream. This was money belonging to traders. He had therefore to refund the sum. After that experience he abandoned the cargo business and seriously engaged in agriculture specializing in fruit trees.

Because he strongly believed in book learning, James Johnson sent his son to school immediately he reached school age. Bishop Johnson writes:[7]

> I learnt very early to give heed to my work at school. I did not like to take a second place in my class and particularly to be outstripped by a girl. Now there was a girl in my class who was rather gifted and it was the wish of the teacher that the girl should take first place. I was determined to disappoint him and that helped me to [pay] great attention to my studies.

When his father saw how studious he was, he arranged with the Headmaster for private lessons for his son. This made him keep ahead of his class all the time. It was during this time while he was doing so well that he suffered the loss of his right eye. He had gone with other boys to collect firewood. On the way, they started throwing stones with slings. Unfortunately, one of the stones caught his right eye and from then on he was unable to use it. He tells us that before the incident he heard a voice clearly saying to him 'Get out from where you are'.[8] But he refused to budge and in less than two minutes the accident took place.

When the pain had subsided, he continued earnestly with his studies because he believed, as he later wrote in one of his well-marked Bibles, that 'we may feed upon the obstacles of our life as a rock-plant does'. And that 'misfortune may be a cancer to the soul or may prove to be the irritating switch in the system to produce the pearl of great price'.

At the age of twelve, something happened in his life which also adds to our knowledge of the training he was receiving at home. He had gone with his father to catch a bull from their herd for slaughter when one of them seemed to charge at him. In trying to avoid it, he fell into a pit.

> At the bottom of the pit and being a dark night I thought I had died and that I was in hell. For I was taught
> Hell is a dreadful place
> Where sinners must with devils dwell
> In darkness, fire and chain.[9]

When his eyes got used to the darkness in the pit, he thought of

Joseph whose envious brethren put him into a pit to kill him but who was later rescued and sold.

These memoirs reveal that before he was twelve T. S. Johnson had received some fundamentalist teaching. He had not only heard of stories like that of Joseph but had the quick mind to associate his conditions in life with biblical or religious personalities and symbols.

At the age of thirteen he sat and passed the CMS scholarship examination which was an entrance examination to the CMS Grammar School. When he was interviewed, the Principal, the Reverend Canon Obadiah Moore, rejected him on the grounds that he was too young. The following year he tried again and passed the examination. At the interview the Principal rejected him on physical grounds—'he was too dwarfish'. Both he and his father were disappointed because his father could not see what a person's physical stature had to do with book learning. The father therefore tried a ruse—to give his son to the Principal as a ward so he could get his secondary school education, but Canon Moore was adamant—he would not have T. S. Johnson as a pupil of the CMS Grammar School on any grounds. When these attempts failed, his father became his adviser and the source of constant encouragement. His father advised him to keep constantly at his books so that he could be as learned as anyone who went to the Grammar School; and, as a good son, he kept his father's advice and acted on it. Then in 1890 something happened that was to change the course of his life. This was the famous 'Five Pastors' Case'.[10]

Among the many things that happened at Benguema during the Five Pastors' Case was the founding of a church school. It was named Bishop's School. This school was situated in the home of James Johnson who was one of the leaders of the Party supporting the Bishop. T. S. Johnson was then eighteen years of age and as he himself remarked, 'good at his books'. The villagers therefore elected him Headmaster of Bishop's School, Benguema. This event changed the course of his life. He saw it as an opportunity to better himself and he did so well that after the case he caught the eye of the Bishop as a good schoolmaster and was transferred from Bishop's School, Benguema to the Cathedral Model School, Freetown. According to Bishop Johnson, he had just taken up his duties as teacher of the Cathedral Model School when his father read an advertisement in the *Weekly News* about scholarships for teacher training at Fourah Bay College. He applied for and won one of those scholarships offered by the Society for Promoting Christian Knowledge. In September 1893 he passed the entrance examination and entered Fourah Bay College in January 1894.

At Fourah Bay he came into contact with the Principal, W. J. Humphrey, who was also the lecturer in Mathematics. Since Johnson loved Mathematics the Principal became fond of him and took special lessons with him as he prepared for the Durham Certificate of Proficiency which he passed in 1895 with distinction in Arithmetic. His success egged him on to greater heights. He diligently applied himself to his studies with the aim of passing the Teachers' Certificate examination. In 1896 he attempted the examination under M. J. Marke who was then Head of the Education Department in Freetown. He came out with a second class and because he was a student at the College, the Government donated the sum of £40 to the College. The Principal called T. S. Johnson, congratulated him on his success, and gave him a special prize of £5 from the amount given by the Government.

Johnson received his first appointment as a certificated teacher at the CMS Mohammedan School then situated at Dan Street, Freetown. While working there, he felt the need for missionary work among the Muslims and started seriously to think of ways and means of tackling the problem effectively.[11] With his assistants, J. N. P. Nicol, Hannah Aitkins, and others, he determined to teach the Mohammedan boys of Fourah Bay about Christ and especially made them learn a lot of Christian hymns. On Sundays he joined with some of the students of the College to conduct open-air services at Fourah Bay.

During the course of these evangelistic campaigns, he saw clearly that one would win over the Muslims if one was respected and also had the necessary theological background. This made him dissatisfied with his second class Teachers' Certificate so he tried the examination again in 1898 and came out with a first class.

Just at the time he got his First Class Certificate the post of Headmaster of St Mary's School, Bathurst, Gambia, was advertised and the Manager, the Reverend S. Hayman, made him the offer. He would have gone but for the advice of Principal Humphrey. He listened to Principal Humphrey and instead of going to Bathurst prepared for the London Matriculation which he passed in 1899. This did not satisfy him so he prepared for the Licentiate in Theology which could give him the theological basis needed for evangelistic work among the Muslims.

In 1900 he passed the first part of the examination and was awarded the Licentiate in 1901 when he passed the final examination. But just at the time he felt himself qualified enough to work among the Muslims of the Dan Street School, he was transferred to be Headmaster of the College School, Cline Town.

While at Cline Town he learnt from students of the College that there was little difference between the Licentiate he was holding and the Bachelor of Arts. The fact was that the Licentiate exempted one from the first-year examination in Arts. He therefore made up his mind to read for the Arts degree. This, time, he was greatly helped by the Reverend E. H. Elwin who had assumed the Principalship of the College after the death of Principal Humphrey in the Bai Bureh War.[12]

Towards the end of the year, 1901, while he was still in the process of helping T. S. Johnson, Elwin left the College to accept the Bishopric of Sierra Leone left vacant by the resignation of Bishop Taylor-Smith who had been appointed Chaplain of His Majesty's Forces. Elwin was at that time *ex-officio* Chairman of the Board of Managers of Cathedral School so he got the Board to appoint Johnson as Headmaster. Johnson willingly accepted the appointment because the Board offered to pay him £5 a month; £1 10s. more than the College school was then paying him.

On 25 January 1902, Elwin was consecrated Bishop of Sierra Leone and in June the same year Johnson passed the examination for the Bachelor of Arts. The new bishop was very happy for his student so he appointed Johnson a member of the Parochial Church Council and gave him papers as missionary to the Cline Town Section.

All these years, from 1893 when he entered the College to train as a teacher to 1902 when he passed the B.A. examination, Johnson was resident in the College. This made him take an active part in parish work at Cline Town. In the course of his work he arranged and paid for the fencing of the church premises—a piece of work which was fully undertaken by one H. B. Macfoy, a blacksmith then resident at George Street, Freetown. Later he became the dedicated Pastor of the Cline Town church. Although the Principal of Fourah Bay College was the *ex-officio* Pastor of the church, everyone knew that T. S. Johnson carried the place.

After obtaining the B.A. degree, Johnson left the College because he was contemplating two things: marriage and the ministry. On 18 February 1903, he achieved the first of his two aims by marrying Miss Marian Konigbabay Johnson, the grand-daughter of Mammy Hannah Green of Holy Trinity fame. Miss Johnson, whose parents returned to Freetown from Nigeria a few years before her marriage, was partly trained in the Girls Section of Cathedral School. On 18 February 1903, therefore, Miss Marian Johnson became Mrs. T. S. Johnson. Out of this union eight children were born, four boys and four girls. Two of the children predeceased the Bishop. Among the six who survived him is the Reverend Evan George Agbogay Johnson who, at the time of writing, is attached to St George's Cathedral.

Johnson's marriage did not dampen his ambition to excel. He continued his studies and in December 1903 became an Associate of the College of Preceptors. This was to give him very good standing in the city as a teacher since the Cathedral and Holy Trinity Schools were the two top schools in Freetown at the time.

After his marriage Johnson started to think seriously of entering the ministry. He therefore applied to the Church for a title, but received no reply to his application. And learning from unofficial sources that his application had been turned down because the Patronage Board considered him dwarfish, he vowed never to become a minister of religion and turned his attention to teaching.

When later Bishop Elwin learnt of the unfair decision of the Patronage Board, he sought ways and means to ordain Johnson. Bishop Elwin got his opportunity a few years after the first Conference of Anglican Bishops in West Africa which was held at Lagos in March 1906. The Conference, under the chairman-

ship of Bishop Elwin, came to the conclusion that the time had
come for the formation of a Province of West Africa. In order
to make their claim more effective, it was decided that each
diocese should reorganize and add more African clergy to the
fold. On his return to Sierra Leone the Bishop selected four
candidates already passed by the Patronage Board for ordination. He persuaded T. S. Johnson to be ordained as the Bishop's
personal chaplain at the cathedral. So on St Luke's Day,
18 October 1909, six years after he had vowed not to be a
minister, Johnson was ordained deacon at Christ Church,
Pademba Road, Freetown together with C. F. Cole, E. H. G.
Nylander, R. L. Pinkney, and B. L. Thomas.[13] Less than a
month after his ordination, on 9 November 1909, Bishop Elwin
died.

The death of Bishop Elwin was a great blow to Johnson. He
felt as if the only friend he had in the city had left him for
eternity. He therefore decided to leave Sierra Leone for Nigeria
to work under Bishop James Johnson who was then the
Assistant Bishop of Western Equatorial Africa. He communicated his intention to Bishop James Johnson but had not yet
received a reply when Mr Denton, the CMS Secretary and the
then Acting Principal of Fourah Bay College, heard of his
intention, and, after advising him not to carry it out, invited
him to join the staff of the College.

Meanwhile, the reply came from Bishop James Johnson
telling him that he was welcome. T. S. Johnson was now on the
horns of a dilemma—Nigeria or Fourah Bay College? He knew
Fourah Bay College, where, since 1908, he had given occasional
lectures in Logic; but at the same time, the CMS had given
notice that they would close down the College after 1911. To
go to the College was therefore like leaving certainty for
uncertainty. The Cathedral Board was willing to allow him
to go to the College on secondment and return to the cathedral
as an assistant priest if the College were closed down. He
writes,[14]

I put the thing in prayer for God to guide me. Everyday I
prayed over it and it was after a period of three months that
the answer came. I was on my knees, it was about 4 a.m.
before daybreak when the answer came: 'Go to Fourah

Bay College'. Like St Paul I must not tell how it came but it really came and so I was not disobedient.

By the time he got to Fourah Bay College, a new bishop had arrived who ordained him a priest on Trinity Sunday, 11 June 1911.

Some people in Freetown started to campaign against the CMS intention to close down the College and T. S. Johnson joined in the fray. He and Denton determined to save the College by all means. And since the finances of the College brought the crisis, Johnson became Denton's right hand man in the management of the finances. He was also placed in charge of catering. Bishop Walmsley, a keen missionary, became sympathetic to the wishes of the people to keep the door of the College open. For this purpose he was able to work out a scheme with the Wesleyan Methodist Missionary Society so that in conjunction with the CMS they could finance and administer the College. This arrangement eased the financial position and the College remained open.[15] T. S. Johnson should be remembered, if not for anything else, for his active part in saving Fourah Bay College.

Having entered Fourah Bay College as a Lecturer, T. S. Johnson determined to fit himself to the post. He took correspondence courses from Wolsey Hall, Oxford, for the B.D. (Durham) degree. In June 1913, two years after he had joined the staff of the College, he got the B.D. and a year later the M.A. was conferred on him *gratis*.

T. S. Johnson's devotion to duty and especially his concrete contribution to Sierra Leone started when he came in contact with many young Sierra Leoneans while he was at Fourah Bay College. He took upon himself to inspire them to greater heights and used his own experiences to inject into them a sense of purpose and dedication to duty. As the one in charge of catering for the students in those days of financial crisis, he constantly tried to convince them that to save Fourah Bay College as an Institution of Higher Learning in West Africa was more important than their eating cheese and mutton. He also pointed out to them that it was a great service to West Africa to eat the cheapest fish available—even cat fish—if by doing so Fourah Bay College could be saved.

T. S. Johnson possessed authority because of his sincerity of service. He matched his precepts with example because many a month he would either take half pay or no pay at all if by so doing he could help the finances of the College. He was wont to say: 'Success does not rest on mere mechanical skill. Call to your aid the unseen powers of mind at your disposal. Reason carefully; then pray; and when you come to the conclusion that one thing is more important than the other, go ahead and do what is more important and use all your energies to accomplish it.'[16]

Johnson's passion for Fourah Bay was unmatched. He spoke of the College with emotion[17] because he considered Fourah Bay College his Alma Mater. He tried to inculcate the love of the College in his students and did everything he could to inspire them to help save it.

It was in one of his pep talks to students that he gave the seven deadly sins of modern society which he later wrote down on the inside cover of his *Notes for Meditation for Daily Use*. These are:

Policies without Principle
Wealth without Work
Pleasure without Conscience
Knowledge without Character
Industry without Morality
Science without Humanity
Worship without Sacrifice

T. S. Johnson made himself available to all students who needed him. He took upon himself to guide, counsel, and help them with their emotional problems. In this respect he became the patron of many, including foreign students. When it was felt, therefore, that something must be done about the training of teachers for the secondary schools of Sierra Leone, Johnson was considered as one who would really contribute a lot to the success of the venture. With that in mind communication was opened with the authorities of Durham for a course leading to the Diploma in the Theory and Practice of Teaching to be held at Fourah Bay. And when Durham required that a member of the then College staff must be qualified for the Diploma, the authorities of Fourah Bay unanimously selected Johnson although he was fifty at the time. He left for Durham in 1923 and passed the examination in 1926. And he writes:[18]

> Whilst at Durham I made the acquaintance of the Reverend J. L. C. Horstead. He was thinking about offering for the Civil Service of the Sierra Leone Government. I tried to put the need of F. B. College to him. He was a devotee of the Student Christian Movement and so had little difficulty to see where he could be of greater use and he chose to come out as Principal of F. B. College.

Horstead's coming coincided with the centenary of Fourah Bay College and plans were made for the celebration. Durham sent out as representative the Reverend Dawson Walker. During the celebrations the degree of D.C.L. was conferred on the out-going Principal, the Reverend J. Denton. The M.A. was conferred on the Reverend H. P. Thompson as the oldest student of Fourah Bay College then alive and on the Principals of the two CMS Secondary Schools—the Reverend Obadiah Moore of the Grammar School and Miss Pilsby of the Annie Walsh Memorial School.

For tuition for the Diploma in the Theory and Practice of Teaching, the first and only student to be enrolled was A. T. Thomas (now Dr Thomas, Chairman of the Fourah Bay College Council). A normal European master was appointed (after T. S. Johnson had trained for the post) as Director with Johnson as his assistant. However, it was plain that apart from lectures, F. A. J. Utting, the Director, depended on Johnson for the smooth running of the Department.

T. S. Johnson was not only dealing with the students of Fourah Bay College. He went about looking for potential teachers and encouraged them. It was on one of his scouting expeditions to the Secondary Schools that he found Canon Harry Sawyerr. Says Canon Harry Sawyerr, 'I was doing science at the Prince of Wales when he sought me out and encouraged me to continue with my studies. He kept in touch with me and later advised me to enter Fourah Bay and, when I did, I directly came under his wing.'

Johnson was looking for men and women to help them so that they could be inspired to build their nation. He strongly believed that 'economic stability is not the sole determining factor of a people ... The best assets of a nation are the men and women it produces. ... We need bread but we also need vision and culture ... [We need the] cultivation of the mind to have a true and proper perspective' on everything we undertake to do.[19]

In 1933 he was offered and accepted the Principalship of the Grammar School. As it was the custom that one must be an old boy of the School before he became its Principal, T. S. Johnson was made to attend classes for a day in order to qualify as an old boy.[20] He took up his duties in September of that year and within a few months most people saw marked changes. He not only improved the discipline of the school but sought to change the curriculum to suit the changing times. For he strongly believed that the aim of education should not be merely to load the child with a quantity of academic stuff, but to prepare him that he might prove seaworthy for the voyage of life. The Bishop of the diocese, G. W. Wright, was so impressed that he created Johnson a Canon of the cathedral in 1934 and when a vacancy occurred with the death of Archdeacon E. T. Cole for the post of Archdeacon of Freetown Johnson was the one the Bishop appointed.

By the time Johnson was appointed Archdeacon, Bishop Wright had nearly completed the arrangements for the separation of Gambia and Rio Pongas as well as North Africa from the diocese of Sierra Leone. When the Bishop left at the tail end of 1935 to complete arrangements with Canterbury, he appointed Archdeacon Johnson as Administrator of the diocese. In 1936 the separation of Gambia and Rio Pongas as well as of North Africa was finally effected. For his part in the creation of the other sees as well as his revision of the 1890 Constitution of Bishop Ingham, Bishop Wright received the Lambeth D.D. from the Archbishop of Canterbury.

Bishop Daly was consecrated for the new diocese of Rio Pongas and Gambia. Bishop Wright chose to go to the new diocese of North Africa. Before his departure, however, he strongly recommended that an Assistant Bishop be consecrated for the Sierra Leone diocese and further recommended that T. S. Johnson be considered for the post. He further suggested that the vacant see of the Diocesan be offered to Horstead who was then Principal of Fourah Bay, Secretary of the CMS, and

Diocesan Canon Missioner. All his recommendations were accepted by Canterbury. Horstead was consecrated Diocesan and on St Barnabas Day, 11 June 1937, T. S. Johnson was also consecrated the first Assistant Bishop of Sierra Leone by Archbishop Cosmo Lang in St Paul's Cathedral, London. Thus by the grace of God, Horstead and the man who convinced him to come to Sierra Leone became the two chief shepherds of the Anglican Communion in Sierra Leone.

Shortly after his consecration, Bishop Johnson was selected as a delegate to the Madras Conference from which he returned with a lot of ideas for the expansion of the work in Sierra Leone. Both he and Bishop Horstead felt the need for young men to enter the ministry and did everything they could to encourage those who were already ordained.

> The days, however, were evil. A generation had arisen who had not the experience of the goodness of God to their race as evidenced in the abolition of the slave trade. Secularism had set in, as in other parts of the world. It was not easy to get qualified candidates for the ministry in the face of the plump stipends offered in the civil and mercantile services.

So wrote Bishop Johnson.[21] The two bishops did not however give up. They saw the situation as a challenge to their missionary zeal. They planned a revival and Bishop Horstead invited Bishop Gelsthorpe of Nigeria to conduct it. Bishop Gelsthorpe was assisted by Archdeacon S. S. Williams, a Sierra Leonean then working in the diocese of the Niger. They also got the assistance of Sister Mary Katherine of the Holy Cross Mission in Liberia. At the end of the revival meetings, the decision cards that were signed showed that the effort was successful.

Bishop Johnson followed the revival with the institution of the Week of Witness campaign. He suggested that a week be set aside in the year when all Christians should give witness of their gratitude to God. In short, it was to be a week when all Christians should become active missionaries. It also became a week of renewal and rededication. Many who know about these campaigns testify that they bore much fruit for the work of Christ in Sierra Leone. And although the campaigns do not take place any longer, the idea of witnessing for Christ is actively being carried on in the various Christian Associations in the country.

Along with the Week of Witness, Bishop Johnson also instituted what he called 'Taking the Church to the People'. This was a weekly affair and not just one particular week in the year. It was a call for evangelists who went from place to place preaching the gospel and explaining the teachings of the Church to people anywhere, including their homes. Pamphlets were printed for the guidance of the evangelists and all who went out on these occasions. Through these visits and the preaching of the gospel, many souls were won for Christ.

But one of the lasting things Bishop Johnson did was the institution of the Early Communion for mourners as well as the combined funeral and memorial service. It was the accepted custom in Freetown especially that after a mourners service, all who attended should retire to the house of the deceased or his relatives to eat and drink. Bishop Johnson found out that on such occasions some Christians forgot temperance and the relatives of the deceased sometimes entered into debt in order to fulfil this obligation. He started to campaign against this excessive feasting and suggested the Early Communion or the combined funeral and memorial service. His reason for the Early Communion was that after the service it would be too early to engage in much drinking; and for the combined funeral and memorial service he argued that the relatives of the deceased may only have to entertain during the wake keeping. Many people hailed these innovations and hid behind them to curtail their expenses. Now these practices are common in Sierra Leone although many do not know from whose fertile brain they originated.

Bishop Johnson's prestige and influence spread over all the country as he continued to inspire and encourage his people to do more for God. His constant theme at this stage was co-operation. 'The time is past, or should be past when one man's business is his own. . . . Today, success spells co-operation.'[22] He stressed the need for Africans to learn how to be altruistic and co-operate because to him 'hell is selfishness consummated and heaven is fellowship perfected'.[23] He appealed for more giving to the Church and got results because his appeals were based on the larger vision of a Church in Sierra Leone that could be a worthy part of a Province of West Africa.

In 1944 Bishop Johnson visited Lagos to attend the third Conference of Anglican Bishops in West Africa. During the conference, he was one of the bishops who took part in the consecration of the Reverend S. C. Phillips as Assistant Bishop of Lagos. It was while he was in Nigeria at this time that he visited Ilesha to confirm the story about his paternal grand-mother.

On his return to Freetown the Bishop continued with his programmes and this time took a very active part in the visitation of the parishes to strengthen and encourage the clergy. In the course of these visitations he started to feel that old age was creeping on him. He therefore decided to retire and give another younger than himself the chance of being the assistant bishop. He gave a year's notice and finally retired in June 1947. In the same year he was awarded the o.b.e.

His retirement opened a new chapter in his life. Convinced that 'every nation has something to contribute towards the complete revelation of the power of the Gospel', and that 'no Church of any age or country has full knowledge of every aspect of the Truth',[24] he started to put down his thoughts in a book wherein he strongly advocated that Christianity in Africa should not be a slavish imitation of Christianity in the West because God has more light which he wants to give to his gospel. Bishop Johnson believed that African Christians can shed light on the truth of the gospel through a systematic analysis of the African background *vis-à-vis* the Christian faith. This is what he tried to do in his book *The Fear Fetish: Its Cause and Cure*, which he published within two years of his retirement.

In this book the Bishop tried to trace why some Africans believe in evil spirits and argued that because they do (and he had ample evidence of Christians going to the 'medicine man' for help) it is better to posit the existence of evil spirits and then show how the gospel could help one to conquer them. He also stresses that it is the African's attribution of spirit to inanimate things that is the key to his fear of dark powers, and since most Africans are at the stage of Animism, it is good to preach the gospel to them with a clear understanding that they believe in such things.

The experience of many, including missionaries, from whom he gathered his evidence perhaps made the Bishop venture to say that because of the mysterious and seeming unscientific nature of some African beliefs and practices

> The African's contribution to world history may not be in the building of material civilization—the achievement of the obligatory standards in science, morals, law or art—but he seems to be gifted in the quest of the Unseen and linking himself to these Unseen Powers.[25]

So that although some African beliefs and practices cannot be proved scientifically, the African is under no delusion that the things in which he believes do really exist because the African also thinks 'that science does not yet know everything'. However he (the Bishop) believed that one can overcome fear through faith in God. 'All we need is a clear life and a great faith in God.'[26]

While writing his book, the Bishop also took part in many activities in the village of Benguema where he intended to spend his last days. He helped to dam the Egadudu stream so that villagers might get more water. He became a member of the Village Area Committee that settled all minor matters in the village and acted as a liaison to the Rural Area Council. He quoted M. C. Warren on a leaf of one of his Bibles as saying, 'If as a Christian you ignore your responsibilities as a citizen, you soon cease to be free to enjoy your privileges as a Christian'; for this reason he thought it his duty to shed light on the political situation. He actively campaigned for J. C. O. Crowther to the Legislative Council and when Crowther informed him that he would no longer stand, the Bishop staunchly advocated the case of R. G. O. King. He thought it his duty to explain the Stevenson Constitution to the people of Benguema village and to as many as would hear him.

When he found the need for a Community Centre in Benguema, he inspired the villagers to build one and helped with his personal funds to see that it was done. Nor was that all. When he found that the roof of the church was leaking, he promised the villagers that he would supply iron sheets for the re-roofing, but while the work was going on, the church collapsed and so they had to build a new church. Since he was the one who set the ball rolling, he felt it his moral duty to supply the funds for the rebuilding and therefore sold some property in Freetown and used the money to rebuild the church.

In the midst of all these activities in the village, the Bishop travelled to Freetown at intervals to do research on the history of the Anglican Church in Sierra Leone. He completed his research and published *The Story of a Mission: The Sierra Leone Church: First Daughter of C.M.S.* in 1953. This book puts him among Africa's church historians.

Some of the villagers in Benguema remember Bishop Johnson as the one who introduced weaving and bought a machine for nut-cracking which every villager was able to use. He made them see the economic value of palm kernels and there are many who have built houses in the village because he woke them to this realization. The Bishop is remembered most in Benguema as a selfless Father in God.

Bishop Johnson was writing a book on Islam and Christianity, spelling out his ideas on how to convert the Muslim, when on 22 October 1955, after a short illness, he breathed his last. He was buried at Benguema.

NOTES

1 Bishop Percy J. Jones was consecrated Assistant Bishop of Sierra Leone when T. S. Johnson retired. The Most Reverend Dr M. N. C. O. Scott, the third Sierra Leonean to be a bishop in his country is, at the time of writing, not only the Diocesan Bishop of Sierra Leone but also the Archbishop of West Africa.

2 Quoted by J. F. Kennedy in *Profiles in Courage* (New York 1961), p. 145.

3 Cf. Dedicatory note in Harry Sawyerr, *God: Ancestor or Creator* (London 1970).

4 Slaves captured on the high seas, often called recaptives, were brought to Freetown and sent to the King's Yard situated above King Jimmy Brook. They were handed over to the Captured Negro Department (Liberated African Department after 1822) which cared for them for at most three months. While in the King's Yard, prospective masters went for apprentices from among them. Some were selected for the Forces and the rest were sent to the villages. On arrival in a village, the men were given tools to farm and build houses; the women were married off and the children sent to school. For further details on how they were sent and the various letters written to the Superintendents see the Government Blue Books now in the Sierra Leone Archives.

5 Cf. T. S. Johnson, *The Story of a Mission* (London 1953), p. 28.

6 Bishop Johnson tells us that the story came vividly to him when he

visited Ilesha in 1944 and met Chief Ajimorkeh II who presented him with a bag woven of beads (a sign of royalty) with the initials of the Chief and his own. Cf. 'Biographical Notes', Mss. now in the possession of the Reverend Evan Agbogay Johnson of St George's Cathedral, Freetown.

7   Cf. Mss. 'Biographical Notes', p. 3.

8   Mss. 'Biographical Notes', p. 3.

9   Ibid., see insertion between pp. 3 and 4.

10 For details of the Five Pastors' Case, see T. S. Johnson, *The Story of a Mission*, pp. 65ff.

11 There is an unfinished manuscript in which T. S. Johnson was developing his ideas on how to convert Muslims. I read the manuscript four years ago, but was unable to consult it for this essay.

12 For a few details see Christopher Fyfe, *A History of Sierra Leone*, p. 566.

13 Cf. Johnson, *The Story of a Mission*, p. 71.

14 Mss. 'Biographical Notes', p. 8.

15 The arrangement with the Methodist Missionary Society was completed in 1917 and by 1918 the Methodists seriously contributed to the funds of the College. Cf. D. L. Sumner, *Education in Sierra Leone* (Freetown 1963), p. 156.

16 These notes came from the back cover of one of Bishop Johnson's well-marked Bibles. The ideas expressed in this paragraph have also been checked and rechecked by the author from many of the ex-students of the Bishop.

17 See, for instance, the insertion between pp. 4 and 5 of his Mss. 'Biographical Notes'.

18 Cf. Mss. 'Biographical Notes', pp. 8–9. It is interesting to note that J. L. C. Horstead took Johnson's advice and became Principal of Fourah Bay College (1926–36); Bishop of Sierra Leone (1936–61); and Archbishop of West Africa (1955–61).

19 Cf. T. S. Johnson, 'New Life For Old' in *SLBR* 8.2, pp. 40ff.

20 T. S. Johnson's name was inserted in red ink between admission number 3653 Eric M. Davies and 3654 Koi Larbi of Accra admitted 25 April 1933. The Bishop was not given an admission number but it was clear that the name was inserted in the Admission Register to grant him the honour of an old boy of the School.

21 Cf. Johnson, *The Story of a Mission*, p. 78.

22 Cf. Ms. Sermon delivered to the West African Students Union, London, pp. 7 and 8.

23 See Random Thoughts set down on the cover of his copy of *Notes for Meditation for Daily Use*.

24 Cf. *The Fear Fetish: Its Cause and Cure*, p. 6.

25 Cf. *The Fear Fetish*, p. 12.

26 Ibid., p. 94.

Towards a Theologia Africana

KWESI A. DICKSON

In the last fifty years or so there has been a marked increase in the tempo of Christian activity in Africa. Three developments, in particular, have led to the marking out of Africa as a continent of special interest to the Christian world. There has been, to begin with, a rapid growth of church membership, a fact which has given rise to forecasts of further phenomenal growth in the not-too-distant future. Along with this, secondly, has gone the development of a total Christian presence. In this connection may be mentioned the establishment of theological faculties and seminaries, the coming into being of the All Africa Conference of Churches which has brought together churches a great number of which have moved away from being 'mission churches', having become independent and autonomous, and generally self-supporting. Of special interest here is the appearance of dedicated Christian leaders who, brought up in the best Western theological traditions, are anxious to relate Christianity to the life of the ordinary man in Africa, and to give the Church the character of an institution which *belongs* in the African world, instead of its being linked in the mind of the African with a Western mode of life and thought. The third development which has been the target of much scholarly probing and evaluation is the proliferation of independent churches, some of which are known to be drawing away people from the historic churches. Many of the independent churches, particularly in southern Africa, have come into being as an avenue by which Africans may express a longed-for freedom; hence these churches have by and large worked out a distinctive ethos which is often a blend of sometimes genuine, and sometimes misconstrued, Christian teaching on the one hand, and traditional African religio-cultural expression on the other.

These three developments have together brought about a new awareness of the Church and its responsibility in Africa. One of the areas of responsibility, recognized as such by both African and Western preachers and writers, is how to relate the gospel to African life and thought. This is the subject of this paper; considering the space available to us we shall do no more than indicate in broad general terms the ideas and trends that have emerged from discussions and related literature.

The starting-point for the discussion of Christianity and its relation to African life and thought is the realization that in the early days of missions in Africa no clear distinction was drawn between the gospel and Christianity. In a recent series of lectures entitled 'On the Feasibility of an African Theology',[1] by Raimo Harjula, a Finnish theologian working in Tanzania, the author draws attention to the need for distinguishing between the gospel, 'the Good News centred in Jesus' death and resurrection', and Christianity as the institutional framework and cultural embodiment with which the gospel is surrounded. In his 1947 Gifford Lectures on 'Religion and Culture'[2] Christopher Dawson demonstrated that religion and culture are often inseparable; for religion cannot escape the necessity of being incarnated in a culture. And Christianity, as it was brought to Africa, was the gospel together with a cultural encrustment of a Western nature. This is clearly illustrated in the words of one of the best-known missionaries to the Gold Coast (now Ghana), Thomas Birch Freeman. Around the middle of the nineteenth century he wrote:

> During the first ten years I often felt a pining after a partici-
> pation in the enjoyment of the rich services of your public
> worship in England, but that has now nearly passed away,
> for Divine Grace has created the same kind of services here.
> For if our Public worship in Cape Coast is not heaven come
> down to earth, it is pretty nearly that of England come to
> Africa.[3]

Freeman, a very discerning man, was acknowledged by the chiefs of the Gold Coast to have a great understanding of Ghanaian customs. He was once slated in the English *Times* by an anonymous writer for admitting into the fledgling Church at Cape Coast converts who were married according to the laws of the land, without demanding that they be remarried according to Christian rites; Freeman's contention was that the Church had no right to consider such conjugal unions invalid. It was this same Freeman who learnt to feel at home at Cape Coast only when the gospel had been proclaimed *and* English forms of service and hymns taught. Of course, it would be foolish to see received forms as being in themselves evil; nevertheless arising as they do from a cultural milieu which may be unfamiliar to the new converts, such forms *can* become an obstruction in the way of a fuller understanding of the realities of the Faith. It was in fact partly this—the realization that the foreign idiom in which the gospel was couched was presenting a barrier against a fuller understanding of the gospel, and partly the growing appreciation of the African cultural and religious heritage, which led to the demand for a reappraisal of Christianity against the background of African life and thought. It is in keeping with the need for this reappraisal that Henry Weman should in 1960 write almost as a rejoinder to Freeman:

> Without doubt the Church has acted in good faith in attempting to bring to life in the Christian congregation that musical heritage which has proved itself to be such a vital factor in public worship within western Christendom. But when experience has shown African and Western music to be two distinct entities, both Church and school ought to recognize African music, and give it a chance to prove itself by the side of the imported music. . . . A service of worship can hardly be the true expression of devotion, praise and prayer if its forms of expression are foreign.[4]

A body of literature has been building up on this subject of Christianity and African culture, an indication of the interest this subject has evoked. An exercise of some significance in this field was undertaken by the Christian Council of Ghana in 1955 when a conference was called in Accra to air views on the subject. The papers presented at this conference were published under the title *Christianity and African Culture*.[5] Some of the contributors made a strong plea for the Church to divest itself of all foreignness in order for it to become part of the African soil. In this connection reference may be made to Busia's contribution in which he argued that the Church should 'come to grips with traditional practices, and with the world view that these beliefs and practices imply'. Before 1955 a number of Western writers had written at length and sometimes passionately on this subject. It will suffice to refer to Bruno Gutmann who in 1925 published his *Gemeindeaufbau aus dem Evangelium*[6] in which, writing about the Chagga of Tanganyika (now Tanzania), he argued that Chagga culture could be accommodated by the Church, and that the Church should see it as its duty to respect the individuality of the Chagga. If Gutmann's thesis was not entirely satisfactory, it was because he did not seem to have any theological basis for the accommodation he was advocating. As Oosthuizen has observed, Gutmann 'takes . . . a stand in the group or tribe instead of in Scripture'.[7] To this point of the need for taking a stand in Scripture we shall return.

Since 1955 there has been a spate of publications on the subject. One might mention such writers as Idowu,[8] Williamson,[9] and Taylor;[10] in 1965 the All Africa Conference of Churches co-sponsored (with the Theological Education Fund) a theological Consultation at Ibadan the outcome of which was the book *Biblical Revelation and African Beliefs*,[11] and most recently, in January 1972, at Makerere University, Kampala, a group of theologians and church leaders held a week-long discussion on the topic 'African Theology and Church Life'.[12] In addition to these there has been a stream of papers and documents on the subject, among which may be mentioned Donald R. Jacob's experimental work entitled *Christian Theology in Africa*[13] which is 'an experiment in the examination of some problems in Theology assuming the presuppositions of African traditional religion'. In his 'Opening Remarks' Jacob notes,

> We have already seen in our study of the traditional religion that there are similarities and many differences between it and what the Bible teaches. Bantu theology has good sociology producing a good culture but it also has weaknesses and it is losing ground rapidly. Traditional Western Christian theology has some weaknesses even for Western needs, and

often has not been seen to be relevant to African problems.
Now we must come to the scriptures to discover God's
answers to our own problems here in our day.

Jacob's words are of interest, not only because of the reference
to similarities and differences between African religion and
Christianity but also because it represents an attempt—and it
does not quite come off—to work out a system of Christian
theology in an African idiom. Reference has already been made
to Raimo Harjula's paper 'On the Feasibility of an African
Theology'; there is, lastly, Harry Sawyerr's 'What is African
Theology?', a paper prepared for the Lay-Leadership Conference held at Kitwe in May 1970.

It is evident from the literature and authors cited above—and
this list does not pretend to be exhaustive—that there has been
a development from the early attempts (some as early as the
nineteenth century) to recommend the use of certain aspects of
African culture, such as music, to express Christian realities, to
present references to African Theology, a term which came into
use not quite ten years ago. In the earlier days, when writers
and preachers drew attention to the need for relating Christianity to the African's world view, there was very little attempt at a
systematic examination of the African system of thought and
Christianity; it was usually a matter of holding up isolated
areas of cultural expression as suitable for incorporation into
the Christian ethos; music, libation, and ancestrology were
seen by some as avenues of meaningful Christian expression.
While some of the protagonists of this approach presented
persuasive arguments in its favour, the championing of this
approach has sometimes been characterized more by emotional-
ism than by sober reason; what was often missing was a serious
examination of the areas singled out in their own context in
African life and thought, and in the light of the total Christian
message. In effect, there was, until very recently, a tendency to
look at African life and thought as serving merely to put a
cultural sheen on church ethos. To be sure, much has been
accomplished in this area. African music is enriching Christian
worship as never before, and much experimenting is going on.
In his *African Music and the Church in Africa*[14] Weman suggests
ways of improving worship services through the use of musical

idiom familiar to the African. Lugira, writing about art, notes that though the Ganda are assimilating Western techniques and methods, yet 'in view of the Ganda aesthetic drive . . . there is surely a rich mine of artistic sense, pattern and design to be usefully and acculturatively exploited by creative minds for the glory of the Most High'.[15]

In more recent years, however, there has been a broadening of the basis of inquiry; a more integrated approach is being urged. There is in fact a quest for an African Theology, an expression which has given rise to a certain amount of misunderstanding. Its suitability has been questioned mainly on two grounds. First, the term has struck some observers as smacking of African nationalism, suggesting as it is held to do an attempt to express theology in ethnic terms without taking account of the existing theological heritage of the world-wide Church. One writer recently commented:

> The question of the reasons why some African Christians are seeking an 'African Theology' deserves to be looked at more carefully. We can say at the outset that since God can be known through His creation, in life and in man, and Africans have always sought after God, the African knows something about God, and with what he has learnt from the Bible, he can produce a theology which can be legitimately called African. On the other hand, it is doubtful whether this can be called Christian theology, since the essential affirmation of Christianity is that the man Jesus of Nazareth, who was crucified under Pontius Pilate, and was raised from the dead, is the fullest and final revelation of God.[16]

This view of the protagonists of African Theology is probably influenced partly by the way writers used to hold up isolated areas of African cultural expression as suitable for incorporation into church ethos, and partly by the fact that, though there has been a stated interest in biblical foundations, there has not been a clear demonstration of this interest.

Judging by their published views, however, it is clear that those who have been seeking after an African Theology fully affirm that Christ is the fullest and final revelation of God. At various gatherings in recent years African theologians have emphatically expressed their faith in the centrality of Christ.

Thus, at the Ibadan Consultation of African Theologians in 1965 there was affirmed 'the radical quality of God's self-revelation in Jesus Christ';[17] or, as Idowu put it,

> We seek . . . to discover in what way the Christian faith could best be presented, interpreted, and inculcated in Africa so that Africans will hear God in Jesus Christ addressing Himself immediately to them in their native situation and particular circumstances.[18]

Admittedly, there has been a tendency, in talking of an African Theology, to look at the matter solely from the point of view of the contribution African life and thought can make, and hardly ever from the point of view of biblical revelation. It is not accidental that the Ibadan Consultation had for its theme 'Biblical Revelation and African Beliefs'; however, it is a matter for regret that in the end, beyond the affirmation of the centrality of Christ, there was very little study done at Ibadan of biblical revelation. In other words, this quest for an African Theology could proceed on the basis of a faulty methodology, that is, by first making a value judgement of certain facets of African life and thought and then seeking sanction from biblical revelation for its incorporation into the expression of the Christian faith. It seems to us that the reverse is the only valid way to build up a Christian theology; if, indeed, the Ibadan affirmation of the centrality of Christ is to be taken seriously—and the participants solemnly and unanimously accepted the affirmation—then it would be inexcusable to fail to give biblical teaching pride of place in this quest. Sawyerr has observed that 'A Theologia Africana must be part of the mainstream of the tradition of the Church whilst attempting to bring fresh insights into man's understanding of the work of God'.[19] At the Makerere Consultation attention was drawn to the need for firmly establishing biblical foundations, though it was acknowledged that the Consultation had not given much time to the discussion of this all-important angle of the subject.

On another ground, the use of 'African' in this connection has been criticized: How can 'African' be used of a variety of peoples ranging from the Arabs of North Africa to the Afrikaaners at the other end of the continent, and of a continent with such a rich diversity of traditional religio-cultural heritage?

As we see it, there is no difficulty here. African Theology, as it is envisaged by its protagonists, is to be fully within the Church's theological traditions, though it will hopefully represent a distinctive interpretation of theological truths. This distinctiveness will arise from its utilizing traditional African concepts. That, surely, would justify the use of 'African'. To quote Sawyerr again, 'The universal theology of the Christian faith will and must always remain one; but interpreted in terms of the ingredients of the African soil, it might correct the present imbalance caused by the stress on Historical Theology among many western theologians.'[20] And such theology need not be worked out by African theologians only, but by theologians, of whatever race, who are versed in African ways and wisdom.

In an editorial on the Makerere Consultation *The Christian Century*[21] reiterates the conviction of the participants that 'unless content were put into that term [African Theology] it might become a mere popular slogan'. But, as Mbiti put it at the Consulation, it would be wrong to suggest that African Theology had not begun to form already. African Theology, argued Mbiti, may be seen in the preaching of the gospel and the variety of responses to it; it is being done in the singing of hymns and songs, in impromptu prayers, and in the independent churches; in short, glimpses of African Theology may be found in the total African response, in word and action, to the gospel. There is no doubt that this is a valid way of measuring and evaluating theological activity; nevertheless, many at Makerere hoped that in the not-too-distant future there would be attempts at 'a systematic reformulation of theology to reflect whatever insights may be gained from a study of the confrontation of Christian and African ideas'.[22]

In the opinion of the present writer we may have to wait for a very long time indeed. Christian worship in Africa has on the whole failed to reflect the concerns which underlie the need for an African Theology, almost as if these concerns had never been expressed. Orders of service remain, as they have always been, an expression of concepts and ideas which are often at variance with African thought, to the extent that the services lose their significance. Thus, several of the sentiments expressed in the Methodist Order of Service for the Solemnization of Matrimony authorized for use in the Methodist Church by the Conference at Newcastle upon Tyne in July 1936 do not have much meaning in a matrilineal set-up where, among other things, children do not inherit the father's property, so that despite the Order's pronouncements, the couple do not become one in the fullest possible sense.[23] It is not only in matters of worship that we see very little evidence of the Church's interest in these concerns; it is a cause for amazement that many theological institutions in Africa have not devised curricula to take account of such matters as are involved in the quest for an African Theology. Though university departments have done better in this regard, Beetham is certainly right when he comments thus on seminaries:

> The curriculum is in most cases too much tied to a traditional Western pattern. Students can still come away from their lecture-room after studying the first two chapters of Mark's Gospel—with its account of the touch of the Jesus of Nazareth on different kinds of illness, including mental sickness— without having come to grips either with the failure of their own Church, despite its hospitals and clinics, to exercise a full ministry of healing or with the success of some Independent Churches in this respect.[24]

The lack of sensitivity seen in this type of seminary training results in the shaping of clergymen who by and large are curiously uninformed about the Church's task in this day and age. Without the leavening of the ministry with the leaven of the quest for the Church's true identity in Africa, discussions regarding the creation of a Theologia Africana will always be associated with a small band of university teachers who would be seen by the church leaders in Africa as at best having misguided zeal, and it will also give rise to all kinds of misunderstanding, such as are mirrored in an article to which reference has already been made.[25]

It would not be inappropriate to sum up this brief review by quoting Sawyerr once again:

> There is a strong case for a Theologia Africana which will seek to interpret Christ to the African in such a way that he feels at home in the new faith. The independent churches have pointed the way to adaptations of Christian worship to suit the African view. But they are unfortunately lacking in

theological understanding. Care must therefore be exercised to avoid both syncretistic tendencies as well as a hollow theology for Africa. To the present writer, the answer lies in the rigorous pursuit of systematic Theology.[26]

And

A Theologia Africana should . . . provide a common medium by which Africans and non-Africans, but even more so, the multiplicity of Christian groupings could begin to think together, first in the African continent, and maybe, in the providence of God, in other parts of the world.[27]

It would be strange, indeed, at a time when the Christian world in general is questioning its role in an increasingly secularized world, for the Church in Africa to continue to wear the garments fashioned a good many generations ago. A certain amount of rethinking of the Church's task in Africa is being done, thanks to the labours of Christian leaders, both African and European. This is as it should be. However, it would be presumptuous of the present generation of theologians to think that the quest could be brought to a successful and immutable end in their time. Each generation will have to re-examine the basis of the quest and restate the issues involved. Christian theology is a growing and progressive science.

NOTES

1 It is understood that Harjula's paper has been published under the title 'Toward a Theologia Africana' in *Svenska Missionstidskrift* (1970), pp. 88–102.

2 *Religion and Culture.* Meridian Books, New York 1959 (second printing).

3 1854 Report of the Wesleyan Missionary Society, vol. XIII.

4 *African Music and the Church in Africa,* Svenska Institutet för Missionsforskning (Uppsala 1960), pp. 112–13.

5 The Christian Council of the Gold Coast, Accra.

6 Verlag der Evang. Luth. Mission, Leipzig.

7 *Post-Christianity in Africa* (London 1968), p. 223.

8 *Towards an Indigenous Church.* Oxford 1965.

9 Kwesi, A. Dickson, ed., *Akan Religion and the Christian Faith.* Ghana Universities Press, 1965.

10 *The Primal Vision,* London 1963.

11 Ed. Kwesi A. Dickson and Paul Ellingworth. London 1969. The French edition is entitled *Pour une théologie africaine*. Editions CLE, Yaounde 1968.

12 It is understood that the papers presented at this Consultation will be published under the editorship of Professor John Mbiti of Makerere University, Kampala, Uganda.

13 This work is in private circulation.

14 See n. 4 above.

15 *Ganda Art*. Osasa Publication, Kampala 1970.

16 E. W. Fasholé-Luke, art. 'An African Indigenous Theology: Fact or Fiction?' in *The Sierra Leone Bulletin of Religion* (1969), p. 6.

17 *Biblical Revelation and African Beliefs*, p. 16.

18 Ibid., p. 16.

19 'What is African Theology?', a paper prepared for a Lay-Leadership Conference at Kitwe, 19–23 May 1970, *Africa Theological Journal* 4 (1971), pp. 7–24.

20 Ibid., p. 21.

21 16 February 1972, p. 185.

22 From the paper 'Towards an African Theological Expression', by the present writer; Working Document, All Africa Conference of Churches Second Assembly, Abidjan, 1–21 September 1969.

23 For a fuller treatment of this see the present writer's article 'Christian and African Traditional Ceremonies' in *Practical Anthropology*, 18.2 (March–April 1971).

24 *Christianity and the New Africa* (London 1967), pp. 106–7.

25 See n. 16 above.

26 Ibid., p. 24.

27 Ibid., p. 23.

Ancestor Veneration and the Communion of Saints

———— ◆•••◆ ————

EDWARD W. FASHOLÉ-LUKE

In his classic work, *The Religion of the Semites*, Robertson Smith took Old Testament studies out of the ivory towers of British universities into the fields of Syria, and also made a crucial point which has often been neglected by Western Christian missionaries in Africa, when he wrote:

> No positive religion that has moved man has been able to start with a *tabula rasa* and express itself as if religion were beginning for the first time; in form, if not in substance, the new system must be in contact all along the line with the older ideas and practices which it finds in possession. A new scheme of faith can find a hearing only by appealing to religious instincts and susceptibilities that already exist . . . and it cannot reach these without taking account of the traditional forms in which all religious feeling is embodied, and without speaking a language which men accustomed to these old forms can understand.[1]

From the outset of Christian missions in Africa, however, Western missionaries unanimously rejected African ancestor cults as pagan superstition, and even the Roman Catholic Church, which has a cult of saints, has forbidden her converts from participating in the rituals of the ancestral cults. It is not surprising, therefore, that it was and still is, at this point, that Christianity has met with the stiffest resistance in Africa, and that several independent African churches are reasserting the ancestral beliefs and practices.[2]

Fortunately, anthropologists have continued to proclaim the fact that ancestral cults are expressions of the family and tribal solidarity and continuity, and there are signs that African churches and even foreign missionaries are beginning to take the findings of anthropologists seriously; they are also wrestling with the problem of incorporating these ideas and practices into Christian faith and practice. But we are convinced that this enterprise will be abortive, unless the Churches develop a theology of the Communion of Saints that will satisfy the passionate desire of Africans, Christian and non-Christian alike, to be linked with their dead ancestors. As Professor Baëta has so aptly expressed it, Africans 'live with their dead'.[3] Is it at this point that the African churches can make a significant contribution to an aspect of Christian theology which has often been neglected in the past by many theologians? In his book *The Primal Vision*, J. V. Taylor sees the significance of this question and points a way to its solution, when he wrote:

> When the gaze of the living and the dead is focused on Christ Himself they have less compulsive need for one another. But need is not the only basis of relationship; and Christ as the second Adam enhances rather than diminishes the intercourse of the whole community from which He can never be separated. Is it not time for the Church to learn to give the Communion of Saints the centrality which the soul of Africa craves? Neither the inhibited silence of the Protestants nor the too-presumptuous schema of Rome allows African Christians to live with their dead in the way in which they feel profoundly to be true to man's nature.[4]

It is now nearly ten years since Taylor wrote these significant words, but there is little sign that either African churches founded by Western missionaries, or African theologians have given the doctrine of the Communion of Saints the centrality which it deserves, even though we affirm our belief in the Communion of Saints in the Apostles' Creed.[5] This paper is an attempt to see how this doctrine can be satisfactorily and adequately expressed, so that African Christians can avoid the dangers of syncretism on the one hand, and the peril of a double existence (accepting the wholesale rejection of ancestral cults intellectually, whilst participating in them to satisfy the deepest longings of their souls) on the other.

But we must pause at this point to examine briefly the vital and controversial question: Do Africans worship their dead ancestors or do they venerate them? This is not a merely academic question, since it involves the problem of whether African ancestral cults are merely idolatrous practices, and also the problem of whether the rituals and prayers offered to the ancestors constitute true worship. We must also ask whether the quality of the so-called worship offered to the ancestors is of the same nature as that offered to the Supreme Being. The question 'ancestor worship' or 'ancestor veneration' is also controversial, because Jomo Kenyatta can boldly affirm that 'the words "prayer" and "worship" . . . are never used in dealing with the ancestors' spirits'[6] among the Kikuyu, but Ulli Beier can also declare with equal certainty that the Yoruba 'worship their ancestors'.[7]

Harry Sawyerr has also made a strong case for the view that ancestral rites, practices, and prayers constitute true worship.[8] But he fails to prove his case, precisely because he does not consider another basic question: Do Africans attach the same quality to 'worship' of ancestors as they do to the Supreme Being? In other words, are there qualitative levels of worship, and do Africans make a distinction between the worship they offer the Supreme Being and the 'worship' they offer to the ancestors? One suspects that the wholesale rejection of ancestral cults and rituals by Western missionaries in Africa was due to their failure to recognize this distinction. Perhaps this problem can be illuminated by the Christian cult of saints.

The basic axiom of the Christian faith is that worship should be offered to God alone; but throughout the history of the Church there have been rituals and prayers offered to saints which sometimes come very close to worship. Critics of the cult of saints and martyrs have often described these rituals as 'Saint Worship', but their practitioners have replied that it is neither Christian worship in a debased form, nor does it contradict the basic Christian premiss that God alone is worshipful. This reply is grounded on the distinction between various qualities or levels of worship, so that a Christian can honestly say that he worships only the true and living God and venerates the saints. This does not mean that veneration of the saints is not genuine; it is merely an acknowledgment that it is at a lower level than worship of God.

We suggest, therefore, that this distinction is equally valid in

African religious beliefs and practices concerning the ancestors and provides us with an adequate paradigm for understanding these rituals and practices: worship of the Supreme Being, veneration of the ancestors. This distinction also provides a genuine basis for the development of a doctrine of the Communion of Saints, which will be acceptable to the universal Church and satisfying to African Christians. Furthermore, the phrase 'ancestor worship' is emotionally charged, conjuring up primitive and heathen ideas of idolatry; but the phrase 'ancestor veneration' is neutral, and does not present us with incompatible alternatives, which the phrase 'ancestor worship' seems to do. Hence the title of this paper: 'Ancestor Veneration and the Communion of Saints'.[9] It would be a distinct gain if African theologians abandoned the phrase 'ancestor worship' and adopted the phrase 'ancestor veneration' in their discussions of the African ancestor cults.

In his excellent book *Oedipus and Job in West African Religion*, Meyer Fortes makes four significant points which must be taken into account in any study of African ancestral cults, even though he deals specifically with the Tallensi. These points are also important for any theology of the Communion of Saints which is to be viable in the African milieu. First, the Tallensi venerate their ancestors, not out of fear, ignorance, or superstition, but 'because ancestry, and more particularly parenthood, is the critical and irreducible determinant of their whole social structure'.[10] Moreover:

> Every important activity and significant social relationship among them is expressed and sanctioned by the ancestor cult. And the pivot of this cult is the key to the relationship in Tale social structure—that is, the relationship between father and son.[11]

Second, the chief filial obligation of sons is the performance of funeral rites for their parents; this duty is supported and upheld by religious sanctions. Thus:

> To fail in it is to incur the everlasting wrath of the ancestors. For the mortuary and funeral rites are the first steps in the transformation of parents into ancestor spirits and the worship of ancestors is in essence the ritualization of filial piety.[12]

Thirdly, the ancestors are the guardians and custodians of the moral values of the Tallensi and Fortes claims that the ancestors

> are the jealous guardians of the highest moral values, that is to say, the axiomatic values from which all ideal conduct is deemed to flow. The first is the rule that kinship is binding in an absolute sense. From this follows the second rule, that kinship implies amity in an absolute sense. The third rule is the fundamental one. It postulates that the essential relationship of parent and child, expressed in the parent's devoted care and the child's affectionate dependence, may never be violated and is, in that sense, sacred. It is indeed the source of the other rules. Tallensi believe that anyone who violates the rules is liable to the mystical penalty of death. For though every death has material causes, no death can occur except by the will of the ancestors.[13]

These rules represent the sacralization of Tallensi filial relationship and the third rule raises for the Christian theologian the question: Who is responsible for death?

But Tale morality is not based simply on right conduct; it is based on right relationships and this is Fortes' fourth point; he writes:

> What the ancestors demand and enforce on pain of death is conformity with the basic moral axioms in fulfilling the requirements of all social relationships; and these are the counterpart, in the domain of kinship, of the obligations posited between persons and their ancestors in the religious domain.[14]

Fortes' points underline two significant truths about ancestral cults in Africa: first, these cults represent the sacralization of family ties, preserve the solidarity between the dead and the living, thus enhancing amity in the community; and second, the cults indicate that the ancestors are the custodians of the morality of the tribe or community; hence ethical conduct is determined by reverence for the ancestors.

The question poses itself: Can some of these ideas be incorporated into Christian theology, and if they can, how can they be validly translated into Christian categories of thought?

The contention of this article is that if Christian theologians in African give the doctrine of the Communion of Saints the centrality which it deserves, it could provide a framework for incorporating African ideas about ancestors into Christian theology. But it must also be emphasized that, though there are points of contact between African and Christian ideas on the subject of the ancestors, nevertheless there are some aspects of African ancestral beliefs which are incompatible with the Christian faith and must be rejected. An obvious example is the belief that no death can take place except by the will of the ancestors. Christian belief states clearly, however, that life and death are in the hands of God and that Christ is the Lord of the dead and the living. In all our theological endeavour, therefore, we must always remember that no people, ancient or modern, have painlessly absorbed Christianity into their systems of thought. Furthermore, the production of culture-bound theologies is a fruitless exercise and would be useless both to the culture for which it is produced and also to the universal Church.

The phrase *Sanctorum Communio*, which is found in the Apostles' Creed, is generally accepted to be a later addition in that Creed and is probably the Western equivalent of the Eastern 'One baptism for the remission of sins'.[15] If this relationship is accepted, then we must also accept the view that *sanctorum* is neuter plural and that the phrase expresses the belief that forgiveness of sins and salvation are dependent upon the sacraments. The phrase should therefore be taken to mean: 'participation in holy things'. But this interpretation of the phrase has not met with universal approval. Kelly, for example, states that the phrase *sanctorum communio* stands 'for that ultimate fellowship with the holy persons in all ages, as well as with the whole company of heaven, which is anticipated and partly realized in the fellowship of the Catholic Church on earth'.[16] This interpretation of the phrase assumes that *sanctorum* is masculine plural. A third suggestion has also been put forward by Karl Barth, though he does not claim to settle the exegetical problems connected with the phrase. He asks 'whether there is not here intended a remarkable ambiguity in a deeper sense', and goes on to suggest that 'only when both interpretations are retained side by side does the matter receive its full, good meaning'.[17] This suggestion provides a useful basis for the development of a doctrine of the Communion of Saints, since it is through the participation in the holy things (*sancta*) that the Christian enjoys that fellowship with the holy people of all ages and the whole company of heaven in this age. Is it probable that the development of a doctrine of the Communion of Saints has been hindered by the dispute over the interpretation of this phrase?

Now it is clear that the spiritual fellowship which is based upon union with God in Christ through baptism cannot be terminated by physical death. On the other hand, it is equally clear that the fellowship between the living and the dead must be carried on under different conditions from those which attend fellowship between the living. Unfortunately, the New Testament is exceedingly reticent about the state of the faithful departed; it is content to declare that they are with Christ. This simple belief was enough while the early Christians regarded the Parousia as imminent and the apostolic Church dwelt on the glorious end of the world, when Christians will immediately receive their crowns of glory. But the delay of the Parousia and the growing number of the faithful departed brought the problem of the condition of the departed to the forefront of Christian thought. The question which clamoured for an answer was: Were the souls of believers received into heaven immediately after death or did they await the general resurrection in an intermediate state?

Tertullian, an African theologian who often crystallized the beliefs of the second-century Church, gives an answer to this question. He declares that 'heaven is open to none, while the earth still stands', and claims that there is an intermediate state, a place of the dead which is divided into two parts: Hades and the intermediate place of refreshment for the souls of the righteous. Tertullian also speaks of the martyrs being nearer to Christ in Paradise and contends that only martyrs enjoy the privilege of being 'at home with the Lord' immediately they leave the body.[18] Tertullian's distinction between the place where departed martyrs are and the place of other departed Christians raises other questions: Do all the Christian dead enjoy, or enjoy at once, the rest and refreshment of the intermediate state? Do they not need further discipline before they can enter into the joy of their Lord? The Greek Fathers of the Church replied that the dead in Christ are in an intermediate state between earth and heaven, expecting the resurrection; some receive discipline, some receive education for the higher life, and others receive further knowledge. As their natures mature and grow under this process, they rise to greater heights and draw nearer to the fullness of their joy. This answer has given rise to the description of the threefold condition of the Church, as the Church militant, the Church expectant, and the Church triumphant. These ideas about the condition of the faithful departed are based on the belief about their relationship with Jesus Christ, who through death has conquered death and provided the link between the living and the dead.

How can these ideas be interpreted in the African situation, especially as many African Christians have ancestors who were not Christians? This question shows that we cannot simply say that the African ancestors can be embraced within the framework of the universal Church and included in the Communion of Saints. We need a more profound appraisal of the situation and a deeper theological interpretation of the beliefs about the fate of the departed, and we would suggest that the interpretation of the phrase *sanctorum communio* to mean fellowship with holy people of all ages and the whole company of heaven through participation in the holy sacraments, gives us a signpost to the road on which our theologizing should travel. At baptism we are made members of the universal Church, and are therefore able to have fellowship with Christians of every age, and are linked with the faithful departed since fellowship within the Church is not limited by time or space and this fellowship is not broken by death. Furthermore, through baptism we are linked with Christ's death, and by our death to sin we begin here and now to enjoy the gifts of eternal life. Death therefore is no longer a dreaded enemy, it is a friend and the gateway to eternal life. But how can those who died without receiving baptism be linked with the living members of the Church?

We must postpone an answer to this question until we have looked at the other sacrament which links us with the departed, namely, the Eucharist. At the Eucharist Christians join with the whole company of heaven, the faithful departed, the angels and archangels, to praise and glorify God. This link is forged by the perpetual memorial of Christ's death, until he comes again. It is at this service that we can and do live with our dead in a way which is profoundly true to man's nature. It is also at this service, where we show forth Christ's death, that Africans can be linked with their non-Christian ancestors. This is so because we believe that the death of Christ is for the whole world and no one either living or dead is outside the scope of the merits of Christ's death. Thus both Christians and non-Christians receive salvation through Christ's death and are linked with him through the sacrament which he himself instituted. This view is supported by the fact that in his roll of heroes of faith, the author of Hebrews includes non-Christians whose faith was not perfect. We would equally affirm that the African ancestors could also be included in the Communion of Saints in this way, since they had a faith which was not perfect; but the death of Christ can make perfect the feeble faith which they had and thus incorporate them into his Body the Church. Furthermore, if they are in an intermediate state between earth and heaven, where they can receive discipline and a fuller knowledge of Christ's work, then at the Eucharist African Christians can pray for their ancestors and plead that the one, all-sufficient sacrifice of Christ may be effective in their case also.

Is it too presumptuous to suggest that Christ still continues to preach the good news to our African ancestors and that they will respond to his call and receive that salvation which will link them indissolubly to Christ and to us their living relatives? No one can measure the extent of the work of Christ; we must therefore not simply dismiss this suggestion as unbiblical. Perhaps, like St Paul, we should, in the face of this problem, simply say: 'O depth of wealth, wisdom, and knowledge in God! How unsearchable his judgements, how untraceable his ways! Who knows the mind of the Lord? Who has been his counsellor? Who has ever made a gift to him, to receive a gift in return? Source, Guide, and Goal for all that is—to him be glory for ever! Amen.' (Rom. 11. 33–6, NEB).

Now any doctrine of the Communion of Saints must consider the question of whether we can pray for the departed and whether they can pray for us, since prayer is one of the vital means of fellowship with Christians who are separated from each other. First then, can we pray for the faithful departed? The biblical evidence for this practice is slight and the New Testament has only one prayer for a departed Christian in 2 Tim. 1.18; this prayer is for his acceptance in the Day of Christ, and not for his well-being in the intermediate state. Furthermore, there is no evidence of prayer being offered for the departed until the end of the second century. The major reason for this was because the departed were regarded as being in a superior state to the living; prayers for them were therefore considered to be superfluous. It was also felt that a person after death has already gone to judgement and that the prayers of Christians for him at this point will be ineffective. However, the catacombs in Rome contained such inscriptions as, 'Remember dear Agatha', 'Jesus, Lord, remember our child', and 'God refresh thy spirit'. These were the simple outpourings of Christian hearts for their departed relatives and did not have the sanction of the Church. But Tertullian tells us that in the church of Carthage (*c.* the late second and early third centuries), a presbyter was called to pray for the soul of the departed between death and burial, and that the Eucharist was offered for the departed on the anniversary of death.[19] Further, in the letters of Cyprian, the offering of the eucharistic sacrifice for the departed is regarded as a common feature of the Christian life.

It is perhaps significant that the North African Church provides us with explicit evidence for the Church praying for the departed and offering the Eucharist on their behalf, an indication of the African concern for the perpetual relationship between the living and the dead. We must note, however, that these prayers were simply meant to commend the departed to God and to request that they be given rest, refreshment, growth in knowledge and holiness. The practice of intercession for the departed continued in the Church until the Reformation, when the use of public prayers for the departed was slowly abandoned by Protestant Churches.

Since the missionary movement to Africa in the nineteenth century was spear-headed by Protestants, prayers for the dead were not encouraged. But this is a necessary Christian duty in Africa and prayers for the dead, that God may grant them rest, refreshment, or a joyful resurrection and merciful judgement are acknowledgments that these things can be given by God alone. Moreover, these types of prayers have the merit of admitting our ignorance of the conditions of the departed and avoiding the presumption that particular persons are already saved, since some people will succeed in concealing their wickedness from their fellow men. African theologians must therefore recover the practice of the ancient North African Church and pray in faith for the departed, both Christian and non-Christian. This will provide the Africans with that link with their dead which they so much desire.

Second, do the departed pray for the living? It is clear that the departed remember in their prayers those whom they knew on earth and take an interest in their well-being; but here again the biblical evidence is scanty, though the writer of the Apocalypse sees the souls of the martyrs interceding with God for the speedy punishment of the persecutors of the Church (Rev. 3.9ff). Furthermore, in the ancient Church it was widely held that the dead pray for the living. For example, Cyprian asks Cornelius, bishop of Rome, when they were both expecting martyrdom, that: 'if one of us goes before the other, let our love for one another be unbroken, when we are with the Lord; let our prayers for our brethren and sisters be unceasing.'[20] If the departed make intercessions for us, can we ask them to pray for us? On this question the Scriptures are silent and the evidence for such practices in the early Church is scanty. But there is no *prima facie* reason why those who believe that their departed brethren are within reach of their words should not ask for the prayers of those who are with the Lord. However, this practice can be abused; the cult of martyrs and the undue veneration of martyrs in the Church of the Fathers is a salutary warning to the modern Church. But we should not discard a useful practice simply because it has been abused and corrupted. For if it does not derogate from the sufficiency of Jesus' intercession to ask a living friend to pray for us, it cannot be wrong for us to request the prayers of a departed member of Christ, who is with him. Indeed, the intercession of the departed who are with Christ is a legitimate consequence of the fellowship in prayer which unites the whole Body of Christ. The invocation of the departed is a practice based upon this truth; it is perhaps at this point that the dangers of syncretism are most clearly seen in the African situation, but it is also at the flashpoint between syncretism and Christian truth that a genuine Christian theology can be produced.

In conclusion, we would suggest that the veneration of the ancestors in Africa and our passionate desire to be linked with our dead in a real and genuine way can be satisfied by the development of a sound doctrine of the Communion of Saints. This doctrine provides for a fellowship in the Body of Christ, which is the Church, that extends throughout the world and continues throughout all ages. This will raise the sights of African Christians beyond their family and clan and would help to solve the problem of tribalism, which is plaguing the continent today. By participation in the sacraments of Baptism and the Eucharist Christians are linked with Christ and so are linked with others not only in different parts of the world, but also with the departed. This is so because Christ is the Lord of the living and the dead. Moreover, the merits of Christ's death are immeasurable, so that even non-Christians can be embraced within the Communion of Saints. Finally, we are linked with our departed through the fellowship of reciprocal prayer: we pray for them and they pray for us. It is also legitimate for us to request the saints to pray for us. Thus in the Communion of Saints, the living and the departed are linked together in an indissoluble bond, through participation in the sacraments that unite us with Christ—so that earth and heaven meet together and already in this life we taste the fruits of eternal life.

NOTES

1 W. Robertson Smith, *The Religion of the Semites* (New York 1957), p. 2.

2 Cf. D. B. Barrett, *Schism and Renewal in Africa: An Analysis of Six Thousand Contemporary Movements* (Oxford 1968), pp. 119ff.

3 C. G. Baëta in *Christianity and African Culture* (Gold Coast Christian Council, Accra, Ghana, 1955), p. 60.

4 J. V. Taylor, *The Primal Vision: Christian Presence amid African Religion* (London 1963), p. 106.

5 See, however, Harry Sawyerr, *Creative Evangelism: Towards a New Christian Encounter with Africa* (London 1968), pp. 92ff and J. Mbiti, *New Testament Eschatology in an African Background: A Study of the Encounter*

between *New Testament Theology and African Traditional Concepts* (Oxford 1971), pp. 147ff.

6   Jomo Kenyatta, *Facing Mount Kenya* (London 1961), p. 260.

7   U. Beier, *A Year of Sacred Festivals* (Lagos 1959), p. 26. Professor E. B. Idowu disputes the claim that the Yoruba worship their ancestors and argues that 'ancestor worship' is a false definition of the relationship between ancestors and their living relatives. E. B. Idowu, *Olodumare: God in Yoruba Belief* (London 1962), pp. 191f.

8   Harry Sawyerr, 'Ancestor Worship ii: The Rationale', *Sierra Leone Bulletin of Religion*, 8.2 (December 1966), pp. 33–9.

9   In a recent article Bishop Peter Sarpong has supported the use of the expression 'ancestor veneration'. P. K. Sarpong, 'A Theology of Ancestors', *Insight and Opinion*, 6.2 (Accra, Ghana 1971), pp. 1–9.

10   Meyer Fortes, *Oedipus and Job in West African Religion* (Cambridge 1959), p. 66.

11   Ibid., p. 30.

12   Ibid., p. 29.

13   Ibid., p. 53.

14   Ibid., p. 53. Cf. Monica Wilson, *Religion and the Transformation of Society: A Study of Social Change in Africa* (Cambridge 1971), pp. 26–75.

15   Cf. S. Benko, *The Meaning of Sanctorum Communio* (Studies in Historical Theology 3) (London 1964), p. 64.

16   J. N. D. Kelly, *Early Christian Creeds* (London 1950), p. 391. Kelly also argues that this interpretation of the phrase is supported by a study of it in its credal setting. He also points out that Nicetas and St Faustus of Riez regarded *sanctorum* as masculine. It will be useful to quote Faustus' comment on the phrase, since it indicates that in the fifth century theologians had seen the difficulty; he writes: 'Let us believe in the Communion of Saints, but let us venerate the saints, not so much in place of God, as for God's honour and glory ... Let us worship the merits of the saints, not merits which they have earned for themselves, but which they have earned for their devotion. Thus they deserve to be venerated worthily, forasmuch as they infuse into us, through their contempt of death, the worship of God and the yearning for the life to come.' Quoted from Kelly, op. cit., p. 391. This situation should serve as a warning to African theologians in their quest for a theology of the Communion of Saints, since veneration of saints could be debased to such an extent that it becomes a substitute for the worship of the true and living God.

17   Karl Barth, *Dogmatics in Outline* (London 1960), p. 144.

18   Tertullian, *De anima* 55 and 58; *Adv. Marcionem* iv.34; *De resurr. Carnis* 43.

19   Tertullian, *De anima* 15 and *De Corona* 3.

20   Cyprian, *Epistula* 60.5.